PRAISE FOR

SOFTPOWER!

"*SoftPower!* is not only important reading for women; it is for all of us trying to move to partnerships based on respect for ourselves and others."
— Riane Eisler, author of *The Chalice and the Blade*

"This wonderful book is chock full of wonderful ideas that you can use to get more success, happiness, and satisfaction out of every aspect of your life. Anyone who is sincerely committed to becoming everything they are capable of becoming, should read and take this message to heart."
— Brian Tracey, author of *Psychology of Achievement*

"*SoftPower!* is a dynamic, well-written book that gives you everything you need to know to effectively assert yourself."
— Pam Butler, author of *Self-Assertion for Women* and *Talking to Yourself*

SOFTPOWER!

How to Speak Up, Set Limits, and Say No Without Losing Your Lover, Your Job, or Your Friends

Maria Arapakis

WARNER BOOKS

A Time Warner Company

"Chambered Nautilus," from *Complete Poetical Works of Oliver Wendall Holmes*. © 1872.

Copyright © 1990 by SoftPower Resources, Inc.
All rights reserved

Warner Books, Inc., 1271 Avenue of the Americas, New York, NY 10020

A Time Warner Company

Printed in the United States of America
First printing: October 1990
10 9 8 7 6 5

Library of Congress Cataloging-in-Publication Data

Arapakis, Maria.
   SoftPower! : how to speak up, set limits, and say no without losing your lover, your job, or your friends / by Maria Arapakis.
      p.   cm.
   ISBN 0-446-39103-4
   1. Women—United States—Life skills guides.   2. Assertiveness (Psychology)   I. Title.
HQ1221.A73   1990
305.4—dc20   90-11988
                                                                                      CIP

Designed by Giorgetta Bell McRee

Cover design by Ann Twomey

This book is dedicated to my mother, Georgia, for putting up with me when I was such a brat and loving me so much as she, herself, struggled to find personal power.

And to my father, George, for giving me the confidence that I could do anything I wanted in my life, and for modeling for me a patient, gentle spirit and unending intellectual curiosity.

I love you both very much and only wish that you were still alive to share this exciting adventure with me. I know how proud you would be.

Acknowledgments

There, of course, are so many people to thank. A giant thank you to Renate Stendhal, my local editor, who worked with me with such professional warmth throughout much of the actual writing of the book and gave me uplifting pep talks when I felt frustrated, exhausted, or just plain sick of the entire project.

Heartfelt thanks to Latonya Mabry, my dear, loyal friend and assistant. Without her help in handling the details of my life, this book would have been impossible.

Love and appreciation as well to one of my closest friends, Cathy Van Berkem. Over the years we have explored together many of the issues talked about on these pages. Her wisdom and wit have influenced my life, my thinking, and my teaching in countless, significant ways.

I am grateful as well to Jeff Salzman, one of my best buddies and professional colleagues, for bringing me business expertise, words of encouragement, enthusiastic belief and support in my work, and a great sense of humor. Our friendship remains one of the true treasures in my life.

Thanks from the bottom of my heart goes as well to my two sons, David and Mark. In a way, we grew up together. I was such a kid when I started mothering that they had to suffer through my maturation process. Along the way, they have taught me, among many other things, that the only thing that really matters in the end is love.

I also want to acknowledge other close friends who have been there for me when I needed a good laugh or a shoulder to cry on: Jeanine Anderson, Bonnie Cox, Karen Klaber, John and Brigitta Houghton, Stuart Karlan, Shanna and Rinaldo Brutoco, my sisters Dede Hirsch and Vicky Gost, Barb Egelhof, and Amy Charles. Thank you for being in my life.

Much thanks and appreciation to Felicia Eth, my agent, and Leslie Keenan, my editor at Warner Books, for believing in the message of *SoftPower!* and for empowering me to bring this book to fruition. You have both been a joy to work with.

Finally, I want to thank the literally hundreds of writers, psychologists, and philosophers whose writings have inspired and influenced me over the years. While I have attempted to always give credit where it was due, I no doubt have unwittingly failed to cite a few sources of ideas or concepts. It is my hope that this book touches lives in the way mine has been touched again and again by the writing of others. Since I was a child, I have been a voracious reader. Starting with *Pollyanna* (her "glad game" was the first mind management idea I ever came across) and continuing to the books I'm currently working my way through, my life has been shaped and transformed many times over by the written word. I am thrilled to be offering at last my own contribution to the world of books.

Contents

Introduction

This Is a Book About You and Your Power

Women have been having problems with power for a long, long time. As we approach the twenty-first century, the problems unfortunately continue. Too much power as a woman and you're pushy and controlling. Too little power and you're a doormat or a victim. While individual power issues are quite varied, we all encounter them and, one way or another, they affect the satisfaction we feel, the success we achieve, and the quality of our everyday relationships.

Given the typical upbringing of a young girl, it should come as no surprise that the female of the species is still struggling with issues of interpersonal power. I remember a booklet handed out by the school nurse to all eighth-grade girls when I was a student at Westbury Junior High School. It was called *How*

to Catch a Teenage Boy and Keep Him and told us in no uncertain terms that the way to a boy's heart and fidelity was
not, as our mothers may have suggested, through his stomach.
It was through submission, subservience, and playing it dumb.
The way to be popular with boys was to act like a pea-brain,
always follow their lead, bone up on their interests, talk about
nothing else, and lose games on purpose to prop up the pre-
sumably frail male ego.

In today's world, thank goodness, such overtly manipulative power tactics are out of style. We no longer bat our
eyelashes and feign stupidity to get what we want. But what
to do instead—in the world of both business and personal
relationships—still remains, for many, a perplexing puzzle.
Traditional sock-it-to-'em male power certainly doesn't hold
much appeal. Those of us who have had a crack at "Games
Mother never taught us" have usually discovered that they're
not even games we want to play. Remember, for example, the
cold-hearted, ball-busting Faye Dunaway character in the movie
Network. If that was what it took to get ahead, we simply
weren't interested.

This book offers you a new and different style of power
called SoftPower™. Part of the appeal and uniqueness of
SoftPower is that it incorporates feminine sensibilities into the
power formula. Whereas most contemporary modes of power
are based on domination and control of others to get your
way, SoftPower is not. Founded on respect for both yourself
and others, SoftPower closes the gap between ethical behavior
and personal power. With SoftPower, you treat yourself at
least as nicely as you treat others, and you treat others at least
as nicely as you would want to be treated yourself. It's a Golden
Rule form of power that lets you operate as a powerful woman
without renouncing deeply felt values of caring and compassion and without wrecking relationships in the process.

SoftPower is based on a practical set of skills and attitudes geared to make everyday life smoother and more successful. With SoftPower, you'll be better able to handle nitty-gritty relationship problems— especially those that crop up at home and at work whenever you need to take a stand, express needs, draw the line, ask for something that you want, or turn others down. A SoftPower approach is neither hard-edged nor wishy-washy. Instead, it's a stand-your-ground, middle-zone solution somewhere between fight and flight.

This Is a Book About You and Honesty

Power and honesty go hand in hand. Telling the truth not only reflects power, it builds it as well. A fundamental premise of SoftPower agrees with the folk wisdom that honesty is— with rare exceptions—the best policy. Dishonesty deadens relationships, distances you from those you lie to, and places considerable stress on you emotionally and physically. Truthfulness, on the other hand, enlivens your relationships, clears the air, helps you discover where things stand, and lets others know where *you* stand. It also makes for greater peace of mind. You don't have to lie awake at night, worried about covering the tracks of your deceptions.

Honesty, however, is not without its risks. When I was deciding on the title for this book, I jokingly suggested to Warner Books that we place an asterisk next to the subtitle (*How to Speak Up, Set Limits, and Say No Without Losing Your Lover, Your Job, or Your Friends*) and note at the bottom of the cover "*But no guarantees!*" There *are* no guarantees. Not every relationship will support or survive your honesty, even when your truth telling is well-intentioned and superbly executed. Instead you may find a relationship has been built on the sands of denial and, if you stop playing ostrich and insist on facing painful realities, the whole thing crumbles before your eyes. When this turns out to be the case, however, it probably wasn't much of a relationship to start with. From a SoftPower perspective, it's better to let go of such tenuous connections and free yourself for healthy, sturdy relationships based on truth and integrity.

Of course, even in rock-solid situations, there are ways and ways to tell the truth, especially when the truth might hurt or rock the boat a bit. SoftPower honesty uses tact and timing. It also uses common sense. You're prepared to take a stand for what you know is right and set limits when enough is enough, but you also know that in certain situations the wisest option may be to keep your mouth shut and do nothing—at least until you've had a chance to calm yourself down and think things through.

This Is a Book About You and Limit Setting

Setting limits is one specific and critical form of honesty. Because limit setting is a central arena of interpersonal power, it is a primary focus of this book. Limits are set in relationships whenever you state your position in the face of potential or existing opposition, express feelings that may provoke disapproval or conflict, or draw the line when something is unacceptable to you. As with other forms of honesty, the ability to set limits both reflects and builds power.

Your limits are (among other things) a function of the fact that you only have so much time and energy—there's only so much you can do. While you may be able to stretch yourself to the max, there will invariably come a point at which you reach a limit and choices have to be made. Because of this, you can never please everyone. Even if you kowtow to the whims and demands of those around you, making one person happy often ends up angering or disappointing someone else.

Limits are also a function of your values and priorities. When you set limits, you demonstrate to others what you believe in, what you stand for, and what you care about the most. At other times, your limits reveal your emotions, desires, and opinions. Setting limits is, therefore, one of the primary ways in which you express your individuality and reveal to others how you are unique and stand apart from them.

Many of us as women (for reasons that will be explored at length in Chapter One) tend to have a great deal of trouble setting limits. We frequently find it excruciatingly difficult to do anything that could alienate us from others or "make trouble"—and setting limits occasionally (but not necessarily) can do both. One of the lessons of SoftPower is that, while keeping your mouth shut may sometimes seem like the safest route at the moment, in the long run it usually jeopardizes relationships and creates more problems than it seeks to avoid.

Women who grow up in dysfunctional families frequently have especially serious problems setting limits. According to Robin Norwood, author of *Women Who Love Too Much*, the degree of dysfunctionality in a family system is not correlated to visible pathology. It's related to how much *denial* there is in that system—how much a family hides from the truth. Thus, a family can appear to the outside world to be a storybook clan, but under the surface it can be built on lies and unexpressed rage. Even when problems do not include overt physical violence, alcoholism, or incest, a family can be a highly dysfunctional one. Not surprisingly, whenever lies and deception are a significant part of a family's dynamics, the children of that family are likely to grow up with severe problems facing the truth and telling the truth—both requirements of limit setting.

When problems with limit setting are extreme, individuals may even shun intimate relationships altogether because intimacy in their minds means relinquishing freedom and individuality. They think that to be close to others requires living a life of lies.

SoftPower Is a Way to Have "Power with Heart"

SoftPower makes it possible to have both intimacy *and* independence in your life. As a caring form of power aligned with love, it is similar in spirit to what Rollo May called integrative power. Here is power that employs kindness, cooperation, and patience and allows you as a powerful woman to be true to yourself *and* close to others.

Women, of course, are not the only ones who can profit from SoftPower. Men and women alike are searching for ways to protect their own rights yet get along with others in the process. In fact, all over the world, humanity is gradually waking up to the reality that, given the state of the planet, power based on violence, domination, and control of others is no longer a viable option. If we are to have peace on earth—for that matter, if we are to have a *future* here on earth—an ethical form of power is urgently needed. Thus, we owe it as much to our children's children as to ourselves to develop SoftPower and become aware, assertive, outspoken members of the human family. Personal power is no longer a personal issue. Self-empowerment is relevant not only to your own future but to the future of our species and the destiny of the world.

Start with Where You Are

Before we change the world, of course, we must first and foremost change ourselves. Luckily, the two go hand in hand. Acting as a model of integrity, self-respect, and truthfulness in your everyday life turns out to be an excellent way to make an impact on the world at large as well.

So let's get right into it and take a closer look at the scope of our problems with power and honesty. What better place to begin then with a description of the kinds of limit-setting headaches that you face everyday—people barging in on you when you're busy, bosses asking you to do things you don't want to do, strangers asking you questions you don't want to answer, friends keeping you waiting after you rushed to be ready, lovers letting you down, and kids giving you no respect.

1

THE PROBLEM
Women and Boundaries

Tina lives in Seattle. She is single, 29, and a personnel manager at a large bank. Tina has trouble setting limits with her boss, Ken.[1] It's 4:15 on Thursday and, just as Tina is winding up for the day, Ken announces that he needs her help in finishing a report due Friday morning. Tina had set aside the evening to shop and cook for a dinner party she's having the next night, but her boss seems desperate. This isn't the first time he's expected her to work overtime without advance warning, but while she has complained a few times about the last-minute assignments, little has changed. Once again, Tina gives in and agrees to help out, but her stomach stays in a knot all evening.

* * *

[1] All names are changed to protect privacy.

9

Louise is 40 years old. She is an executive vice-president for a large insurance company and the mother of a four-month-old son. Louise is upset because Karyn, the young woman taking care of her baby, plays with Greg all day instead of putting him down for an afternoon nap as Louise has asked her to do. Louise had hoped that her pediatrician would back her up on the wisdom of getting the baby used to napping at an early age, but unfortunately he didn't. Now she's afraid of offending and perhaps losing Karyn (who is otherwise wonderful with the baby) if she orders her to follow directions on the nap. Louise's insecurity as a new mother doesn't help. So, even though she's an experienced, highly competent manager at work and believes in her heart of hearts that she's right about the nap, she says nothing.

Carolyn is an attractive 17-year-old. She lives with her mother and stepfather in Dallas. On numerous occasions, her stepdad has barged into her bedroom without knocking, sometimes catching her half-dressed. Once, in the kitchen, on the pretense of horsing around, he "felt her up." When she told him to knock it off, he teased her, saying she was too sensitive. Carolyn hasn't mentioned anything to her mother because she's afraid it would only make trouble.

Janice, 43, is a secretary in her hometown of Albany, New York. She has three teenagers and a 20-year marriage to her high school sweetheart. Janice has trouble being honest with her mother. A number of times each day her mom calls the office to chat (*"Hi, it's me. What are you having for dinner?" "Chicken? Again? I thought Annie doesn't eat chicken"*). Janice tries to be patient because she knows her mother is lonely and well-intentioned. Eventually, however, she snaps, *"Mother, I'm busy—I can't talk with you now."* Then, of course, her mother becomes hurt and defensive (*"Fine, I won't call you at all. It's too bad you don't have time for your family"*). Janice shakes her head in despair as she complains, *"If I'm nice to her, she calls a hundred times. If I'm honest, she sulks for days. I give up."*

Joanne, in her early fifties, is a dynamic and successful professional speaker. Recently, while on the road for an engagement, she went out to dinner with John and Leslie, old friends she hadn't seen in more than twenty years. During dinner, John drank too much and became loud and unpleasant. Although he was in no shape to drive, when his wife tried to convince him to hand over the keys he refused. The two of them proceeded to have an ugly argument while Joanne stood by awkwardly, uncertain whether or not to "interfere." Finally, the wife gave in and the two women climbed reluctantly into the car and let John drive unsteadily back to Joanne's hotel.

Beth is 32 and lives in a Cleveland suburb with her husband, Paul. She is unhappy with their sexual relationship but doesn't know how to ask for what she wants. Paul's style of lovemaking leaves Beth totally unsatisfied. But as Beth confides, *"Where do I start? He expects me to turn on instantly. He doesn't seem to have a clue that I'm so miserable. I'm afraid if I tell him how I feel he'll think I've been deceiving him all along and we'll end up in a huge fight."*

Helen is an operating room nurse in a Chicago hospital. On several occasions she has suspected that a respected surgeon was physically manipulating unconscious patients in inappropriate ways. At first she couldn't believe her eyes, but after several episodes she became convinced that he was getting a few cheap thrills with unknowing patients. While personally and professionally horrified, she is reluctant to speak up for fear of jeopardizing her job. Why would anyone believe her word against his?

While clearly these scenarios run the gamut from petty to profound and from annoying to traumatic in terms of the implications and impact each would have on an individual's life, they all revolve around either an inability or an unwillingness to be truthful in an emotionally difficult situation.

HOW ABOUT YOU?

Where in your life do *you* have trouble speaking up or setting limits? Is it at home with the kids? At work with the boss? On dates with men? In stores with strangers? How directly, comfortably, and effectively would you handle the following?

The couple behind you keep whispering during the movie.
A house guest overstays her welcome at your home.
Someone wants to "small talk" when you're in a huge rush.
Your boss fails to follow through on an important promise.
Someone in your family reads a private letter after you told him or her not to.
You're blamed at work for something you didn't do.
Your husband calls you a liar in front of friends.
You're given an impossible deadline to meet.
The salesmen in the office stand near your desk telling sexist jokes.
A colleague spreads a nasty, untrue rumor about you.

Someone you manage goes over your head for a decision.
A close friend violates a confidence.
A co-worker takes unfair credit for your idea.

In the coming pages, you will be given specific ways to handle these common sorts of relationship problems. But, before we move into these SoftPower remedies, let's get a better sense of what lies at the core of such problems—the issue of limits and the concept of boundaries.

Setting Limits Is an All-Encompassing Issue

The need for establishing limits within relationships pops up whenever you work together, live together, play together, or even temporarily share time or space with others. From the kitchen to the bedroom to the boardroom to the grocery store, there's no escaping the necessity for occasionally turning others down, stating needs, resolving conflicts, and airing differences. These are power issues you face each and every day of your life in all relationships, from the most casual to the most intimate.

Considering the pervasive nature of the issue, you'd think we would all have developed a certain level of mastery in handling such encounters. Unfortunately, this is hardly the case. Most of us have serious ongoing problems with limits. We are reluctant to set them in the first place, afraid and awkward in the process if and when we do set them, and discouraged by the disappointing results we reap from our hesitant and bumbling attempts.

A lot of our troubles with limit setting can be traced back to the families and schoolrooms in which we grew up. As

children, we typically witnessed three styles of handling conflict: 1) push people around to get what you want; 2) back
down and keep a low profile to avoid getting pushed around;
3) go underground to get your way by devious measures. In
other words, the choices were: Act like a bully, act like a wimp,
or act like a sneak. To make matters worse, women were pretty
much restricted to the latter choices of wimp and sneak.

There's no doubt about it. Women have unique challenges
to surmount when it comes to setting limits. Men have their
share of headaches in this area as well, but throughout this
book we'll consider the issues of power and limits from the
particular perspective of women. Let's take a look at five special
dimensions to the female side of power and setting limits:

1. Power is considered unladylike. "Out in the open" power
has long been considered the exclusive domain of men. Consequently, women who exert personal power in relationships
do so at the risk of being labeled or shunned. Yet, everyone
—man, woman, adult, or child—wants to experience a sense
of positive power and control in life. When we feel powerless
or don't know how to express our inborn natural power appropriately, this drive for power becomes distorted. The dis-
tortions range from the deceitful to the self-defeating to the
downright dangerous. For women, this has translated at the
extremes into Scarlett O'Hara feminine wiles, Joan Crawford
misplaced rage, and Marilyn Monroe self-directed destruction.
These are, granted, the extremes. But even if you don't resort
to such drastic measures, when you feel powerless it's easy to
engage in minor-league versions of these same distorted power
plays of manipulation, misplaced fury and frustration, or self-
abuse.

Few of us were raised to know what healthy power looks

like in a woman. Instead we saw that women who did have clout were frequently ridiculed, ostracized, or punished. If, like Bella Abzug, you didn't match male pictures of what a woman was supposed to look like, you were turned into a joke. If, like Gloria Steinem, you had the nerve to speak out against the status quo, you were branded a man-hater. Back in the bad ol' days, some who stepped out of line were even burned at the stake

Because of such long-standing social taboos against powerful women, many of us understandably opt to keep a lid on who we are. We stay safely silent and try to maintain a low profile. By so doing, we avoid the potential of censure and rejection.

2. Women have a natural bias for relationships. Women seem to have an inborn (and subsequently culturally reinforced) bias for relationship. We are, as a result, usually reluctant to do anything that may jeopardize our ties with others. In her book *In a Different Voice*, Carol Gilligan, a professor at Harvard University, explores this feminine disposition to affiliation and comes to some interesting conclusions.[2] From her developmental studies of young girls and boys, Gilligan notes one indisputable way in which the two gender groups differ. As women, we are born out of a female body and are almost always raised by other females. Because of this, our primary sense of ourselves as females of the species develops from an experience of "I'm the same as you," "I'm connected to you," "I'm in relationship to you." Men, on the other hand (born male out of a female body and also raised by women),

---

[2] Carol Gilligan, *In a Different Voice*, Harvard University Press, 1982. Gilligan was named Woman of the Year by *Ms.* in 1985 for her ground-breaking research.

have to establish their male identity through a process of separation—"I'm different from you." "I'm *not* connected to you."

According to Gilligan, this undeniable difference in heritage predictably produces grown-up women who are at home with intimacy and connection but ill at ease with autonomy and separation. It just as predictably produces men who are comfortable with independence and self-reliance but less secure with togetherness and sameness. Of course, Gilligan is talking in generalities. On an individual basis, you can find women who are highly independent and not particularly relationship oriented. And there are men who crave relationships and feel insecure on their own. But, on the whole, the female of our species seems to be more invested in creating and maintaining relationships than the male.[3]

3. Women are raised to be people pleasers. As women, we are encouraged from an early age to cater to the needs of others and place ourselves last on the list. Little girls to this day continue to be culturally programmed to operate as "pleasing machines"—*"Put others first." "Your opinion doesn't count." "Don't be selfish." "If you want to be popular, you shouldn't argue." "If you don't have something nice to say, don't say anything at all."* The importance of the sanction of others is reinforced from all sides. As a result, many of us end up as adults choreographing our every move to audience applause and approval. Marching to our own drum and getting out of step with the crowd are clearly not part of this approval-seeking dance.

There is another less direct way in which people-pleasing

[3] There continues to be, however, a never-ending "nature-nurture" debate on the genesis of this difference. There are those who argue that all gender differences are due to socialization (nurture) and those who claim they're all due to genes (nature).

programming inhibits our limit-setting behavior. Such social training carries with it an implication that females are second-class citizens, worthy only if others think we are. This damages our budding sense of self-worth and makes the threat of rejection and disapproval (both real risks of limit setting) especially hard to bear. If someone doesn't like us it becomes a confirmation that the worst is true. We're not good enough. We're not lovable enough.

4. Motherhood complicates the picture as well. In our role as mothers, we encounter yet another factor that makes it hard for us to set limits. Motherhood sets up a unique relationship of dependency within which establishing boundaries for personal needs and desires is extremely challenging. We participate, as mothers, in the closest of human ties. At the start, there is literally no boundary between a woman and the baby who comes to life within her. At birth and during infancy, our children rely on us for their very survival. The mother-child bond remains a highly dependent one for years.[4] With such dynamics at play, it is an understandably complex challenge for a mother to establish boundaries for such personal needs as time alone or time to be with friends. Failure to do so can become one of the biggest crosses a woman bears. A neighbor of mine who has two little ones under the age of five put it this way, *"I don't even know who I am anymore. Everything I do in my waking hours is for the kids. The person I was has disappeared."*

Ironically, you do your children an enormous favor when you learn to set limits. They need to learn how to set limits in their own lives as much as you do in yours. As their mother,

---

[4]Obviously, I'm referring here to the vast majority of the situations in which the mother is the primary caretaker.

you can model this behavior for them. Child abuse prevention programs frequently do just this by specifically teaching youngsters how they can say no to friends and strangers. The children learn that they have a right to decide who touches them and how they are touched.

Small children are not the only ones who need the skills of limit setting. A UPI story reported that a Baltimore sex education program for teenagers produced surprising results. Whereas the community initially feared the program would encourage promiscuity, it instead accomplished just the opposite—the young women who took the program ended up having sex *less* often (and stayed virgins longer) because they learned it was okay to say no and were shown how to do it diplomatically.

As mothers, we convey a similar message when we demonstrate to our children a willingness and ability to draw the line with others. When we protect our own privacy and need for solitude, when we say no to unacceptable or abusive behavior, when we stand up for our rights or for a cause we believe in, in appropriate and responsible ways—all of these behaviors provide our children with excellent examples of positive power.

5. Professional women are supposed to fit in without a fuss. In the world of work, there is often little tolerance for "uppity" women who disagree with the status quo. Despite the considerable progress and social changes of the last few decades, we continue to be surrounded in corporate America by pervasive chauvinism. This means it is riskier for us than it is for men to speak up in the work place.

As relative newcomers to the game of business, women are expected to play by the existing rules and not mess things up. In *Feminine Leadership*, Marilyn Logan points out that the prevailing attitude still greeting women at the doors of many organizations is "Sink or swim—don't expect help, don't expect favors, and don't make a fuss." As the commandant at West Point told the first women cadets who attended the academy, "Nothing's going to change around here but the plumbing."[5]

Examples of double standards are everywhere. In a 1985 *New York Times* article, "Women's Near Liberation," Kati Marton lamented, "How many times have you heard male colleagues praised to the skies for their family involvement and concern for their kids? It's seen as a sign of a sensitive, caring soul. If a woman, on the other hand, calls in to say she must stay home with an ill child, more often than not she's written off as someone not interested in her job."[6]

Feeling out our muscle in the business arena, many of us have tried hard to fit in without making trouble but have found the price too high. Fitting in has frequently felt like forcing a round peg into a square hole because much of the advice to us instructs us to leave important aspects of our nature—the sensitive, intuitive, flexible, compassionate parts—at home with the kids and lunch boxes. This puts us between a rock and a marshmallow. Sell out on ourselves, our values, and our true priorities to make it professionally, or settle into a Donna Reed/Father Knows Best storyline.

There is a sad irony to corporate America's reluctance to accept true feminine power. When, as women, we come to the workplace with all of who we are intact, we offer to the business team advantages that are frequently missing. Women offer fresh, expanded choices that round out stiff, old-fashioned organizational styles. A solid sense of relationship ethics

[5] Marilyn Loden, *Feminine Leadership*, Times Books, 1985.
[6] *New York Times*, June 12, 1985.

is one of our strengths. Increased flexibility is another. As Gilligan's studies on comparative morality systems have demonstrated, the female perspective on rules is usually more adaptable than the male view. Little girls are frequently willing to bend or break rules if relationships are in jeopardy. Winning at any expense is not the only thing that matters.

Unfortunately, traditional businessmen rarely welcome the changes in the status quo that are suggested by women. Thus, when a woman recommends new rules or violates the old ones still being played in "hardball" upper echelon executive chambers, she must have considerable courage and a readiness to be booted out of the game.

The Philosophical Implications of Limits Are Profound

Aside from the particular problems with limits that women experience, the issue of boundaries is an equally critical one for men and women alike. It is an issue that strikes at deep, universal human chords having to do with our integrity as individuals, our fears, our guilt, and our need for satisfying relationships with others. D. H. Lawrence describes it beautifully:

> In every living thing there is the desire for love, or for the relationship of unison with the rest of things. That a tree should desire to develop itself between the power of the sun, and the opposite pull of the earth's center, and to balance itself between the four winds of the heaven and to unfold itself between the rain and the shine, to have

roots and feelers in blue heaven and innermost earth both, this is a manifestation of love: a knitting together of the diverse cosmos into oneness, a tree.

At the same time, the tree must most powerfully assert itself and defend itself, to maintain its own integrity against the rest of things. So that love, as a desire, is balanced against the opposite desire to maintain the integrity of the individual self. Hate is not the opposite of love. The real opposite of love is individuality.[7]

Lawrence's description of the two complementary faces of reality—connection to others and autonomy—is eloquent. I take exception, however, to his conclusion that individuality is the *opposite* of love. I think it is more properly considered another form of love—*self-love*. Asserting your integrity against the "rest of things" demonstrates that you care about yourself, respect your right to be different, and feel comfortable with a certain level of autonomy.

Boundaries both protect and express your unique individuality. Unless you live as a recluse in a Himalayan cave, there are bound to be times when, like D. H. Lawrence's trees, you must distinguish yourself from others. No matter how tolerant or easygoing you are and no matter how much you love others unconditionally, you will not always agree with what those around you say. You will not always choose to do everything they ask. You will not always want to put up with all that they do.

Individuality, depending on how it's experienced and expressed, can be either the bane or the blessing of the human condition, but one thing is for sure: Without a well-developed

[7]This excerpt is from D. H. Lawrence, "Love Was Once a Little Boy," *Phoenix II: Uncollected, Unpublished, and other Prose Works*. Viking Penguin, 1959.

willingness and ability to express your distinctiveness, you run the risk of ending up like a bonsai tree, your own true nature pushed, pulled, and misshaped by the demands and pressures of others. While such a contrived form may be attractive to some, it is always a pruned version of what was possible, a fraction of your full potential.

Some would argue that boundaries are undesirable, that openness and sameness are the superior states. They preach, "Be flexible," "Don't be negative," "Be agreeable," "Stop being stubborn!" But, as you'll see, the message of SoftPower is that limits (and the individual differences they reflect) are neither good nor bad. They just are. The question is how you live with them, how you communicate them, and how you respond to the limits of those around you.

We now know from modern physics that at certain levels of reality boundaries disappear, revealing an underlying unity where we all become part of a cosmic web of sameness. This universal oneness is an exciting realm to visit, but it's not the level of reality at which most of us work, play, and brush our teeth. Day to day, we exist for the most part in a world of real differences. You don't smoke; your officemate does. You like going to bed at ten; your new lover is a night owl who stays up half the night. You're a neatnik; your kids are slobs. Although way down deep inside we are all the same, there always exists concurrently another equally valid side of the cosmic web where we are vastly different and unendingly unique from one another. It is a province that can be both exciting and maddening.

When you set limits, you are expressing to others this arena of differences. You are saying, *"I have integrity as an individual and sometimes I am unlike you. Sometimes I don't want the same things you want. Sometimes I find your behavior unacceptable.*

Sometimes I won't be able to help you out or give you what you want."

Setting limits, however, does not always mean saying "No." It can just as frequently be a way to say *"Yes, but," "Yes, and,"* or *"Yes, if."* Boundaries versus togetherness is not an "either/ or" question. Part of the beauty of SoftPower is that it shows you how you can express individuality while maintaining intimacy, how you can draw the line without walling off, and how you can express a position without closing down to creative compromise.

Limits Are Like Fingerprints

Like fingerprints and snowflakes, your limits are one-of-a-kind, unique unto you. This is what makes them such an intriguing area of personal power. What drives you to distraction may be no big deal to someone else, and vice versa. You may, for example, see drop-in company as the height of rudeness while your surprise guests consider an unannounced visit spontaneous and fun. For this reason, you can never safely assume that others will know when they've done something that upsets you. Nor will you necessarily know when *your* behavior is upsetting to someone else. Forthright honesty therefore remains the best bet for straightening out problems and preventing more of the same kind of trouble down the line (*"It was great seeing you Sunday, Mom, but, in the future, would you please give me a call first before dropping by? It's nothing personal—Bob and I just like knowing ahead of time when someone's coming by"*).

Unlike fingerprints (and like snowflakes), limits change constantly. They are highly unstable. Not only do they vary dramatically from person to person, they shift *within* each of us from situation to situation. They change over time, place, person, and circumstance. What is acceptable to you today may be intolerable tomorrow. What you can live with in the privacy of your home may humiliate or infuriate you in public. What you relish from one man is despicable from another. What is considered assertive in America is a gross insult in Nepal.

Part of the challenge of limits revolves around this complex relativity. Your limits at any particular moment depend on a host of factors and are, as a result, never fully predictable. Knowing where you stand and what you want to do about a situation is rarely a black-and-white issue. For this reason, in the coming chapters a good deal of attention will be paid to how you can better "read yourself" as you assess problem situations that you face in your life.

Because limits are relative, they are also, to some degree, arbitrary. In other words, they're entirely up to you. Not only do you determine where you draw the line, you decide whether or not the line is flexible—whether it's time to stand strong and not budge or whether it's time to yield. At times it may make sense to "surrender." Perhaps the issue at hand is not all that important a matter. Or maybe you've had your way on a number of occasions and now it's your turn to give in. At other times, flexibility will be out of the question and a limit will be nonnegotiable. Under no circumstances will you be willing to move an inch.

Given the changeability of limits, communicating your limits to others is a job that is never finished. Throughout your day, throughout the year, throughout your life, you'll change your mind, your feelings, your desires, your priorities, and your thresholds of tolerance. And, to avoid conflicts and misunderstandings, many of these changes will need to be shared.

My Mother Was a Model of How Not to Do It

One of the reasons why the issue of boundaries has fascinated me for years is that, during my childhood, I witnessed my mother's struggles with the matter. She followed the pattern of long-sufferer (I called it major-league martyr). My mother would have given you the shirt off her back, washing it and ironing it before handing it over. I watched her time and again, in the face of the smallest sign of opposition, relinquish her own desires and opinions. *"No problem, sure I can do it for you." "You know, you're right. My idea was stupid. Let's do it your way." "Anything you want is fine."*

But everything wasn't fine. For my mother kowtowed to others so constantly that her ability to know what *she* wanted—independent from the desires, pressures, and expectations of everyone else—eventually atrophied.

My mother's style with boundaries was more complex, however, than simple nonassertion. Within the family, she vacillated between martyr and bully—too little and too much. Depending on her mood and a host of other variables, she went to one extreme or the other. Sometimes she blew up at us, sometimes at herself. Outsiders never saw the explosive, unhappy person we knew. Publicly she behaved herself and "blew in" instead, the tension imploding. Her body paid a heavy price for keeping it all in and putting up with so much. Possibly as a result, she suffered (and usually ignored) health problems much of her life and ultimately died of cancer.

My mother's problems with limits reflect the misguided and all too common view that self-sacrifice is the path to appreciation and approval from others. While sometimes this may turn out to be at least superficially true, the long-term toll is almost always destructive. The recipe club at St. Paul's Greek Orthodox Church may have regarded my mother as a saint, but those in the family knew the misery, sickness, and frustration attached to this brand of nonassertive selflessness. The price she paid for approval was high indeed.

THE PRICE OF THE PROBLEM

Even if your difficulties with limits are less severe than my mom's, they can cost you plenty. Here are some ways in which a reluctance to exercise power through honesty can work against you:

When you fail to set limits, problems repeat themselves.
When you fail to set limits, you rarely get your way.
When you are less than truthful, you tend to manipulate to get your way.
When you fail to set honest limits, your relationships suffer (even if you don't manipulate).
When you can't say no, you spread yourself too thin.

To better understand why it's so important to be more truthful in relationships, let's look at these various "costs," one by one.

When You Fail to Set Limits, Problems Repeat Themselves

A few years ago, two friends of mine, Stan and Julie, took a long-awaited vacation with another couple to enjoy the autumn colors of New England. Unfortunately, their travel mates turned out to be aggressive, dominating decision makers. As a result, what was supposed to have been a relaxing week doing the bed-and-breakfast circuit turned into a miserable, stress-filled marathon. The entire time, my friends rushed around at too fast a pace, stayed at inns they didn't like, and spent scarcely a minute alone. The surprising thing about this story is that my friends are anything but nonassertive individuals. Both are successful professionals who are outspoken and in command in other areas of their lives. Yet, in this social setting neither of them wanted to ruin the trip with a fight, so they said nothing (and instead ruined the trip with tension).

Silence implies consent. People are not mind readers. While bringing a concern out into the open never guarantees a resolution, saying nothing almost always guarantees more of the same. Instead of one lousy day on the trip, an entire week is wrecked. Instead of suffering one sexist joke, you hear dozens. Instead of an occasional problem with lateness, you're kept waiting time and time again.

When You Fail to Set Limits, You Rarely Get Your Way

Another consequence of an inability to establish boundaries is that you'll predictably suffer frequent episodes of disappointment and dissatisfaction. In other words, you will fail to get what you want in a lot of situations. My friends—because of their unwillingness to speak up—got a lot of what they didn't want (rushing around, etc.). And they also missed out on what they *did* want—a chance to slow down and relax.

Many of us shortchange ourselves and sell out on our priorities on a regular basis with our failure to be honest. We go out for the evening when we'd rather be home watching TV. We take on added responsibilities when what we really need is a rest. We end up eating Chinese when we're craving a pizza. Sometimes, in fact, *nobody* wins because *everyone's* telling lies. I've known couples who took vacations neither wanted; friends who went to movies neither cared to see; lovers who made love when both wanted to go to sleep—all because no one was willing to tell the truth.

When You Are Less Than Truthful, You Tend to Manipulate to Get Your Way

We all have needs and desires and, one way or another, we seek to get these met. When you're not up-front about what you're after, it can be tempting to stoop to underhanded tactics to get what you want. You may try false flattery to seduce someone into cooperating (*"You seem like a caring, considerate person. I thought you'd want to help out on this"*). You might pretend to agree to something knowing full well you'll sabotage or withhold in the end (*"Fine, let's do it your way"*). Or perhaps you criticize your partner (*"You're neglecting the children. You should spend more time with them"*) instead of being honest about about your own needs to have time away from the kids.

Resorting to indirect or sneaky moves can sometimes work in the short run, but the fall-out of such manipulation almost always comes back to haunt you in the end. Deviousness sets up deviousness in return. Those with half a brain soon figure out they're being duped and, once they see the phoniness, they resent it and find a way to get even.

When You Fail to Set Honest Limits, Your Relationships Suffer

When you silently tolerate abuse or say nothing about unmet needs, relationships are bound to fill up with tension and resentment. While the cumulative effects of dishonesty can be considerable, even one tiny white lie can produce significant repercussions. A story from my own life is an example:

A number of years ago, I went on a trekking trip in the Himalayas with my older son, David. Some months before the trip, during a phone visit with a new friend, I made mention of the upcoming adventure.

"How exciting!" she responded enthusiastically. "Wouldn't it be wonderful if I could join you there? I have vacation time so I'll bet I could do it. Wouldn't that be great?"

It was an awkward moment. What could I say—"No, it wouldn't be great"? Or, "I'm not sure if it would be great"? (which was closer to the truth). I hadn't even thought about anyone else coming along. Instead, I heard my mouth reply, "Oh, yeah, that would be great."

Once off the phone, however, I knew immediately that I

had no interest in her joining us. What was I going to do? I considered telling her that the trekking group had filled up even though, in fact, there was no limit to the group. As I contemplated lying, however, I realized that I couldn't do it. I knew that, were I to have lied, something dramatic would have occurred in my relationship with her. There would suddenly have been a distance between us. I would have felt tense and uncomfortable talking with her—not only during that particular conversation, but afterward as well. I would have been constantly worried that she might ask, "Is there a waiting list for the group? Have things changed?"

Because I cared about the friendship, I had to tell her the truth. At first I was afraid that if I told her I didn't want her to come on the trip she would take it as a personal rejection. But as I thought some more, I realized that, in fact, it wasn't a rejection at all that I was communicating. It was an assertion of what I wanted (which, in fact, had nothing to do with her). It was a declaration of my desire for time alone with my son, the mountains, and myself. With a friend along, I knew the dynamics of the trip would change significantly. Seeing the situation in this light made it easier for me to talk with her, and I was ultimately able to clear up the matter with ease.

Telling the truth in relationships, by the way, doesn't mean you blurt out everything indiscriminately. A SoftPower style takes into consideration the appropriateness of honesty, not only regarding what you say but when you say it and how you say it. In some cases it may be more fitting to keep your opinions or feelings to yourself. There was no need, for example, for me to mention to my friend that, even if I had wanted someone else along on the trip, I doubted that I would have chosen her.

When You Can't Say No, You Spread Yourself Too Thin

In addition to creating distance between you and others, failure to set limits can damage your relationships in yet another significant way. When you overload yourself and run yourself ragged because of an inability to turn others down, those you care about the most end up with the leftover crumbs of your time and energy.

Unfortunately, the media regularly presents to us images of women who supposedly do it all and have it all. The new female success symbol seems to have no limits. Not only does this dynamo run her own multimillion-dollar business, she is gracious wife and hostess to the corporate executive husband, is raising four well-adjusted, school-age children, is president of the PTA, runs marathons, has multiple orgasms, and bakes whole-wheat bread in her spare time.

The problem is that on closer inspection such success stories often reveal a workaholic who has sacrificed on the altar of success her ability to play, hang out, hang loose, and smell the roses. Not long ago the *Washington Post* referred to a study in the *American Journal of Psychiatry* and reported that, "Women with MBAs are paying a heavy price for participation in the corporate world." The study revealed that women with business degrees were suffering significantly more from stress, depression, nightmares, and feelings of being on the verge of a nervous breakdown than were their male counterparts. The price you pay for life in the fast track can be high indeed.

In a profile on actress Kate Jackson, *TV Guide* described the price she paid on the road to success. In the name of success, she sacrificed friendships, physical health, and emotional peace of mind. The toll it took forced Jackson to reevaluate the meaning of success. She discovered "It's not how much money I have, although I'm sure a farmer about to lose his land would disagree. But money doesn't make you happy—I know that. I swear the bottom line is how well you handle the relationships with the people you love." As the article wisely summed it up:

"Healthy success has to do with balance. Obsessive success reflects the simplistic belief that career success is the same thing as success in life. Yet only when you admit the distinction will you strive for *internal* success as well as external—where you *feel* as good as you look."[8]

As Kate Jackson's story demonstrates, the Type-A, workaholic, heart-attack-prone lifestyle that has for so long been the prototype of the male ideal wrecks both relationships and health. And "success," be it the entrepreneurial or the corporate version, frequently mandates such a frenetic pace. Those who live at this kind of dizzy rate suffer headaches, heartburn, high blood pressure, and hemorrhoids. They usually haven't been to a concert in years or gazed at the stars in longer.

Unfortunately, corporations have not yet figured out that, in the long run, the rat race does not serve the bottom line. Ultimately, the human being who balances professional obligations and personal relationships with appropriate, healthy limits is the one who is most productive at the office. Instead, we find Felice Schwartz in a 1989 *Harvard Business Review* article suggesting to corporations that they adopt a "Mommy Track" for women who want to have both careers and families. While Schwartz subsequently denied coming up with the concept and insisted she did not mean to imply that women involved in raising children are a corporate liability, many took

[8]*TV Guide*, September 1988.

the idea to mean that mothers are not worth as much to a business as those women who do not have a family to worry about.

Despite such prejudice against human values, there are some hopeful signs that change is afoot. The *Wall Street Journal* reported not long ago in an article, "Stepping Off the Fast Track," that many employees—men included—are starting to turn down promotions when a move means disrupting their families. Other statistics show that women unwilling to sacrifice personal values and priorities in order to "make it" are leaving corporate America in droves to work in small businesses or start up businesses of their own.[9] In such changed circumstances, they may still work long hours, but at least they maintain more control over their schedules.

MEN HAVE ALL THE POWER, RIGHT?

What about men? Do they, as commonly assumed, have it all worked out with regard to power?

Hardly. In the last two decades, it has become increasingly clear that men have as many problems with the issue of interpersonal power as we do. Warren Farrell, in *Why Men Are the Way They Are*, tells of how his notions of power and success changed drastically after meeting Ralph, a member of his men's group who seemingly "had it all" but privately was filled with despair:

> I had always assumed power meant having status and access to income, influence, and external rewards. Ralph

[9] And, by the way, are succeeding at rates more than double that of male entrepreneurs.

had all of them. Yet up close he didn't seem very powerful. I started asking whether power meant, instead, the ability to control one's own life. If we redefine power as the ability to control one's own life, Ralph probably had less power than anyone in the group. Ralph had given up the ability to control his life by spending his life doing what he was programmed to do. Ralph had lost real power by trying to gain the appearance of power. He looked like a leader yet he was, in fact, following "a program for leaders," so he was really a follower. He had reached a high level, but he had done so by adapting to his boss and his boss' boss. He was, as he put it, a "high-level mediocre."

With the accusation that "men have all the power," women reinforce the belief that external power is all there is to power. The more they see the limits of external reward power, the more they will stop saying "men have the power."[10]

THE SOLUTION? SOFTPOWER!

Obviously, old-style "external reward" power is not the answer. This traditional masculine power is not what most of us are after. It violates too much of what we hold dear. On the other hand, "power behind the throne" isn't the way to go either. We aren't about to throw in the towel and retire to the kitchen, not only because of simple economics but because of deeply felt personal commitments to make a difference in the world outside the picket fence.

SoftPower, the power we'll be exploring on the coming

[10]Warren Farrell, *Why Men Are the Way They Are*, McGraw Hill, 1986, p. 8.

pages, offers you what is needed—a mid-zone where you can be firm without being forceful, say no without walling off, and be self-respecting while still respecting the rights of others. With a SoftPower attitude and approach, you find that an open heart and a clear mind bring you much more than a clenched fist or an anxious, furrowed brow ever could.

Part of the beauty of the SoftPower solution is that it is not a cookie-cutter cure that assumes all women are alike or want the same thing. A SoftPower style of power can be easily customized to different lifestyles and personalities. It is equally useful for the secretary in Des Moines, the manager in L.A., the business owner in Chicago, the student in Dallas, the housewife in South Dakota, the masseuse in Marin, the mother in Tampa, and the engineer in Fairbanks.

As you read the pages that follow, keep this idea of customization clearly in mind. If I suggest something that you know in your bones doesn't fit for you, don't use it. Take what suits you. You are the expert on what risks you're ready to take. You are the expert on what is suitable to you. You are the expert on you. This, in fact, is one of the central messages of SoftPower.

2

I'M JUST A GIRL WHO CAN'T SAY NO

Why Women Have So Much Trouble Setting Limits

Women are famous for excess. According to legend, we give in too much, take on too much, put up with too much, and love too much. Unfortunately, as we saw in Chapter One, this image of the woman who can't say no is more than social stereotyping. It's a reflection of a reality that many of us know all too intimately and live with every day.

On the other hand, some of us can say no, but we don't do it very effectively. Instead, we set limits so timidly no one takes us seriously. Or we do it so combatively we damage or destroy relationships in the process and lose more than we gain.

What are *your* patterns? To begin the process of shifting to a SoftPower style, it helps to first understand your current habits.

IT'S TIME TO BE HONEST WITH YOURSELF

There are basically two places where you can be truthful—with yourself and with others. *Self-awareness* is telling the truth to yourself. *Speaking up and setting limits* is telling the truth to others. You need the first kind of honesty (self-awareness) before you can effectively engage in the second (assertion).

Despite the fact that we all claim to want honesty, deception is usually a daily part of our lives. And although lying to ourselves makes no sense at all, self-deception is a sizable part of the problem. As someone once remarked, "Sure, the truth shall set you free, but first it may make you damn mad." Or depressed. Or frustrated. Consequently, when situations are not to our liking, it's easy to indulge in a little self-delusion.

In facing the truth about your current patterns, you will undoubtedly find both good news and bad. There will be areas of strength where it's easy as pie for you to turn someone down and clear problems up. There will also be weak spots—times when you are vulnerable to losing your courage and your cool.

Perhaps, for example, you tend to be meek with friends and family but aggressive with strangers—you let family and friends walk all over you (*"Okay, okay! We'll do it your way"*), then holler four-letter words on the freeway or snap impatiently at salesclerks who are slow or incompetent (*"Would you speed up? I haven't got all day!"*).

Or maybe your aggressive tendencies come out mostly with your kids. I remember that, as a young mother, I used to scream and yell at my two sons when they didn't listen to me. At my wit's end, I resorted to bully tactics (*"You do it or else! Why? Because I said so!"*). Although I wouldn't have dreamed of subjecting grown-up friends to such behavior, I let myself blow up with my kids.

Maybe you're beautifully assertive with professional peers but wither in the presence of authority figures or "experts." When dealing with someone who has a big title, snazzy office, impressive credentials, or more know-how than you do, you become tentative and docile (*"I'm sorry. It must have been my mistake. How dumb of me"*).

Or perhaps you become a jellyfish when you fall in love. You meet a man you're interested in and suddenly you're insecure as a teenager—agreeing with things you don't really agree with (*"Oh yes, I loved the play, too"*), putting up with things you don't like (*"You're going to be two hours late? No problem"*), and doing things you don't want to do (*"Anything is fine—whatever you want"*).

As you identify your personal disabilities, don't feel discouraged if you find lots of room for improvement. Rest assured we'll soon be looking at many skills that will help you change your ways.

WHERE ARE YOUR WEAK LINKS?

The following three-pronged analysis is designed to reveal your personal and professional vulnerabilities in setting limits. It does this by reviewing the who, when, and what of your problems. You'll identify the individuals you have the most struggles with, the times you are most susceptible to confusion or upset, and the kinds of situations that are most bothersome for you. You will get the most from this exercise if you actually put your lists down on paper. But even if you fail to do this, by merely considering these questions you will heighten self-awareness of your everyday personal patterns.

Let's Start with the Who

There are no doubt a handful of select individuals in your life with whom you find it especially hard to be honest. Who are they? With whom do you hold back too much (or come on too strong)? Is it with your husband or boyfriend? Your boss? Your secretary? Your best friend? List everyone you come into contact with on a regular basis. Include members of your immediate family, relatives, friends, neighbors, and acquaintances (for example, people you know at church or your tennis club). List those with whom you interact at work—people you manage, support staff, colleagues both inside and outside your company, clients or customers, vendors and authority figures (your boss, his or her boss, other executives of your organization). Write down categories of people as well—men, women, older people, younger people, salespeople, waiters and waitresses, physicians, accountants, lawyers, service people, and strangers (individuals you interact with on the street, at social events, on a plane, etc.).

Once you've finished, circle those individuals (or categories) with whom you have the most trouble setting limits. Then look for patterns. Are most of your problems at work or at home? Are they primarily with family, professional colleagues, or personal friends?

Now On to the When

This step of the assessment process investigates the when of your problems. Mentally review your usual routine and break your lifestyle into morning, afternoon, and evening "event segments." These might include:

Getting ready for work in the morning
Getting kids dressed, fed, and ready for school
Eating breakfast
Commuting to work
Arriving at work
Staff meetings
Preparing dinner
Evenings at home
Leaving the kids with a baby-sitter
Doing weekend chores
Making love

Identify those times when you are most susceptible to being short-tempered, ill at ease, or impatient. Do you tend to be edgy in the morning while trying to get your kids off to school? Do you experience tension at most staff meetings? Are you feeling frustrated and disappointed with the lovemaking side of your marriage? Consider if there are other predictable situational factors that interfere with your ability to handle stress. For example, is it especially hard for you to deal with conflict when you're overtired or feeling sick?

Wind Up with the What

The last angle of your self-assessment focuses on the "what" of your problems. What sorts of mistreatment are the hardest for you to handle? What feelings (or desires) are most difficult for you to express or respond to? This list might include:

Interruptions
Being ignored
Being yelled at
Rudeness
Lateness
Criticism
Sexual harassment and chauvinism
Expressing anger
Responding to anger
Expressing hurt feelings
Responding to tears
Expressing disagreement
Responding to disagreement
Asking for what you want
Asking for help
Asking for favors
Asking for information
Asking for privacy
Asking for more time with someone
Delegating work
Giving criticism
Turning down work
Turning down requests for help or favors
Returning an unsatisfactory meal
Asking for store refunds

Six Common Dysfunctional Styles

Knowing the who, when, and what of your problems is a good start, but it's equally important to understand the *nature* of your difficulties as well. In what way do you go to extremes? Are you the one who is usually overpowering or overpowered? Are you impulsively honest and brutally frank? Or are you more often tentative and tongue-tied when trying to talk over a problem or express a need? Following are several common styles of excess. Which are familiar?

Style #1: You don't set limits enough. You rarely open your mouth when something bothers you. Instead, you keep a stiff upper lip. To avoid trouble, you let things pass or give in easily (*"No, I'm not upset." "Everything's fine"*). In your attempts to preserve the peace, you permit others to mistreat you and take advantage of you. It may seem to everyone that you're easygoing, but privately you are tense and long-suffering.

Style #2: You set limits excessively. You frequently confront, complain, request, or demand. Lots of things are "big deals" that bother you (*"I don't like your tone of voice." "I don't like the look on your face." "I hate it when you pick your teeth"*). You make a fuss over issues that would have been better dropped than dealt with. You're easily annoyed, difficult to please, and impatient a good deal of the time.

Style #3: You set limits too late. You hold things in until you've had it. Eventually you speak up but, because you're at the end of your rope, you overreact (*"I'm not finished, dammit! Would you stop interrupting!"*). Frequently you suffer physically in the process (*"Now I have a splitting headache!"*). Many times, you procrastinate to the point where your limits do no good. The damage has been done and there's no undoing it.

Style #4: You set limits too soon. You fly off the handle without understanding the full story or considering all your options. Because you act without forethought and before all facts are in, you come to half-baked conclusions (*"You said you'd call—I'm tired of your lies"*) and say things you later regret.

Style #5: You set limits too meekly. You make a half-hearted attempt to set things straight. Afraid of starting a fight, getting rejected, or hurting someone's feelings, you tiptoe around an issue as if it were a live grenade (*"I kind of have a little bit of a problem with this, but it's no big deal. Oh, let's just forget it"*). You hope others get the hint from your silence, tone of voice, facial expression, or body language.

Style #6: You set limits too harshly. You're forceful in what you say and how you say it (*"You're a slob! Your room is a pig pen. Clean it up immediately or else!"*). In the name of getting what you want, you are at times demanding, condemning, pushy, stubborn, rude, inconsiderate, or abrasive (*"This is the last straw—I can't take this mess one more day!" "I've had it! This time you've gone too far!"*).

In general, aggressive personalities favor the too-much, too-soon, too-forceful styles, and nonassertive types lean toward the too-little, too-late, too-meek ones. If you're like most people, you at times slip into all six of the styles but tend to use one or two of them more than the rest. My mother, for example, could go in the blink of an eye from "I'm fine, don't worry about me" expressions of long-suffering to "I've had it!" explosions. This particular kind of flip-flop is a common pattern. Someone upsets you; you try to be patient and say nothing. They do it again; you continue to be restrained. They keep it up; you lose it and explode ("*Damn it, cut it out!*").

My mom had another tendency that is commonplace. She acted out one extreme (too little) in public and its correlate (too much) in private. The bully boss is often a wimp at home. The person who's unable to stand up to the bully boss at the office can be a tyrant with loved ones.

You Can't Speak Your Mind If You Don't Know (or Haven't Made Up) Your Mind

There is a second kind of self-awareness that is as important as awareness of your communication patterns. *In the heat of the moment* you need to be aware of what's going on inside of yourself. You need to know what you want, what you don't want, where you draw the line, and how you feel. The degree to which you'll be self-aware in the midst of an interaction will vary, of course, from situation to situation. Sometimes you'll be clear as a bell. At other times you'll find yourself in a complete muddle. Most of the time you'll be somewhere in between.

Complete oblivion. With zero awareness, you won't have a clue about what's going on internally. Desires, opinions, and feelings will all be stuffed "down under" where you don't have to deal with them. What you don't know can't hurt you, right? Well, not quite. As I mentioned in Chapter One, repression of this sort usually hurts plenty—in the form of headaches, backaches, bleeding ulcers, high blood pressure, and cancer. Cancer research, in fact, frequently describes the cancer-prone personality as someone who family and friends view as saint-like. She is the person who always does for others, puts up silently with things that bother her, and makes untold sacrifices in the name of keeping the peace. Unlike a saint, however, this person is not letting her unspoken disagreements and disappointments go. She is simply doing the proverbial ostrich act, refusing to face her own unhappiness or deal with others about potentially contentious differences.

Clearly with such limited self-awareness, you are seriously handicapped in the area of limits. Unwilling to tell the truth to yourself, you certainly cannot be honest with others.

"Part of the puzzle" awareness. More typically, the situation is not so drastic. With partial awareness, you are aware of some things, unaware of others. For example, you may know without a shadow of doubt that you don't want to accept a work assignment, but you're uncertain about why you feel the way you do.

Knowing part of the puzzle is better than nothing. It's certainly an improvement over total oblivion. But because you still don't understand all of what's going on, any attempt on your part to be straight with others will be limited by what you don't know.

"After the fact" awareness. Sometimes awareness hits you after an interaction has taken place. You hang up the phone and think, *"Wait a minute—I don't want to do this. Why did I say yes?"* You walk away from a conversation and think, *"I don't like how I was treated! I should have said something."*

Like partial awareness, delayed awareness represents prog-

ress, a start in the right direction. Better something than nothing and better late than never. Even after the fact, you may
be able to undo (or redo) what has taken place. If nothing
else, you've got the advantage of having a chance to calm down
before handling the situation.

Confused awareness. When a lot's going on at once or
when things happen suddenly, conflicting feelings or desires
may tug at you from every side and be hard to sort out. If
you're invited to give an important presentation, it's possible
to feel flattered, overwhelmed, and scared—all at once. If
someone makes a joke at your expense, you may feel insulted,
afraid to confront the person, and embarrassed because you're
blushing. Experiencing a multitude of emotions simultaneously may make it hard to speak up—it's not easy to communicate when you feel emotionally scrambled inside.

Conflicting desires (wanting incompatible or contradictory
things) can also be hard to figure out. One part of you may
want to stop working but the rest of you knows you need to
meet a critical deadline. Your body may want to have sex with
a new beau, but your mind argues for holding off until you
know him better. Pulled in two directions, it's easy to give in
against your best interest to the desires and demands of others
or get sidetracked by lesser priorities of your own.

GET TO KNOW YOURSELF BETTER

There are eight dependable ways to increase and maintain the
self-awareness necessary for successful limit setting. Ideally,
these strategies will enable you to know not only *that* you're

upset but why you're upset and what your options are regarding a problem at hand.

1. Use Your Body as a Barometer

Physical cues can alert you to the fact that you're upset, that a situation is provoking frustrations and needs your attention. In fact, for many people physical reactions are the first clue that trouble is brewing. Discover what symptoms your body favors. Do you hold your breath when you're nervous? Do you tighten your stomach when upset? Once you know your tendencies, you'll be able to spot even subtle physical reactions that function as early warning systems. Such faint signals tip you off to problems while they're still at early, more manageable stages. When you notice low-level reactions, you no longer need to make yourself sick before realizing, "*Something's wrong, I've gone too far!*"

The following physical states are common signs of trouble:

Sudden tightness: Tightened fists, furrowed brow, clenched jaws, tense muscles, pursed mouth, tight stomach

Changes in your breathing: Quickness of breath, constricted breathing, holding your breath, hyperventilating

Increases in body temperature: Flushing, sweating, getting hot all over, blushing

Aches and pains: Queasiness, indigestion, sudden headache, back or neck pain

Body reactions can also assist you in discriminating between those times you sincerely "don't care" about something and those times when you're fooling yourself with rationalizations. For example, your mind may insist, "It doesn't matter," but if your stomach stays in a knot, listen to your stomach, not your mind. Your mind is likely to deceive you, your body is not. Barbara, a professional speaker who contracts with a national seminar company, tells of a time she listened to her body instead of her mind:

"Last February, Eileen called from the meeting planning department to ask if I would fill in three dates for another speaker in Michigan. At first I thought it would be no problem. My brother and sister-in-law live near one of the cities, so I figured I could even manage a visit with them in between programs. I told her that I'd be glad to do it.

"As soon as I hung up, however, I noticed that my body felt horrible. I was tight as a spring and felt like I would burst. I realized instantly that my body was saying, 'No way! I do not want three more days of work and I definitely do not want to fly all over upper Michigan in the middle of winter!' I knew I needed to turn down the dates. I called Eileen back immediately and told her that I'd changed my mind."

It would be great, of course, if the interpretation of bodily reactions was always such a cut-and-dry matter. It's not. An uptight feeling can mean any of a number of things. Sometimes it indicates, as in Barbara's case, that you've agreed to something you don't want to do. At other times it reflects your own unreasonable thinking turning a demanding but acceptable situation into a nightmare. In a third case, the uptightness merely means you're coming down with the flu. If you're confused about the meaning of a physical reaction, turn inward and take a reading of other indicators as well. What are your thoughts on the matter—are they reasonable or off the wall? What do you sense intuitively—do you have a gut sense of the situation? If so, what is it? What are your desires and priorities? Are they being honored or violated?

2. Use Your Feelings as an "Alarm System"

Your emotions are another personal "barometer" useful in monitoring situations. Reflect on what's happening to you emotionally. Do you feel anxious? Angry? Annoyed? Instead of being angry at yourself for feeling angry, use your emotions to better understand what's going on and what needs to be done. We'll be looking in depth at how to do this in Chapters Four and Five. The goal of such increased awareness is to better understand yourself, not necessarily to act on your feelings. With increased awareness, you can better comprehend how you get all worked up and what you get worked up about. You can also track mounting tensions—small upsets that by themselves seem insignificant but in fact represent the tip of a growing emotional iceberg.

Unfortunately, many of us pay attention to emotions only when they reach extreme levels. We "stuff" our feelings and wait for a state of rage, panic, or massive depression before taking due notice. Train yourself to be sensitive to even subtle emotional experiences. The following states deserve particular attention because they frequently indicate a problem with limits:

Anger—from mild annoyance to full-blown fury
Fear—from low-level anxiety to total terror
Embarrassment—from minor upsets to major humiliations

Disappointment—from fleeting frustrations to devastating letdowns

3. Take Stock of What's Important for You

By writing down your long- and short-term goals on a regular basis, you can clarify what truly matters to you in the larger scheme of things. What do you really want to accomplish? What are you really after? Sit yourself down for an old-fashioned goal-setting session, and commit personal priorities to paper. What do you want to achieve in an upcoming day, week, or year? Don't get hung up on formal rules of goal setting that have you quantifying everything so it's measurable. This is not a grant proposal for federal money. It's a list for your private use and can be as informal as *"I want to spend time with the kids this weekend"* or *"I want to finish my report by Monday morning."*

With a clear sense of priorities, it becomes easier to turn down off-course obligations and invitations. If a friend asks you to go away for the weekend, you'll feel less torn about setting limits effectively (*"I'd love to join you, but I need to work on a report, so I'm afraid I can't"*). Aware of your priorities, you'll be better able (and more likely) to choose the right path instead of the path of least resistance.

Once you write goals down, stay close to them by reviewing your list daily. It won't do you much good to write goals down only to lose the list five minutes later in the mess on your desk and never look at it again. Seeing your goals in black and white keeps you constantly aware of what counts the most. Post them on the refrigerator, bathroom, mirror, and desktop.

If you habitually cater to others, you will probably need to do more than make a list to discover your natural will. Be creative. For example, one woman who felt confused about her sexual drive asked her lover to conduct an experiment with her. She explained to him that because she was always responding to *his* sexual needs, she had little sense of her own. They struck an unusual agreement—for six months, she alone was the one to initiate sexually. This gave her the chance to know her desires, independent of his—how often she wanted no sex at all, how often she wanted to "jump his bones" three times a day, and how often she was somewhere in between.

4. Pull Back Periodically and Spend Time Alone

Alone time invariably increases self-awareness. Getting off by yourself gives you a chance to catch your breath, put things in perspective, and discover your natural will.

Solitude will be especially important for you if you're the kind of person who is overly eager to please or is easily intimidated by others. By yourself, you can sort out what *you* want from what everyone else wants. A friend of mine describes how this worked for her when she took her first vacation alone:

"Waking up my first day in London, I was shocked by the realization that I could do exactly what I wanted without consulting or considering anyone else. If I wanted to, I could waste the entire day in bed with a novel, wander the streets of Soho till dark, or spend the whole day at the London museums.

"At first, confronted with this carte blanche of choice, I felt more confused than ever. Having always looked to others for the lead, I didn't have a clue as to my own personal inclinations. Soon, though, as I relaxed into the freedom of solitude, my personal desires began to emerge, and I had the time of my life. This chance to be 'solo' has even helped me in knowing what I want when I'm with others."

A number of years ago I started a tradition with myself. At least four times a year, I take myself away for what I call a solo retreat. On these getaways, I stay for a night or two at a bed-and-breakfast inn out in the country. Any peaceful place will do, but somewhere near unspoiled nature—the mountains, the ocean, a lake, a river, or the desert—is best. If you don't have the time, interest, or resources for a long trip by yourself, try one of these solo minivacations. The benefits are countless: An opportunity to unwind, communicate with your deeper self, and recover a clarity of purpose are just a few.

If you can, coordinate your retreat with the changes of the seasons to celebrate nature rearranging herself. Solo retreats are wonderful at personal passage times as well. When you face a turning-point decision, an important birthday, or a significant ending or beginning in your life, a chance to slow down and be with just yourself can bring you a fresh perspective and vastly expanded creativity.

For cold-weather retreats, seek out a place with a fireplace. I suggest choosing a retreat destination that you can drive to. The solitary driving time is a perfect transition from your busy daily life. Select a scenic route, if possible, even if a back-road approach takes longer. Plan a relaxing drive where you feel free to stop for a picnic, some fruit, or a short stretch.

Once you arrive at your destination, do as little as possible. Keep activities low-keyed and introspective: journal writing, walking in the woods, reading inspirational books, lying in a hammock, spending time with the stars, watching the sun rise or set. Connect as much as possible with the silent pulse of nature—water, wind, wildlife. A completely *silent* solo retreat can be a powerful experience (I discovered this once when I had no choice because of laryngitis). If an extended period of silence doesn't appeal to you, at least consider reversing your usual mode. If you're ordinarily gregarious, keep to yourself. If you're shy, reach out and initiate conversations with those you encounter. In either case, resist the temptation to call friends. And let your family know you want to be called only in emergencies.

If the idea of a retreat seems impossible because of the constraints of time, money, or kids, be creative. Stay at an inn where you have kitchen facilities (or use the time for juice fasting) to save money. Ask a friend with a cottage on the lake if you can use it for a night or two. Exchange childcare with someone. If you budget for your retreats on a monthly basis, you'll be able to make them happen.

5. Learn from the School of Hard Knocks

Experience is a great teacher. Each time you allow your limits to be violated, learn what you can from the episode, to prevent similar problems in the future. For example, when you have a fight with someone, see what you can glean from the situation about your limit-setting patterns. A friend of mine told me about a quarrel she had with a new boyfriend, John. They had spent a terrific weekend together skiing. The next night— a Monday evening—he came over to her place after work to drop off her skis. One thing led to another, and they ended up walking to a neighborhood restaurant for dinner despite the fact that she really wanted to take care of personal chores (which she ordinarily would have handled over the weekend).

When they returned to her apartment, they watched a movie on television. At one point, John commented on how antsy she seemed. She became defensive, he got mad, and they parted in a huff.

In hindsight, she realized what had happened. After spending so much time with John, she needed time alone—or at least time to take care of her own needs. Had the relationship been an established one, she probably could have taken her "space" with him around—he could have watched the movie while she did her chores. In fact, this would have been ideal because she would have enjoyed the company while she worked. That was one of the reasons she hadn't said, "I need time alone tonight." A part of her wanted him to hang around—she just didn't want to have to entertain him or sit with him in front of the tube all night. When they talked things over a few days later, he assured her, "I would have been fine watching the movie alone while you did what you needed to. You should have just told me." Next time she will.

6. Talk Things Over with a Friend

Venting a problem to a friend is another way in which you can see a situation in a new light. A productive airing session frequently helps you unravel your reactions and consider all options. When you talk over a problem with someone, however, be sure the person is a good listener. Good listeners do not minimize or discount your feelings (*"Calm down—it's not that bad"*). Nor do they hand out cheap advice on what you should do (*"Tell him to go to hell!"*). Or respond with "me, too" stories that match or beat yours (*"You think you've got problems—wait till you hear about mine*"). Good listeners pay careful attention to what you say, then they feed it back to make sure they got it straight ("*It sounds like you felt caught in an awkward bind when he asked you that in front of his parents*").

A commonly used term for good listening is "active listening," a phrase coined by Thomas Gordan. Active listening creates a self-correcting feedback loop. If someone active-listened to you, it would work like this: You say something. The listener tries to grasp the gist of your message. He (or she) then checks it out with you to make sure he understood correctly. To do this, he paraphrases what he heard. You verify if he read you accurately ("*Exactly*") or clarify if he didn't ("*No, I didn't feel caught in a bind. I felt humiliated that he talked to me that way in front of others—especially his parents*").

When you air a problem in this way, you are given a chance to further define the nature of the situation that you're grappling with. You are also usually better able to understand your reactions to the problem and the options you have for straightening things out. Out in the open, problems become more manageable. And even when a problem continues to seem enormous, the mere process of being heard helps to subdue out-of-control emotions. Plus, when you talk out a problem, you frequently come up with ideas and options you would never have thought of on your own.

Although the process of active listening is a simple enough concept, it's not an easy skill to master. Consequently there aren't many people around who know how to serve as sounding boards. Most are too quick to hand out advice, change the subject, or switch to talking about their own problems. If no one you know seems able to active-listen to you when you need it, learn the skill yourself, then teach it to a friend. Read Thomas Gordan's *Parent Effectiveness Training* and *Parent Ef-*

fectiveness Training in Action.[1] Or better yet, take an evening course in communication skills at your local high school or college. Many include instruction in active listening.

During serious crises, of course, you may need more than a friend's ear to sort things out. When this is the case, consider professional counseling. Don't be shy about asking for references from friends and colleagues. Revealing your vulnerable state to a caring co-worker or relative not only deepens such relationships, it can bring you good leads as well. Thankfully, we're beyond the era when admitting you need therapy is socially taboo.

7. Conduct a Private Investigation

Pose a number of questions to yourself and view your problem from a variety of angles. One fresh insight about what's going on can make all the difference in the world. If there is a lot at stake (a dispute with the big boss, a serious upset with a close friend), you may want to write out a thorough assessment of the situation. The following questions may stimulate your thinking:

What specifically is bothering you about this situation?
What are you basing your reactions on?
Is the information you're using flimsy or substantial?
Do you need to find out more?
Are any of your assumptions questionable?

[1]Thomas Gordan, *Parent Effectiveness Training*, McKay Publishers, 1970. Thomas Gordan, *PET in Action*, Bantam, 1984.

What are you so angry about?

Are you feeling guilty and, if so, what about?

How might you be getting yourself unnecessarily worked up?

What are you afraid will happen?

How likely is it that what you fear will actually occur?

What could you do to minimize this risk or be prepared for it?

What do you want to have happen, and what can you do to help it happen?

How important is this anyway?

Will it matter to you a month from now? A year from now? How can you put this in proper perspective?

What are all your choices for dealing with this problem?

Which of these options make you feel alive? Which feel deadening?

If you follow your best instincts, what would you do?

How would an "ideal assertive you" handle such a situation?

What can you learn from all of this for the future?

8. Write a Letter

In general, putting things down on paper fosters greater self-awareness. Letters in particular can help you better comprehend a situation. Write a fiercely frank letter to the person you're upset with (just don't mail it!). Express *all* your feelings, no matter how irrational or extreme they seem. Get everything out of your system. Then look over what you've written and see if you can distinguish appropriate concerns from exaggerated ones. Reread the letter until you can find humor in the situation and chuckle at yourself for getting so riled up.

As you calm down, write a more "enlightened" letter—one that reflects your clearest thinking, most positive intentions, and highest self. Consider actually sending this letter, or use it as a written rehearsal for what you'll say in a face-to-face interaction.

Write a letter to *yourself* as well. Talk to yourself as a wise adviser and friend would. Or write separate letters to conflicting *parts* of yourself. Send one to the part of you that wants to speak up about a problem and another one to the side of you too scared to confront. Or write a letter *from* these parts, so that each gets a chance to have its say.[2]

FEAR FREQUENTLY BLOCKS HONESTY

Many emotions may be stirred up when there's a problem in a relationship, but feeling scared is clearly the primary one that holds us back from being truthful. Unfortunately, in some situations, a certain level of apprehension may not be entirely inappropriate. Telling the truth *can* entail risk. Turning a friend down can start a fight. Bringing something that's bothering you out into the open can lead to tension, anger, tears, or withdrawal. Asking for what you want can bring disappointment, disapproval, or a door slammed in your face. Depending on the circumstances, by being honest you could even get fired, destroy a friendship, or end up in divorce court.

----

[2]These and a few of the other diary techniques I'll be mentioning are inspired from ideas in Tristine Rainier's excellent guide to journal writing, *The New Diary*, J. P. Tarcher Press, 1978.

As if all that's not bad enough, you may be fearful for less catastrophic reasons as well. Perhaps you're afraid you'll bother others if you make a special request. Maybe you're worried you'll hurt someone's feelings by speaking the truth. Ironically, though, when you look closely at such other-directed concerns, more often than not you find self-interest in disguise. They usually have as much to do with wanting to spare *yourself* the misery of having to deal with someone's hurt or angry feelings as they do with offending others.

When telling the truth seems too scary, remember that risk is always two-sided—with every risk of loss, you risk gain. While telling the truth may create temporary tension in a relationship, honesty from the heart can just as easily bring about a new level of intimacy and harmony. While being frank might hurt someone's feelings, done diplomatically it can clear the air and straighten out misunderstandings. And while letting others know what you want might lead to disappointment and despair, it also can lead you to your heart's desire.

Remember Your Rights

Staying aware of your rights in a given situation is one good way to reduce both ahead-of-time jitters and after-the-fact guilt. A number of years ago at a Hyatt Regency tea dance (an old-fashioned ballroom dance), I had an experience that brought home to me how this works. A man I didn't know asked me to slow dance. It was obvious from the start that he wanted to dance closer to me than I wanted to dance to him. He was after a cheek-to-cheek, feel-your-partner's-heartbeat kind of experience. I was not. For the first few minutes of the dance, we engaged in a noiseless struggle. I stiffened up and away from his grasp; he strong-armed me in. Suddenly he stopped dancing, stepped back, and snarled, "I know your type! You're one of those women who has to control everything." With that, he stomped off the dance floor. Shocked, I found my way out of the crowd and sat on the sidelines, where I could digest what had happened. A number of things ran through my mind.

First of all, I realized that his assessment of me had some truth to it. To a certain extent, I *was* trying to be controlling. While I had no interest in controlling everything, as he claimed, I *was* trying to control how closely we danced together—and I had a perfect right to do so. Had I reminded myself of this right during our dance, I would have had the courage to be more direct about my needs. Instead of a silent tug-of-war, I could have said, "Excuse me, I'm not comfortable dancing this closely."

Remembering my rights *after* the incident was still a help. For one thing, it made me feel better about my attempt to handle the situation, albeit unsuccessful. Instead of sitting there worried about whether or not I was a controlling woman, I felt assured that I had had a right to set limits, whether he liked it or not.

Of course, I wasn't the only one who had rights in this scenario. My dance partner, obnoxious as he was, had rights as well. He had a right to want to dance lovey-dovey. He also had a right to be unhappy about what happened. But he did not have the right to force himself on me against my will. Nor did he have the right to treat me abusively (which I felt he did).

You always have a right to your own opinions, values, feelings, priorities, and, within certain legal and ethical limits, actions. So does everyone else. Remembering what rights you and others have helps you evaluate options. A roommate has a right to be sloppy if she wants. You have a right to find a new roommate if the mess she creates bothers you enough. A friend has a right to ask for a favor even if it's a totally unreasonable request. You have a right to turn him down. Your husband has a right to be emotionally closed. You have a right to get a divorce if you find his lack of openness unacceptable.

Remember Your Responsibilities As Well

In addition to having rights in any given situation, you also have responsibilities. Reminding yourself of your own accountability for straightening out conflicts can motivate you to speak up when you would otherwise stay silent. The meek are destined to put up with a lot. *You* are destined to put up with a lot if you say nothing about problems that crop up in your life. You are responsible for teaching others how you want to be treated. You are responsible for letting others know what's acceptable and not acceptable to you. If you suffer without a peep, don't blame others if problems continue (or reoccur at a later date).

You also have a responsibility to *act* responsibly if and when you do speak up about a problem. Acting responsibly means you speak your mind in a nonabusive fashion. You don't have a right to blast others with anger, persecute them with revenge, or respond in cruel or underhanded ways.

The tricky part about responsibility is that what is deemed responsible is strictly a matter of opinion. It's relative not only to the individual evaluating a situation but to the specifics surrounding the situation. While breaking a promise and leaving a friend in the lurch would be considered irresponsible by most, if you have a compelling reason for canceling out (like a death in the family), your action suddenly becomes completely acceptable.

Aside from such relativity issues, there are, of course, accepted norms regarding responsibility. Seeking revenge, embarrassing someone in front of others (when you could have handled an interaction in private), turning someone down on a life-and-death request because it's a minor inconvenience— all of these would be seen by most as clearly irresponsible actions.

When you act in a responsible fashion, it becomes easier to speak up without guilt. You know you're doing your best to be fair and decent and, as a consequence, you can feel more comfortable being frank. While this doesn't mean others will be any happier with what you do, you'll at least have a clean conscience about your own behavior.

There May Be Payoffs for Acting like a Wimp (or a Bully)

There's one additional consideration to be aware of as you look at your habits regarding limit setting. Be alert to those times when you end up *rewarded* for selflessness or selfishness, for such reinforcement can hold you in old patterns and block your intentions to change.

There are a number of social rewards for nonassertion. Backing down (*"I think I'll keep quiet and avoid trouble"*) can make you feel protected. It's a way to avoid having to deal with unpleasant responses that your honesty might provoke. Sure, your stomach may stay in a knot, but at least you don't have to endure someone's anger, tears, or withdrawal. Staying silent can also earn you a reputation for being polite and easygoing.

Blowing your lid can have payoffs as well. It can make you feel powerful ("*I showed him!*") and reduce internal pressure by allowing you to release steam. A temper tantrum can also spare you the experience of more vulnerable emotions of hurt, embarrassment, disappointment, and sadness. What's more, by strong-arming others, you may end up getting your way—which can be the biggest reinforcement of all.

Look at Long-Term Effects

Ultimately the price for acting like a wimp or a bully is far greater than any payoff—in the end, you lose more than you gain. While you may feel temporary satisfaction by exploding or backing down, eventually you sacrifice self-respect, damage relationships, suffer physical tension, and experience mental turmoil.

When tempted to seek the safety of retreat, consider the long term cost of such self-protection. Is it really the best bargain in the long run? When you're at the brink of blowing up or about to force others to do it your way, ask yourself what the implications will be for your bully behavior. It is possible you'll destroy the very thing you're after—that even if you win the battle you'll lose the war? Would honesty (expressed in a responsible fashion, of course) be the better bet?

* * *

Stereotypes regarding women and excess are not always fair, but there's some truth to them when it comes to setting limits. Many of us do go to extremes when it's time for honesty. We tend to speak up too little, too late, or too tentatively. Or we do it too much, too soon, or too forcefully.

Two major causes for such excesses are lack of awareness and lack of courage. Appreciating your own patterns is a key step in changing self-defeating habits. Staying aware of personal needs, desires, and emotional responses as they change from moment to moment is equally important. With increased awareness, you'll be ready to carry out the SoftPower solutions we're about to explore and discover that, using a SoftPower approach, the truth not only sets you free, it deepens and enhances your relationships as well.

The first of these strategies involves taking charge of your mental home. As you'll soon see, with SoftPower mental housekeeping, you can stay calm and clearheaded even when the going gets rough. You can feel confident and optimistic even after setbacks and defeats. You can also prevent many needless misunderstandings and conflicts from occurring in the first place, which will spare you considerable unnecessary misery and grief. Interested? Good. Let's get right into it then and take a close look at how you can clean up your mental act.

3

MENTAL HOUSEKEEPING
Keeping Your Mental Home in Good Shape

When you look at the world all you see is your mind. Philosophies through the ages have affirmed—and Einstein's physics has more recently confirmed—that your view of reality is constantly being fashioned by your mind. Your mental state operates as an ever-changing set of filters that perpetually colors, shapes, and (at times) dramatically warps your sense of what's real. In addition to determining your overall experience of life, this mental filtering system influences virtually all of your limit-setting behavior: your perceptions of problem situations, whether or not you speak up when there is a problem, what you say if you do speak up, and *how* you say what you say. Because of this direct, cause-effect correlation between what happens in your mind and how you view and deal with interpersonal problems, we are going to continue our exploration of power and honesty with an exploration of the mind. We will examine not only the workings of the mind but how you can develop a Soft-Power frame of mind. Such a mental framework will serve you in a number of ways. Among other benefits, you'll be able to recognize and eliminate faulty mental filters (irrational thoughts, negative beliefs, and unnecessarily restrictive thinking) that distort reality and have you seeing problems where none exist, misunderstanding (or overlooking) those that do exist, and magnifying petty concerns into exaggerated proportions.

This mental cleanup will in turn significantly affect your limit-setting behavior. If you believe, for example, that people are inherently bad, you'll accuse others of malice even when they're innocent. On the other hand, if you believe most individuals are basically decent, you'll allow for the benefit of the doubt and find out more before jumping to the conclusion that someone was up to no good. If you're convinced that you are unworthy and deserve punishment, you'll accept verbal abuse as something you had coming to you. If, however, you appreciate your own inherent loveability you'll refuse to tolerate abuse in a relationship. Instead you'll stand up for yourself and your rights.

You are either captive or captain of your mind—take your pick. As captive of your mind, your thinking runs wild on you. It can tie you up in knots. It can scare you stiff. It can enrage you and make your blood boil. As captain of your mind you manage your thinking, monitoring it for errors and reining it in when it takes you off the deep end. With a well-managed mental home, your thinking calms you down instead of riling you up, encourages you when the odds look grim, and reminds you of your best when you're feeling at your worst. You alone decide if unruly thoughts lead you to mediocrity and despair or if, positively directed, they lead you to excellence and brave acts.

The SoftPower mental housekeeping that we're going to

look at in this chapter is more than simplistic positive thinking. Slapping a happy face on rude reality to rid yourself of self-defeating beliefs is a start in the right direction, but by itself it's incomplete—like putting on clean clothes when what you really need is a shower. For lasting results, you need to go beyond surface tidying of your mind to deeply ingrained mental habits. You must correct underlying faulty-thinking patterns and alter self-sabotaging attitudes if lasting change is to occur.

DON'T CONFUSE YOUR THINKING WITH "THE TRUTH"

There are many hurdles you encounter when you enter the realm of the mind, but one of the biggest is confusion between your individual point of view and the truth. For this reason, one of your first housekeeping tasks is cultivating an appreciation for how frequently any mind—your own included—makes mistakes. Once you do this, your own thoughts and beliefs (and everyone else's as well) will seem less sacred.

In reality, your thinking is occasionally accurate, sometimes grossly inaccurate, and—more often than not—somewhere in between. A certain level of suspicion toward what happens inside your mind is, therefore, warranted. Such skepticism helps you break the habit of unilaterally accepting all of your mental output as accurate (*"She doesn't like me. I know it!"*). Instead, you play devil's advocate (*"But, then again, maybe I'm misunderstanding what's behind this. Perhaps she's just shy"*). This keeps you open-minded and fosters a flexible, creative point of view.

Staying clearheaded, however, involves more than mere recognition of faulty thinking. It also means that even when you are convinced that your beliefs coincide with what is true, you know that there are many versions of "the truth." You know truth is strictly a matter of opinion. If you want proof that this is so, listen to a dozen eyewitnesses of an accident give descriptions of what they saw. Or read, side by side, irate and glowing letters to the editor in reaction to the same magazine article. Or stand on a street corner and take a survey on the best way to thread the toilet paper. Everyone's got an opinion, and everyone thinks his or her opinions, priorities, and perceptions are right.

In addition to maintaining a distinction between your thinking and the truth, a SoftPower frame of mind recognizes that you and your point of view are separate from one another as well. If you overidentify with your thinking, you'll be convinced your mind *thinks you*—which means you are indeed captive, with little or no choice about what happens to you mentally. In fact, *you* think your mind. While you may never escape the effects of your mental filters, the filters themselves are choosable and changeable. At all times, under all circumstances, you can elect to change your mind and clean up your mental act. You are *not* what you think.

It's time to take charge of your thinking. To do this, you need to understand the two primary ways in which your mind interferes with limit setting. For simplicity's sake, we're going to explore each of these interferences—1) misunderstandings, and 2) closed-mindedness—on their own, even though in reality they overlap. Misunderstandings can be the result of closed-mindedness, and closed-mindedness can be a function of misunderstanding.

UNDERSTANDING MISUNDERSTANDINGS AND LEARNING TO THINK STRAIGHT

Any mind is an imperfect operation. Like a computer, it occasionally bombs. While the sophistication and complexity of the mind puts the most dazzling computer to shame, the comparison to a computer is otherwise not a bad one. The most technologically advanced computer depends on bug-free software programming to work properly. Garbage in, garbage out. If there's a "bug" in the program, the biggest and best machine will crash and spit out gobbledygook. Your mind is no different. It, too, is "programmed." It, too, stores and manages information. And like a computer, when there's a bug in the program, the brightest, healthiest, best-informed mind in the world can become a flawed operating system and fill itself with gobbledygook.

We all suffer from buggy mental software. But, once you discover where the bugs lie, it becomes possible to straighten things out so that your thinking serves and supports you instead of leading you astray. We'll be looking at some of the most common mental bugs that mess up our minds shortly.

The Mind Is Basically a Guessing Machine

The mind sees its job as figuring things out. While many views of thinking refer to it as a logical, sequential, and orderly affair, it isn't quite that simple. To do its job, your mind brings in information through various perceptual channels, mixes it with a variety of internal data, and processes everything cognitively. The resulting point of view depends on a mix of factors from past, present, and future—prior experiences, memories, and beliefs, current perceptions, expectations, emotions, circumstances, future aspirations, intentions, and goals. All this (and more) seasons the complex workings of your mind.

In its ongoing effort to understand what's going on, your mind churns out endless guesses about what things mean. You make up your mind with such conjectures a thousand times daily. These assumptions have an extraordinary amount of influence on your life, governing virtually all of your behavior. At times, they propel you to act: *"I assumed you wanted me to." "I thought I was supposed to." "I assumed it would be all right." "I thought I could." "I assumed you'd want to know."* At other times, they hold you back from action: *"I assumed you didn't want me to." "I thought I wasn't supposed to." "I didn't think I could." "I didn't think you wanted to know."*

A well-known creativity puzzle demonstrates the restrictive aspect of assumptions. The task of the puzzle is to connect nine dots that are placed in a three-dot by three-dot square configuration on a piece of paper (Figure A). To do this, you are allowed to use only four straight lines and are not allowed to retrace any line or lift your pen or pencil from the paper:

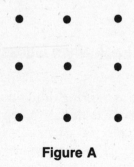

Figure A

Most people who attempt the problem make an immediate (and unconscious) assumption that the four connecting lines have to be confined to the boundaries of the dots. Working within this mental constraint, they fail to solve the problem (Figure B):

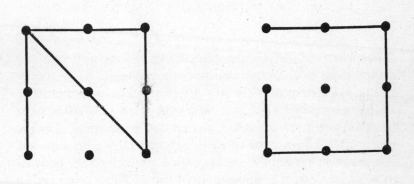

Figure B

To find a successful solution, you must first recognize that you are free to extend the lines beyond the dots. In other words, you must challenge the unspoken assumption that restricts you to the outline of the dots. With extended lines, a solution becomes possible (Figure C):

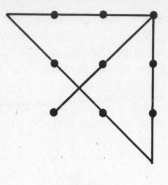

Figure C

The motto of the puzzle—"Break out of your nine dots"— is a reminder to challenge assumptions, especially when you're feeling stuck or powerless. It's a lesson relevant not only in creativity workshops but in everyday life. To follow the advice, however, you first need to know what you're assuming. Awareness is a prerequisite for conscious change. If you're unaware that you're assuming you must confine yourself to the boundaries of the dots, it's unlikely you'll think, "Wait a minute— I can make the lines as long as I want."

Unfortunately, we are unconscious of many (if not most) of the assumptions we make. For every "out in the open" assumption created, we hold dozens of others with little or no awareness. When these unverified, unchallenged "down-under" assumptions are inaccurate, needlessly limiting, or misleading (as many of them are), they can make for a lot of trouble. In fact, some of them are downright dangerous. They lead to conflicts, crossed wires, disappointments, resentments, and occasionally even tragedies. You assume your boss won't mind if you leave early on Friday because you worked late three nights last week. You assume it's okay to borrow your roommate's car without asking because she didn't mind the last time you needed it. You assume the baby-sitter knows what to do in a fire because "doesn't everyone?" As the old saying goes, to assume makes an "ass" out of "u" and "me."

Given the frequency and risks of mistaken assumptions, it's easy to see why a central goal of SoftPower mental housekeeping is the reduction of misunderstandings. To accomplish this, you need to be perpetually on the watch for faulty assumptions. Your own misunderstandings are only half the problem. Erroneous assumptions that others make can be equally problematic. Consequently, as we look at the various forces behind mental mistakes, we'll consider not only how your own mind makes bad guesses but how you may be setting up the likelihood of someone else misunderstanding *you*.

It's easy to be confused by nonverbals. A great deal of communication takes place without words—acceptance is expressed with a nod, gratitude with a gift, anger with a pout, hurt with silence, desire for revenge with a no-show, eagerness to help with money. Sometimes such indirect communication does the job, but it just as often leads to misunderstanding and conflict. The reason is simple. Nonverbals are highly ambiguous. Tears can mean grief, anger, or happiness. Or they can mean a cinder in your eye. Folded arms can mean someone's closed to what you're saying, or they can mean a person's feeling chilly. So while misinterpretations are possible under the best of circumstances, they dramatically increase whenever your mind tries to figure a situation out via nonverbals.

Mixed messages are a good example of how nonverbals can be confusing. A typical mixed message involves someone saying one thing and doing another. For example, your boss insists she's interested in what you're saying, but she keeps glancing at the clock every few minutes as you talk. Or you swear you don't mind when a friend cancels out on a date, but your voice sounds hurt and angry. Like someone shouting, "I'm not mad!" or a welcome mat placed next to a "Pit Bull On Guard" sign, mixed messages can be both baffling and maddening. Without more information, it's hard to know what's up.

Don't be so sure of yourself. Whenever you deal with ambiguous situations, make it a rule of thumb to remind yourself that you don't know for sure. Keep assumptions tentative and hypothetical until you find out more. Make up your mind after you get additional information (and be ready to change your mind as new data rolls in).

One way to evaluate the accuracy of your thinking is to trace backward to what led to your assumptions. Ask yourself, *"What makes me think this?"* Then determine if your thinking is based on flimsy, questionable nonverbals or on clear-cut, substantial evidence. If you find that you've concluded someone is bored with what you're saying solely on the basis of a few glances at the clock, question your deduction. What else could this behavior mean? Perhaps the person has an appointment to keep or a plane to catch. Maybe they need to make a phone call at a certain time. Ask pointed questions if you need to know more. *"I notice you're watching the time. Is this a bad time for us to talk?"* And when your confusion is a function of a mixed message, bring the discrepancy out into the open: *"You said you don't mind changing our plans but you sound upset about this. Are you?" "I'm confused—you promised to do this but the job is still not done." "If you're not mad, why are you yelling?"*

Don't trust the grapevine. Another policy that helps you prevent misunderstandings is maintaining a healthy skepticism of secondhand information. Remember the "telephone game" we played as children, in which one person whispered a message to a second person, who passed it on to a third, and so forth? Remember what a crack-up it was when the last person in the line stated out loud what she had heard? Somehow, in the transmission, the gist of the message always became convoluted beyond recognition. Hearsay, rumors, and reports of someone else's experience are no more reliable or trustworthy than the end product of the telephone game. When accuracy is imperative (and it's feasible to do so), go to the first source and experience it for yourself. The following story from General Patton's war memories illustrates:

> I visited the troops near Coutances on the twenty-ninth and found an armored division sitting on a road, while its Headquarters, secreted behind an old church, was deeply engrossed in the study of maps. I asked why they had not crossed the Sienne. They told me they were making a study of it at the moment, but could not find a place where it could be forded. I asked what effort they had made to find such a place and was informed they were studying the map to that end.
>
> I then told them I had just waded across it, that it was not over two feet deep, and that the only defense I knew about was one machine gun which had fired very inaccurately at me. I repeated the Japanese proverb, "One look is worth one hundred reports," and asked them why in hell they had not gone down to the river personally. They learned the lesson and from then on were a very great division.[1]

[1] Ken Keyes, *Taming Your Mind*, Living Love Publications, Coos Bay, OR, 97420.

With important matters, go directly to the river and find
things out for yourself (*"I heard you're angry with me over what
I said at the meeting. I wanted to find out if that's true"*). Operate
like a court of law and refuse to accept gossip and scuttlebutt
as proof of anything.

What are you expecting? Holding expectations—assumptions about what will happen next—is another natural, normal
operation of the mind that is a hazard area for misunderstandings. The first step necessary for better management of expectations is to ask yourself whether expectations are necessary in
a given situation and, if they are, what function they will serve.
Under some conditions, expectations will be essential and extremely useful. This can be the case whenever you are trying to
coordinate multiple schedules. Because members of a team need
to know what to expect from each other before intelligent planning can be done, clear-cut, out-loud expectations make a lot of
sense. In fact, as a rule, whenever the needs and desires of more
than one person are involved, formalized expectations (such as
agreements, contracts, and plans) can help everything run more
smoothly.

On other occasions, expectations may not be all that critical.
They're a "nice to have," not a necessity. For example, when
you start a romance, while it's reassuring to know how often
you can expect to hear from your new beau, you can function
just fine without this information.

And, of course, there are even times when knowing what's
going to happen will ruin everything. These are occasions
when you want to be surprised. Many of life's joys and ad-
ventures are a thrill primarily because they were not antici-
pated.

Expectations become fertile ground for misunderstandings
when, relative to a situation, they are naive, unclear, unspoken,

unnecessarily negative, or inflexible. Then they can lead to disappointment, fear, confusion, or conflict. If you expect, for example, the same cooperation from a three-year-old that you would receive from an adult, you're headed for sorry disillusionment. Or if you convince yourself you'll be receiving an engagement ring for Christmas from your boyfriend and he shows up instead with a bottle of perfume, your holiday could be ruined.

In situations where misunderstood or conflicting expectations could spell trouble, pay especially close attention to who's expecting what from whom. Here are some useful questions to ask yourself:

"What am I expecting in this situation?"
"Are my expectations clear enough and realistic enough given the circumstances?"
"How attached am I to my expectations?"
"Am I feeling loose enough about my expectations to accommodate surprises?"
"Have I been clear enough with others regarding what I'm expecting?"
"Which of my expectations are better kept private?"
"If I want to ensure accurate expectations, what do I need to find out?"

When precise expectations are called for, ask for specifics. If you have a deadline to meet, find out exactly what you can expect regarding delivery from your vendors ("*Can I count on receiving these by Wednesday noon?*" "*Is it safe for me to assume you'll be able to meet the Friday deadline if I don't hear from you otherwise?*"). If you're cooking a Julia Child dinner for friends, inquire about when everyone's planning on arriving and request they call you ahead of time if they're going to be late.

Don't assume someone will know the soufflé will be ruined if he shows up at 7:20 instead of at 7:00. If you're evaluating a job offer, ask directly what authority, resources, and responsibilities you'll have if you accept the position. You have a right to know what you're getting into. If a prospective employer is turned off by your questions, you're better off knowing that ahead of time, too.

Some situations, of course, demand more precision than others. The trick is to know which are which. When you're going to pick up a friend at the airport, you need to be exact about where and when the rendezvous will take place, but the degree of specificity needed will vary depending on the situation. "I'll pick you up outside the terminal" may be adequate in Timbuktu but not in San Francisco. In the latter case, you'd better specify lower level, Terminal One, by the United Three sign, outside the doors, inside in bad weather, half an hour after landing time, etc. Otherwise your friend could end up freezing her tail off in howling wind and rain upstairs outside Terminal Two while you search futilely for her in bumper-to-bumper traffic downstairs at Terminal One. Not a great way to start a visit—you with a splitting headache and her dripping wet and miserable.

In most cases, even ambiguous clarity ("*I don't know for sure when I'll be arriving.*" "*We're not sure yet what the job will entail because the position is brand-new*") is useful. At least then you know what you don't know, which enables you to better estimate what range of contingencies to plan for.

Beware of "black hole" thinking. Occasionally your mind becomes so absorbed by what's wrong (or could go wrong) that it loses sight of the whole. Such a mental distortion can plummet you into misery, rage, or despair. Preoccupation with negatives is especially common after an episode of criticism, rejection, or failure. Even if you hear dozens of compliments and only a handful of criticisms, it's possible to walk away from an interaction with a mind consumed by just the bad news. You can obsess over the negative feedback for days despite the fact that it was, in reality, a small fraction of the whole.

There are other less obvious ways in which your mind can exaggerate the negative side of life. Sometimes it discounts the positive (*"He didn't mean that compliment. He just said it to make me feel better"*). At other times it somersaults a neutral into a negative: The absence of a compliment becomes an insult; the absence of feedback becomes disapproval; the absence of a phone call becomes a rejection.

To bail yourself out of mental black holes, you need to restore the bigger picture by reminding your mind of the rest of reality. The old-fashioned advice to count your blessings still has value. Bringing positive aspects of your life to the foreground of your consciousness helps you put negatives into proper perspective. A personal example illustrates:

During the first few years of my career as a speaker, I was extremely sensitive to the slightest hint of professional criticism. I would become terribly upset by even one isolated negative evaluation in a stack of hundreds of wildly enthusiastic ones. I remember in particular my reaction after a seminar in Chicago. As I read through some 400 evaluations, I came across three intensely hostile ones. They were so negative I felt I had been slapped in the face. After handing the pile of forms back to the program manager, I left the hotel and proceeded to the airport to catch a plane to the next city on my tour. All that evening, I was in a foul mood—I felt as if the day had gone terribly and I had failed miserably. Then I realized what was happening. I was letting those three evaluations out of 400 "pollute" me. They were ruining my entire evening even though they were only 3/400 of the whole!

I made a decision that night to carry with me on future travels a collection of "warm fuzzy" evaluations received over the years. For a long time I did just that and, whenever I found myself overreacting to isolated criticism, I hauled the pile out and stuck my nose in them. They reminded my mind of what else was real. In every instance, it worked like a charm. In a matter of minutes, I was able to restore a healthier, more realistic sense of perspective.

IRRATIONAL THINKING—HOW MUCH ARE YOU OVERREACTING?

There is one kind of thinking that causes so much ado about nothing and breeds so many misunderstandings that it deserves special attention. It is usually referred to as irrational thinking. In general, irrational thinking distorts reality and exaggerates the importance of events. It does this through a variety of maneuvers, including the maintenance of underlying false beliefs and viewing events from a "poor me," victim perspective. At other times irrational thinking involves rationalizing, catastrophizing, personalizing, always-never thinking, and must-have thinking. Let's look more closely at each of these irrational mental tendencies. Once you're familiar with them you'll be better able to straighten out such thinking before it wreaks too much damage.

Underlying Irrational Beliefs: Do Some of Your Beliefs Make No Sense?

All thinking that occurs on the surface of your mind is influenced by a vast network of underlying, unconscious beliefs. While you are usually aware of a good deal of your top-level thoughts, you may be oblivious to the under-the-surface beliefs that give rise to your thinking. When these unconscious beliefs are false or unreasonable, they get you in trouble by leading to faulty, misleading assumptions and conclusions.

Following are a few examples of some irrational beliefs that are relevant to setting limits. Under each is a description of how the belief might affect your thinking, emotions, and behavior.

"If things don't go my way, it's just terrible and I can't stand it." When you're convinced that not getting your way is intolerable, you'll feel despair or rage whenever things don't turn out the way you want them to. If you sink into depression, you become immobilized. If you work yourself into a frenzy, you end up stubbornly battling for what you want.

"Emotions are caused by circumstances and are, therefore, uncontrollable." If you believe feelings happen "to" you as a result of externals beyond your control, it becomes easy to excuse yourself for either holding back from honesty (*"I can't help it—I'm too scared to say anything"*) or exploding (*"I can't help it—I'm so angry!"*).

"People who harm me or do unfair things should be punished." When you believe thoughtless, incompetent, or cruel people

deserve to be punished, you'll feel justified setting limits abusively (*"Why should I be nice? They don't deserve it." "Of course
I was rude to her. She asked for it"*).

"When others pressure me, I always end up giving in." If you're
afraid that you won't be able to stand your ground in the face
of opposition, you may surrender from the start to save yourself an argument (*"Fine, we'll do it your way"*). If you're a more
aggressive sort, you'll stubbornly fight for your position or
refuse to hear the other side (*"I don't want to talk about it—
I've made up my mind!"*).

To uncover the underlying faulty beliefs that affect your
response to a problem, stay aware of your thinking as it occurs
in terms of a specific situation. When you notice your mind
going off the deep end (*"I've reached my limit!" "This is the last
straw!"*), trace back to root beliefs behind the thinking (*"If
things don't go my way, it's just terrible and I can't stand it"*).
Then switch to a more reasonable mental track by talking to
yourself differently (*"I don't like this and I can handle it"*). If
your mind continues to run wild despite attempts to rein it
in, you can at least discount such thinking. You don't have to
take everything your mind tells you so seriously.

Sometimes thinking happens so fast you have little or no
awareness of what has transpired until after the fact. But even
after the fact, when you suspect irrational thinking is at work,
review your thought process retroactively. That way you can
use the experience to prevent more of the same kind of problem
thinking in the future.

As you evaluate thoughts and beliefs, you may find that
some of your thinking seems so bizarre or neurotic that you're
embarrassed or horrified by it. There's no need to be ashamed
of what happens in your mind. Better to get it all out in the

open—if not to others, than at least to yourself. When held private and unexamined, irrational thoughts have enormous power, but, in the light of awareness, your worst fantasies and fears can be miraculously diminished in their impact. Trouble-making thinking can be seen for what it is, challenged for what it falsely assumes, and transformed at will into thoughts of courage and confidence. Maybe you'll even be able to laugh at the dramas your mind creates. Just don't act on such thoughts. Cool out before doing or saying things you could later regret.

Certain American Indian tribes had a ritual called the Eater of Impurities, which promoted the kind of mental self-acceptance I'm describing. The tribe's high holy person would sit with everyone in the tribe, one by one. He would ask them to describe all the despicable inner experiences they could recall, including thoughts, feelings, and fantasies they considered totally unacceptable or abnormal. The result was an amazing healing and purification process. When the previously inadmissible was shared in an atmosphere of trust, compassion, and good humor, it became a bridge for love and understanding.

Victim-Tripping: Are You Feeling Sorry for Yourself?

Many irrational beliefs confuse responsibility with blame and thereby act as demoralizing influences. Pointing the finger of fault at externals perpetuates feelings of helplessness and hopelessness:

"I didn't do this. I didn't want this."
"I'm not responsible for this."

"It's out of my control."
"You did it to me."
"He did it to me."
"My parents did it to me."
"The system did it to me."

A victim perspective and the feelings of impotence that it engenders render limit-setting behavior either limp or desperate. Instead of communicating from a healthy stance of self-responsible power, you become "poor me" or "enraged me" being "done to."

The minute you point the finger of blame at others and whine, *"I'm not responsible for this,"* you give away your power. In reality, even when others seem to hold all the cards and situations appear completely outside your control, you are never completely stuck. You are the one who decides what attitude you hold toward what is happening to you and what actions you'll take in response. This means you always have choice, no matter what the circumstances.

From a SoftPower point of view, responsibility is a function of choice, not blame. Dropping a victim perspective and claiming responsibility for your life reflects a recognition that, throughout your life, your are perpetually making choices. You know that how your life turns out is to a large degree a reflection of all the choices you make. There is a direct cause-effect relationship between the choices you make and the results you reap. Therefore, if you don't like what is happening to you, you can do something about it. You can make different choices today and get different results tomorrow.

Under ordinary circumstances, when a situation is not to your liking, you have a number of options to choose from. If you're in a rotten marriage, you decide whether or not to stay in it. If you leave, you decide whether you build a new life for yourself with optimistic good cheer or whether you spend your days crying in your beer. When others ask you for favors, you decide whether to say yes or no. When you wake up in the morning, you decide whether to drive to work or take the bus. And while you may not choose to be rear-ended at a red light, should an accident occur you choose how you'll respond mentally, emotionally, and behaviorally—which means you significantly influence what happens to you as a result of the accident.

Rationalizing: Are You Talking Yourself Out of Being Assertive?

A third common way in which irrational thinking can undermine your power is via rationalizations that convince you a situation doesn't matter when, in fact, it does (*"It's not that important if I have an orgasm. I don't want to make a big deal over it." "So what if he's stood me up once or twice? It's not worth an argument"*). If you are a nonassertive sort, you may need to be especially careful about this bad habit. Those who are timid about confrontation often talk themselves out of assertion with "It's not worth it" arguments or overly rigid prerequisites for action (*"I'll do something about this when he's in a better mood." "I'll handle this when I don't have my period." "I'll wait until the kids are in college and then I'll get a divorce"*).

Of course, some issues *are* better dropped than dealt with. Not every problem is worth a confrontation and occasionally nonaction is the smartest choice for reasons of strategy or safety. If a suspicious-looking stranger on the street offends you, you may wisely decide to ignore the behavior instead of challenging him directly.

But under ordinary conditions, doing nothing is usually a cop-out. So be careful not to let your mind talk you into being a wimp. As I said in Chapter One, the price for staying silent when the truth should be told can be a steep one:

Problems tend to repeat themselves.
Your rarely get what you want.
You resort to manipulation to get what you want.
Unspoken tension damages your relationships.
You spread yourself too thin and neglect top priorities.
You suffer wear and tear physically.

Catastrophizing: Are You Getting All Worked Up over Nothing?

Another way irrational thinking can handicap you is by blowing problems out of proportion. Instead of downplaying what's occurring with "It's not important" rationalizations, your mind exaggerates the significance of a situation, turning molehills into mountains and mountains into Mt. Everest. These mental overreactions can lead you to meekness (*"I don't dare!"*) or feistiness (*"How dare he!"*). In either case, your thinking functions like a runaway train that takes you over the edge. (*"If I complain to my boss I could lose my job! If I lose my job, I'll never find another one! If I confront him, I'll end up a bag lady!"*).

Typically, we're most prone to catastrophizing when we're already out of sorts about other matters. In an off-balance state, a minor irritant that would be overlooked at other times can be the last straw. On a really bad day, we can have a nervous breakdown over a broken nail or scream like a wild banshee over a glass of spilt milk.

Ranting and raving (*"I've had it! He doesn't give a damn about me—this is the last straw!"*) may make you feel better temporarily because it releases tension, but in the long run it works against you. Catastrophizing produces a physical state of crisis alert that pumps your adrenalin and elevates your blood pressure. It also narrows your thinking to either-or, fight-flight options. In a steadier mental state (*"I'll do what I can to change this. If I'm unsuccessful, I'll consider what choices I have at that point"*), you'll be far more able to solve problems creatively than you would be in an "all worked up" one. Here are examples of affirmations (present-tense, positively phrased statements) designed to calm down your mind:

"I can handle whatever happens."
"I have the courage and confidence to deal with this."
"I can clear up this situation with poise and composure."
"I have a right to say no even if she doesn't like it."
"I can disagree with him without starting a fight."
"I'm able to stay calm even if she loses her temper."

When your thinking is making a situation worse than it need be, use such affirmations to help yourself reframe the problem and see it in a new light. No matter how upsetting something seems at first glance, you can choose to look at it differently. Remember that all of your thoughts, conclusions, expectations, judgments, and opinions are subject to change. You can think anything you choose. If a colleague at work blames you for something you didn't do, you can take it as a personal character assassination and become outraged. Or you can see it as a misunderstanding of some sort and stay calm and professional about the charge. If your spouse calls you a liar in front of friends, you can choose to let the incident ruin the whole evening or you can decide to put it on a mental back burner and deal with it in private the next day. This is one of the main advantages of a relative universe: We're free to change our perspective whenever we want. If one frame of reference toward a problem is unnecessarily upsetting, we can pick and choose from others that are less so. We can convert *"This is terrible, I can't stand it!"* into *"This is bearable and I'll make the best of it."* Reframing situations in this way doesn't mean denying unpleasant facts or suppressing appropriate emotions. It simply means putting the facts (whatever they may be) into the most reasonable light possible and finding the brightest outlook feasible for a given set of circumstances.

Personalizing: Do You Believe the World Revolves Around You?

The tendency to overpersonalize events reflects both an egotistical and an irrational frame of mind, for it presumes that you're the center of the universe and everything happening around you is a function *of* you. A friend doesn't show up for a date—you see it as a rejection. Someone's late picking you up—you take it as proof that the person doesn't respect you.

More often than not, what we think is personal has nothing to do with us. You find out the next day that the friend who stood you up had to leave town because her dad had a heart attack. You learn that the person who was late was tied up by an accident on the freeway. Once while Christmas shopping I encountered a gift-wrap clerk who was clearly out of sorts. She was muttering under her breath and banging the packages around as she worked. I was sure she was mad at me because I had made a special request regarding the wrapping. But, when I asked her if this was the case, she looked up startled and exclaimed, "*No, no, I'm sorry. I've just having a real bad day. It has nothing to do with you.*" She proceeded to launch into a litany of miseries—her car had broken down, her ex-husband had lapsed on the child support, her request for time off after Christmas had been denied. And that was just the beginning.

To make matters worse, by taking things personally you risk not only one misunderstanding but a chain of them. For example, had I privately continued to take the clerk's behavior personally, I would no doubt have reacted in kind, with annoyance and impatience. This in turn would have convinced her that I was yet another demanding customer, something she certainly didn't need. Then this, of course, would have only made her angrier, which would have increased *my* annoyance, etc. The following story that a friend related to me illustrates how misunderstandings can snowball when you take things too personally:

"While lunching with a colleague, I spotted Pat, a woman I know, at a nearby table. When Pat looked over at me, I smiled and waved at her. She stared at me blankly, then continued talking with the women at her table. I felt like a fool. It's awkward to wave at someone when you're ignored in return. The next time I saw Pat, I gave her the cold shoulder—if she was going to be aloof with me, I wasn't about to go out of my way to be friendly with her!

"Then, a few weeks ago, Pat phoned and asked, 'What's the matter? Are you angry with me?' When I mentioned to her the restaurant incident, she told me that she had been to her optometrist that morning and that he had put eye drops in her eyes. Her vision was so blurred, she couldn't see across the table, let alone across the restaurant!"

This sort of vicious cycle of misunderstanding can happen in the best of relationships and, if uncorrected, can even destroy one beyond repair. I know of a couple who almost split up because she decided his failure to call for a week meant he was losing interest in the relationship when in fact he was in the middle of a job crisis. Taking his lapse personally, she responded by her own withdrawal, which *he* took as a sign that *she* didn't care about him anymore—and just at a time when he needed her the most. Hurt and angry, he backed off himself. Then, of course, she responded with increased distance of her own. Later she told me that at one point she had herself convinced that he had fallen in love with some sweet, young thing and was happily planning the wedding. Thank goodness, she had enough self-awareness and courage to talk with him about the situation. Once things were out in the open, they were able to straighten the mess out before it was too late.

Adopting a wait-and-see attitude is a good way to combat a tendency to take things personally. The idea is to stay neutral and curious. Make curiosity a policy when dealing with snippy salesclerks, aloof strangers, or preoccupied co-workers. Instead of assuming their behavior is personal to you, postpone making up your mind until you know more.

Needless to say, this advice will be easier to follow with strangers and casual acquaintances than with those near and dear. It's hard to stay neutral and curious when the impertinence is coming from your 15-year-old, the impatience from your boss, or the indifference from your husband or lover. But even then (in fact, *especially* then), it's smart to reframe *"This is about me"* into *"I wonder what this is about?"* If it's appropriate, ask directly for information (*"You seem upset. Is there a problem?"*). Then listen carefully to what's said in response. Find out what's really going on. You'll probably be amazed at how seldom things are about you. (Just don't take *that* personally.)

Always-Never Thinking: Are You Overstating Your Case?

Always-never thinking is another way in which an irrational mind misleads you with inaccurate generalizations. Social stereotypes are examples of this tendency to think in black-and-white terms: *"All men are cads." "Women are sneaky—they're back-stabbers." "All blacks have rhythm." "The Irish are big drinkers."*

Even if you pride yourself on being free from such bigoted beliefs, you may be boxing yourself in with other sorts of more personal stereotypes: *"I always have bad luck." "I never do it right." "She always breaks her promises." "You never admit you're wrong." "He only thinks of himself." "You never listen to me." "You always want your way." "He's never on time."*

One of the problems with always-never thinking is that it tends to generate emotional flooding on both sides of an interaction. *"You always do this," "You never do this"* accusations provoke high defensiveness and heated arguments (*"I am not always late! I was on time two weeks in a row!"*). Defensiveness is understandable, given that absolute statements are invariably exaggerations. We do not live in an always-never, black-white world. We live in a world of degrees, not absolutes. Even in the physical universe, what seems like the purest of whites has an imperceptible amount of black in it (and vice versa). In the complex world of relationships, absolutes are all the more rare. While your husband may be late most of the time, it's highly unlikely he's *always* late. While a friend may frequently fail to listen to you, it's improbable she *never* listens to you.

Awareness is the best remedy to always-never thinking. Reread journal entries and listen to yourself as you talk to others about problems. Ask close friends to point out "always" or "never" statements that you make about either yourself or someone else. Whenever the terms "always" and "never" creep into your thinking or speaking, replace them with specifics: *"You've been late twice in the last week."* Even when the words "always" and "never" are absent, watch for implications of absolute thinking. Comments like *"I cry whenever I get angry"* or *"He doesn't care about anything I do"* also reflect black-white, either-or ways of looking at a situation.

Must-Have Thinking: Are You Locking Up Your Mind with Insistent Demands?

When your mind is convinced you must have something "or else," you paint yourself into a corner of very restricted choice. A desire for things to be a certain way is not the problem. Believing you *must have* them a certain way in order to be happy is. Must-have thinking cramps your limit-setting style. It provokes a forceful, rigid attitude toward conflicts. It also makes it harder to deal with situations that don't work out your way.

To maintain freedom and emotional equilibrium, try to hold preferences instead of demands. For example, it's fine and good to seek fair, respectful treatment from those you deal with. Just don't base your well-being or peace of mind on being treated fairly. If you do, you set yourself up for anguish or fury when something unjust occurs. If life were fair, birds wouldn't eat worms, people wouldn't eat chickens, and earthquakes and floods wouldn't wipe out thousands of innocent victims. When you operate out of preference, you know there will inevitably be times when you won't get a fair shake and you can live with it when an occasional inequity is unavoidable.

Holding a mental state of preference enables you to let go and move on when you can do no more about a problem. You stop wasting your time over what's unchangeable (*"But she doesn't deserve the promotion. I do. It's unfair!"*) and focus instead on clarifying how you can take care of your needs in spite of injustices (*"I want to sit down with my boss and find out what I need to do in order to ensure getting the next promotion that comes along"*).

We've looked at a variety of strategies for increasing personal power by decreasing misunderstandings. Let's review these mental housekeeping principles before moving on:

1. Distinguish between your thinking and "the truth."
2. Keep assumptions tentative and hypothetical, especially those based on nonverbals.
3. Be suspicious of all secondhand information.
4. Clarify expectations and adjust those that are unrealistic or restrictive.
5. Focus on the bigger picture, not just the negatives of a situation.
6. Challenge and change unreasonable, inaccurate beliefs that mislead and upset you, especially those that see you as a victim to circumstances.
7. Stay on an even keel by neither downplaying (with rationalizations) nor overplaying (with catastrophizing) the significance of events.
8. Resist the temptation to take what others say and do personally, and instead stay neutral and curious until you know more.
9. Recognize the basic fallacy of all-or-nothing, always-never thinking.

10. Upgrade must-have thinking to the freedom of preference.

CULTIVATING OPEN-MINDEDNESS

Mental accuracy and flexibility are closely related to a third important characteristic of a SoftPower frame of mind: open-mindedness. Staying open-minded gives you an enormous advantage during difficult confrontations. Without open-mindedness, you may overlook or refuse to incorporate data that could shed new light on a situation. Instead, with a mind that's all made up, you risk staying stuck in narrow, rigid, off-base, or otherwise counterproductive positions. All of the ten SoftPower strategies just reviewed promote open-mindedness as well as mental accuracy, but here are a few more ideas for keeping an open, adaptable mind:

Expect the Best and Stay Open to the Unexpected

Negative expectations close down your mind. When you dwell exclusively or predominantly on bleak possibilities (and overlook the ways in which things could work out smoothly), you doom yourself to self-fulfilling, self-defeating prophecies. Pessimistic "futuring" is especially common when risks are high (which is ironically just when we could most use an optimistic outlook). But even when the odds are in our favor, many of us habitually narrow our thinking to the worst of potential outcomes. Then, because we're dwelling on what could go wrong, we lose our nerve. Or if we do make a move, we're either overly timid or feisty and ready for battle—either of which sets up the very failure we're afraid of.

When your mind puts you through the mill with gloom-and-doom, "what if" thoughts (*"What if I lose my job?" "What if he thinks my idea is stupid?" "What if I can't do it?" "What if I blow it?" "What if he blows up?" "What if he never calls again?"*), help it to relax by stretching your perspective with a few positive visions of end results. What if he thinks your idea is workable? What if you *can* do it? What if everyone stays calm and composed? What if he loves your spunk and proposes marriage? Carrying upbeat expectations (or at least the most favorable ones feasible for a given situation) establishes a positive atmosphere in which you're more likely to be easygoing. This increases the chances that those you're dealing with will be cooperative and pleasant as well.

Occasionally, optimistic expectations may be farfetched and inappropriate. Expecting a deranged person to treat you decently is foolhardy. But this kind of situation is the exception, not the rule. In most encounters, negative expectations work against you and positive ones serve you.

Don't Be So Picky

Judgments are another way in which we make up (and therefore close down) our minds. Like many other functions of the mind, judgments are neither good nor bad—they just are. By nature, we are judgmental creatures. Even our indifference is a form of judgment—we've simply judged that something is not worth an opinion.

As with other mental processes, the question is not whether or not you make judgments but whether your judgments serve you or not. Are they functional or dysfunctional? Functional judgments are a part of a discriminatory spirit that lets you appreciate quality and aesthetics and decide what suits your fancy. Dysfunctional judgments, on the other hand, are blaming, rigid, and pervasively negative. You lose personal power and freedom when you are crabby about a million things, condemn things you don't like as "wrong," or are so stubborn about your opinion that you shut down to opposing but equally valid views.

One way to evaluate your own judgmentalness is to ask yourself the following questions:

Are you so picky you rarely find things to your liking?
Do your complaints usually outnumber your positive observations?
Are you able to lower your standards when necessary?
Can you have your opinions yet feel comfortable keeping them to yourself or having others disagree with you?
Do you express your judgments with poise, grace, and flexibility or do you act on them with arrogance, defensiveness, and anger?

"Shoulds" are a specific form of judgments used by your mind to establish a sense of right and wrong. Observers of human behavior have long disagreed on the usefulness of "shoulds." Karen Horney, a psychoanalyst who wrote extensively on human nature, thought they produced nothing but strain and disturbance in relationships. Wayne Dyer, in *Your Erroneous Zones*, lobbied for their complete eradication. He says "shoulds" restrict us to a robotlike existence of unbending rules. Psychologist and writer Carol Tavris, however, views them as "governing agreements" that can add to the health of a relationship.

I agree with both Dyer and Tavris. Mental dictates can fence us in unnecessarily and, at other times, "shoulds" are quite useful. There *are* things that, in my opinion, you and I should and shouldn't do. But these self-regulatory mandates need to spring from freely chosen personal values, not from rules crammed down our throats by overcontrolling parents, dictatorial teachers, or repressive societies.

"Shoulds" become debilitating when you live by someone else's rules without checking to see if they are personally appropriate to you. They also breed problems when you try to force *your* standards on someone else or when you adhere religiously to a set of "shoulds" regardless of extenuating or changed circumstances. The litmus test of a "should" is whether it feels right and congruent to you deep inside. I know deep down that I should be kind to people, supportive of friends, and loyal to loved ones. I know deep down that I should not be cruel, dishonest, or rude. Unfortunately, such personal ideals are no guarantee of enlightened behavior 100 percent of the time. They're merely private standards I have deemed worth shooting for.

Like everything else in the world, "shoulds" are a relative matter. What one person considers the height of rudeness may be perfectly acceptable to someone else. What's more, there will be times when what is ordinarily seen as rude suddenly becomes acceptable because ordinary measures are not working or an emergency calls for abruptness.

Stretch Your Point of View Through Empathy

One final way to foster open-mindedness is to develop empathy—an ability to walk in another person's shoes. Empathy means appreciating what someone else is going through or has gone through. It is not the same thing as sympathy, which usually implies agreeing with another's experience. Empathy is compassion not agreement. An ability to feel empathy reaps many rewards. If, for example, relatives arrive late for Thanksgiving dinner after you expressly asked them to be on time, an ability to empathize will help you avoid a holiday fight. If you only have room for your own annoyed point of view (*"How come they haven't at least called?"*), when they finally show up, the first words out of your mouth will be an accusing, *"What happened? Why are you so late?"* With empathy, you realize they may be sitting in bumper-to-bumper traffic on congested holiday freeways with frazzled nerves and growling stomachs. Then you'll be ready to convey a warm, welcoming, *"Come on in, I'll bet you're starving"* when the gang finally arrives. And you'll at least wait until they get their coats off and have a glass of eggnog before asking questions about the delay. Of course, if you find that the lateness was not due to extenuating circumstances, you may then choose to express your feelings about this. For that matter, even if the delay was unavoidable, you might mention that you would have appreciated a call. But with open-minded empathy, you know that many things (like calling from the road) are easier said than done and no one is perfect.

There are three possible ways to empathize with others. All use shared human experiences to bridge individual differences:

Level #1 empathy. At the highest level of empathy, you are able to strongly identify with another person's experience because you have gone through something virtually identical yourself. There's nothing like writing a book to help you understand a colleague who is cranking out a manuscript and no longer has time for long, leisurely visits with you. There's nothing like having lost a spouse to comprehend the pain a friend feels over the death of her husband or her need to talk about him nonstop as she goes through her grieving process. But however close your own experience seems to someone else's, no two experiences are completely alike. Therefore you can never know exactly how others feel. While you may fully understand a large part of their situation, in other respects you could be completely off base. So resist the temptation to think you know exactly how someone feels and stay open as well to the ways in which the experiences of others are unique unto them.

Level #2 empathy. With level #2 empathy, your experience is more like a close cousin to someone else's. Maybe you haven't written a book, but you've written a doctoral dissertation or a term paper. Having been through something similar, you can appreciate the pressures of a writing project's deadline looming ahead, the necessity for setting limits, and the challenge of getting creative juices going on command. Or maybe you haven't lost a husband, but you've lost a parent or child. From this experience of profound loss, you know firsthand the stages of disbelief, denial, and anger common in adjusting to the death of a loved one.

Level #3 empathy. A lesser but still helpful level of empathy occurs when despite the fact that you haven't had any comparable experience yourself, you know firsthand the generic feelings or desires that another person is going through. You know what it's like to feel overwhelmed by something that has to be done by a certain date. You know the despair and rage that can result from suffering a personal loss.

At all three levels, it's easier to feel empathy for those similar to yourself. The challenge increases, however, when you need to identify with those who are radically different from you. When this is the case, consider seeking additional information. If you can find some common ground, you may be able to enlarge your perspective to include more of theirs. Abraham Lincoln once remarked to an aide at a diplomatic gathering, "See that man across the room? I don't like him. I need to get to know him better." By moving closer and finding out more, you may be able to understand individuals who at first glance seemed totally alien or despicable to you.

In the book *At a Drop of a Veil* (the true story about an American woman's life as a young wife in an Arabian harem), there's a good example of how increased information can bridge differences. The author tells of her initial reactions to the custom of wearing a veil. At first, because she couldn't fathom how Moslem women subscribed to this tradition, she assumed they must be privately hating and resenting it (or accepting it only out of ignorance or fear). Then she discovered that, to most Arabian women, the veil was considered proof that their men respected women and wanted to protect them. It was seen as a badge of love, not a demeaning restriction. With this information, a despicable foreign habit became more understandable even though it remained personally unacceptable.[2]

In today's world, empathy is a necessity if we are to survive. Millions of us who differ drastically in values and behavior share one small, interconnected planetary home. Thousands of us who differ in radical ways share social communities.

[2]Marianne Alireza, *At a Drop of a Veil*, Houghton Mifflin Co., 1971.

Dozens of us share one office and handfuls of us share single households. Crammed together on a planet at the brink of destroying itself, it's essential that we be able to appreciate and respect other perspectives—especially those with which we vehemently disagree. Even if you are totally opposed to the position of those who are against abortion, in favor of capital punishment, or planning a nuclear war, it's important to make an honest attempt to understand the fears, desires, and needs that lie behind such stands. Everyone, from the lunatic terrorist to the tyrannical boss to the deceitful child to the submissive wife, is convinced that his or her way is right. No matter how extreme the position, to each of us our own position makes complete sense.

Let me stress that empathy does not mean agreement or compliance. Understanding the Moslem view of veils doesn't mean you change your own mind about the practice of veiling women or don a veil yourself. You can fully understand and empathize with someone else's point of view, yet continue to be in total disagreement with it and even lobby vigorously for change. Nor does increased empathy mean you acquiesce to abuse or intolerable circumstances. You can still speak up and set limits. But, with empathy for the other side, you can do it with caring and compassion for all involved.

SoftPower mental housekeeping involves preventing misunderstandings from occurring in the first place and clearing up those that do occur before they wreak too much havoc. It means living with a rational, positive, flexible, open frame of mind.

With a well-managed mind, many would-be problems disappear in front of your eyes. Or, if they don't vanish entirely, they become reduced to manageable size. With a well-tended mental home, you stay clearheaded in the face of danger and lay the groundwork for the next important characteristic of SoftPower—emotional freedom.

4
EMOTIONAL FREEDOM
Don't Bite the Bait

Emotional sensitivity can be a tremendous asset, a serious liability, or a bit of both. As an asset, turbulent emotions serve you as a personal alarm system. They reveal a need to either take action or change your thinking. As a liability, emotions flood you and knock you off balance. Out of control, you are at the mercy of your anger, guilt, or fear. To maintain positive power and an ability to set limits successfully, you need a new kind of relationship with your emotions, one where you run them instead of them running you.

In general, circumstances that call for limit setting are emotionally charged experiences in and of themselves. Usually, such situations involve an upset of some sort—disappointment over a broken promise, annoyance because someone cuts in front of you in line, impatience with slow service, embarrassment over a joke at your expense. Then, to make matters worse, these initial emotions are frequently compounded by fears of rejection, resistance, or reprisal. No wonder that emotional management is a prerequisite for SoftPower limit setting.

The case of a battered woman is an extreme example of how emotions can at times block us from resolving problems in relationships. When an abused woman is asked why in heaven's name she didn't do something to get out of the abusive situation, her responses reflect the immobilizing and debilitating effects that all emotional upheaval potentially has. There is the paralysis of hopelessness (*"It wouldn't have done any good"*), fear (*"I was afraid it would only get worse." "He's all I have. What would I do without him?"*), embarrassment (*"I was too ashamed to tell anyone"*), and guilt (*"It was my fault. I must have deserved it"*).

WE ARE ALL "BATTERED" TO SOME EXTENT

The same feelings that so debilitate a battered woman exist in milder form within all of us and lead to the inertia in which we find ourselves stuck from time to time. We've all had occasions when we've put up with much too much out of fear of losing a relationship or when we've held our tongue out of a sense of hopelessness, wondering "what good would it do anyway?" My friend Paula's story illustrates:

A few years ago, Paula moved into an apartment not far from where I live in Oakland, California. She asked me over for a visit shortly after getting settled. The minute I arrived I knew something was wrong. Paula quickly filled me in.

"I'm going to have to move," she exclaimed, close to tears.

"What? You haven't even unpacked your boxes! Is there something wrong with the apartment?"

"No," she continued, "There's something wrong with my neighbor. He plays hard rock music at all hours—day and night. I haven't had a good sleep in a week. I can't take it any longer."

"Isn't moving a rather drastic solution?" I asked. "Have you tried to do anything else?"

"Yeah, I tried." She shook her head slowly to show that her attempts had been in vain.

"What did you do?" I asked when she didn't go on.

"I gave the guy a dirty look in the elevator. I thought he'd get the hint."

If Paula hadn't looked so unhappy I would have laughed out loud. Talk about the subtle approach! She then added that she had heard another neighbor across the hall pound on the guy's door and curse him out. She certainly wasn't going to act like that. Her only recourse, she was convinced, was to move.

Like a battered woman, Paula held herself back from being more direct with her neighbor because of fear (*"I don't want a fight"*) and a sense of hopelessness (*"He's not the cooperative kind. I can tell"*). These emotions confined her to one pathetic, unsuccessful attempt. Happily, however—unlike the tale of most battered women—Paula's story has a happy ending. She did not end up moving. Instead, with a little encouragement, she asked her landlord for help in resolving the problem. The landlord sent a letter to the neighbor advising him to buy headphones (which he did), and Paula finally got a good night's sleep.

By the way, emotions don't always act as inhibitors. In fact, a certain level of emotional response can be a positive force in getting you off the dime. It can motivate you to finally do something about a problem instead of just griping about it. But when emotions run high, they almost always handicap you. Your thinking becomes jammed, your perceptions distorted, your intuition blocked, and your behavior disabled. Flooded with fear, you retreat at the first sign of trouble or chicken out and never try at all. Flooded with anger, you either clam up for fear you'll blast some poor soul with your wrath, or blow up and say things you later regret. Hot emotions invariably interfere with attempts to effectively resolve problems.

"Leftover" emotions that linger after the dust has settled can also be a problem. Even if you handle a situation successfully, you can sweat for days over imagined repercussions (*"I wonder if I came on too strong?" "I hope she's not mad." "I'll bet he'll try to get even with me." "I should have kept my mouth shut"*). You can toss and turn for nights with endless reenactments of an argument or diabolical plots for revenge (*"I don't believe she had the nerve to say what she said—I'll show her—I'll turn in that report late." "If that's the way he's going to be, I'll be stubborn too"*). You can beat yourself up for weeks with guilt over turning someone down (*"I should have never said no—she really needed my help." "Maybe I should call and give him the money. After all, he is my brother"*).

ALL EMOTIONS ARE "DO-IT-TO-YOURSELF" EXPERIENCES

SoftPower emotional management is based on one simple fact: Every feeling you experience—be it happy or unhappy, intense or mild—is self-induced. No matter how much it seems to you as if somebody else has "made you mad," anger is your own creation. So is fear, guilt, boredom, loneliness, disgust, depression, and any other feeling that you experience. This means that just as you can choose to take charge of what happens to you mentally, you decide what happens to you emotionally.

The fact that you are responsible for your emotions does not mean feelings are bad or that you should never be upset. Nor does it mean you'll suddenly feel emotionally composed in all situations. It simply means you know you have a choice about who upsets you, what upsets you, and how upset you get.

Mind management and emotional management go hand in hand because what you feel is directly related to what you think. As Wayne Dyer puts it: "You feel what you think and you can learn to think differently about anything if you decide to do so." It works the other way around as well. You think what you feel. When you're already mad (from anger-provoking thoughts), your mind tends to continue thinking angry thoughts. When you're already blue, your mind tends to continue to fill itself with depressing thoughts that perpetuate your despair. Like the proverbial chicken and egg, it can be hard to tell which comes first, the thought or the feeling. Mind and emotions feed and fuel each other.

To gain a better handle on your emotions, you must stay continually aware of the self-manufactured nature of feelings. Aware, you know that you have the power to influence the cause-effect, mind-feeling connection at any point. You not only decide whether you become upset in a given situation, you decide how upset you become and how long you stay upset. The following story is a perfect example of the self-induced nature of emotions:

Gloria and Nancy work in the same office and walk to work together each day from neighboring apartments in downtown St. Louis. Most mornings, they stop off at a small restaurant to get coffee and croissants to take to the office. One day, the pleasant young man who ordinarily waited on them was gone and in his place was a new employee—a sullen, rude older man who grunted an unfriendly response to their hello and practically threw the change at them.

By the end of a week, Gloria was fed up with the way she was being treated (*"Who does he think he is? I don't need this first thing in the morning!"*). To give him some of his own medicine, she started acting rude and unpleasant right back to him. Nancy, on the other hand, continued to be warm and friendly. Every day, she offered a cheery "Good morning" despite the fact that the man never once returned her greeting.

Finally, Gloria could stand it no longer. "How can you treat that guy so nicely when he's treating us like dirt?" she asked her friend one morning as they were leaving the restaurant.

Nancy stopped walking for a moment and looked at Gloria with surprise. "Why should I let some stranger's behavior determine how I act this morning? Why should his mood ruin mine?"

When you recognize the self-manufactured nature of feelings, you establish emotional independence from others. You stop relinquishing your peace of mind and feelings of self-worth to the dictates of others. Let's look at what happened in Gloria and Nancy's case, for example. Where did Gloria's vexation come from? Or better yet, where did it *not* come from?

For starters, Gloria's unhappiness was not a function of her desire for decent treatment. Of course she would want to be treated pleasantly by someone with whom she was doing business. Nor was her vexation a function of her failure to take action to remedy the situation. While taking her business elsewhere or talking with the man to see if she could improve the situation would have been smart, assertive moves, Gloria's distress was not about behavior. She could have made all the right moves and still been upset. Or she could have done absolutely nothing and felt perfectly content like her friend Nancy. Gloria's distress sprang from what happened *in her mind* in response to the man's behavior. At some level—either consciously or unconsciously—she had herself convinced that in order to feel happy and have a nice morning she needed this man to be friendly toward her. This conviction alone was the source of her emotional misery.

ARE YOU GIVING AWAY YOUR POWER AND YOUR PEACE OF MIND?

The waitress is snotty; you're snotty back. Your boss is in a rotten mood, you lose your good one. Your partner acts cold and distant, you pull back and are distant, too. Each time you let the actions and moods of others dictate your own, you lose power.

It doesn't have to be this way. You have a choice about how you feel and how you act. So do I. And so did Gloria. As Eleanor Roosevelt put it, "No one can make you feel inferior without your consent." No one can make you feel guilty, angry, insulted, bored, afraid, embarrassed, disappointed, impatient, or anything else. For others to "make you feel" some emotion, they must have both your permission and your participation. You have to "bite the bait."

Part of the challenge of emotional management is that certain bait may seem irresistible. To add to the challenge, others often know the kind of bait you love, and they dangle it in front of your nose to lure you into reacting. Your kids no doubt have it all figured out. They know what gets you going (*"You love Sara more than me"*). In fact, anyone close to you will know what makes you jump. So when they want to liven things up, all they have to do is put out the bait (*"Have you put on a few pounds?"*) and watch the show. The results, they know, can be quite entertaining.

But you're the one who decides if there's going to be a show. And, if you so decide, you can refuse to perform. In fact, with practice, you can learn to stay composed in situations that would formerly have sent you through the roof or driven you to despair.

Stop Being a Slave to Circumstances

The importance of recognizing that feelings are self-induced cannot be overstated. Once you know that emotions are the result of what happens within you (rather than what happens around you), the locus of control and power in your life shifts dramatically. In effect, you are freed from emotional bondage to circumstances. Instead you know that, no matter how bad things get or how few degrees of freedom you have, by changing what is going on *inside* yourself you can change how you feel. By changing the way you talk to yourself, by challenging beliefs and assumptions you hold to be true, by modifying how badly you want or believe you need something, and by shifting the way you look at a situation, you know you can spare yourself unnecessary grief, pain, and rage.

Of course, in the heat of the moment emotional freedom is easier said than done. When things get cooking, enlightened notions about feelings being your own creation can suddenly disappear. Instead, emotions seem to spring directly from circumstances, and it seems as if the only way you could possibly feel better is if the situation itself were to change:

"If only I had a baby, I'd be happy."

"If only I had more money, I'd feel confident."

"If he weren't such a bully, I wouldn't feel so intimidated."

"If she'd quit the sarcasm, I'd calm down and not be angry."

"He told me he wants a divorce. Of course I'm depressed."

Use Your Emotions as an "Alarm System"

Upset feelings are best used as warning signals that, like the negative indicators in your car, tell you when something is wrong. When your gas gauge lights up, you know there's a problem that needs attention (you need gas), decide on a remedy (pulling off to get gas), and take action (you take the next exit to find a service station). Self-awareness of emotions can work in a similar way. Imagine yourself, for example, rushing out of the office at the end of a busy day to get home early. Now imagine that, as you hurry out, someone from a neighboring department approaches and starts a conversation. You like this person and want to be friendly, but you also need to be on your way. So there you stand pulled in two directions—leave and tend to your own needs or stay and attend to hers. If you're uncomfortable setting limits, you no doubt take the path of least resistance—stand there and talk. But as the clock ticks on, your restlessness grows. Finally, you notice your impatience. This is your signal. Your restlessness conveys to you the need for a decision. Either set limits and leave (*"Excuse me, Connie. This is not a good time for me to talk. How about coffee in the morning?"*) or change your priorities and stay (*"This is important for me to hear about. It doesn't matter if I get home a little late"*). Used in this way as a signal, your emotional response nudges you to make a change and improve the situation—or accept it as it is.

In real life, of course, feelings are usually much more complex and mixed up then this scenario implies. As Carol Tavris puts it: "Our emotions are not especially distinctive. They tend to come in bunches, like grapes, and it is very rare to find a single emotion causing trouble on its own."[1] Consequently when emotional bells and whistles go off, you won't necessarily receive the kind of clear-cut directions you get when your gas gauge lights up. Instead, you may feel emotionally scrambled, lost within a host of feelings going on all at once. Thus, if your teenage son is late arriving home, you can feel anger (*"He damn well better have a good reason"*), fear (*"Maybe he's been in an accident"*), regret (*"I should have told him to call before leaving the party"*), and embarrassment (because your guests see how upset you are)—all at the same time. Or if your boss offers you a promotion, you may feel simultaneously flattered (*"He thinks I can do the job"*), scared (*"Can I do the job?"*), sad (*"I don't want to leave my friends"*), and excited (*"This is going to be great!"*).

When You Feel Confused, Buy Yourself Some Time

If you need to sort out mixed-up emotions, resist rushing into a hasty response. Back off and take a breather. In the middle of upsetting circumstances, it may be impossible to determine how you feel or why you feel the way you do. Buying yourself time gives you a chance to better understand what's happening

[1] Carol Tavris, *Anger: The Misunderstood Emotion*, Simon & Schuster, 2nd Edition, 1989.

to you emotionally and what range of options you have. The ideas in Chapter Two for getting to know yourself can help: Check out your bodily responses, assess your desires, look at the situation from a variety of angles. When circumstances allow (or an issue is particularly significant), take the time to talk things over with a friend or write about what's happening in your journal. Ultimately, of course, you want to be able to respond effectively on the spot. But as you acquire better skills in setting limits, build in "delay time" between initial reactions to a problem and any attempts to handle it. This disrupts habitual knee-jerk responses that in the past have failed to get you what you want.

In certain situations, a delayed response can be an especially smart strategy. Whenever you face a potentially explosive or critical situation, this will almost surely be the case. At moments of crisis, the tendency is to restrict yourself to "survival thinking." You see only two choices—fight or flight. If you can step back from the fire, however, and calm yourself down, you see all sorts of possibilities you'd never consider while freaking out.

Buying time is also a smart move if your limit-setting style tends to be excessive or forceful. With a chance to put things in perspective, you realize that many problems are better dropped than dealt with and that an easygoing, low-keyed approach can frequently work better than a tough, no-nonsense one.

When a situation involves making a promise or assuming a responsibility, taking a break can also let you review other commitments before saying yes or no. This keeps you from getting roped into obligations you have no time for or activities you have no interest in.

Sometimes, of course, there will be no chance to buy time. If your boss drops a last-minute assignment on your desk as she runs out the door at six o'clock, taking a break to think things over isn't going to work. Unless you immediately say, "Wait! I've got a big date tonight," she'll disappear into the sunset and your evening will be ruined. But even if you sit there tongue-tied as your boss flees, all is not lost. At the very least, you can learn from experience and prevent more of the same from happening the following week. Instead of bitching about what an inconsiderate boss you have, devote your energy to a "best you" rehearsal—an imagined version of how the "best you" would handle a situation, were it to happen again. Or, better yet, imagine how you'll talk over what happened with your boss so there is no next time.

Thankfully, most situations are not now-or-never propositions, and you will be able to delay responding for at least a few minutes. If nothing else, excuse yourself to the bathroom where you can count to ten. Or ask a few questions or take a few deep breaths to stall for time.

With certain chronic problems, you might want to make buying time a policy. For example, if you usually have a hard time turning down social invitations, it makes sense to have a delay tactic at the tip of your tongue—something like, "*Thanks for the invitation. I need to check my schedule before saying yes. When do you need to know?*" Here are other examples of responses for buying time:

"I'm not sure how I feel. I need time to think about it."

"I'm upset by this. I'd like to take time to think things through before I respond."

"This is not a good time for me to discuss this with you, but I could talk with you tomorrow. When would be a good time?"

"Before I say yes, I need to check a few things."

"I need to look over some other deadlines before taking this on. How about if I call you later today?"

"I'd like to look over my other commitments before promising anything."

"You've caught me by surprise. I want to sort this through before responding. I'll give you a call this afternoon."

How Would the "Best You" Handle It?

Rehearsals—both imagined and enacted—are one of the best ways to cope with crippling emotions. By envisioning how the "best you" would deal with a troubling situation, you calm yourself down in the moment and give yourself a blueprint for change in the future.

Rehearsals work after the fact as well as before. After the fact, a replay lets you dwell productively on a problem, then lay it to rest with the assurance that you've grown from the experience and will do better next time. Beforehand, "pre-play" rehearsals establish both an emotional and a behavioral groove in which to move once you're in the actual situation. While you may not be able to pull off the ideal response, chances are good that when the real-life drama rolls around, you'll be closer to this optimum level than you would be if you went in cold.

There are at least three ways in which to rehearse "best you" scenarios:

1) See the "best you" in your imagination. Your mind is a private rehearsal room where you can try out alternative ways of responding. In the seclusion of your imagination, you can practice dry runs before engaging in the real thing. All it takes is closing your eyes, relaxing, and picturing how a "best you" would look, sound, and feel. As a song I once heard proclaimed: "If you can see it in your imagination, you can have it in real life."

2) Act out your "best you" rehearsal with a friend. If you are more visceral and learn best by doing, role-playing may be the best way for you to rehearse. Acting out a confrontation can even provide comic relief. But the most important benefit of a role-play is the kinesthetic dimension of the experience. Going through the motions gives you a chance to try on emotional and behavioral responses. If you have no one to role-play with, do it by yourself in front of a mirror. Or take a long, leisurely drive and practice both sides of the interaction out loud as you drive.

3) Script out your rehearsal on paper. A third way to stage a rehearsal is to write a "best you screenplay." In *The New Diary*, Tristine Rainier calls this process giving yourself a second chance. As an example, she tells of a woman who became so unglued by the sight of a cockroach in an apartment where she was staying in New York City that she packed her bags and left town. To reexperience the incident with more composure, she wrote the following in her journal and dated it with the day of the real upset:

> I was walking over to the sink when I saw it, a three-inch cockroach. I was terrified. I got a broom and tried to hit him, but he scuttled under some boxes. That made me angry. I found the lye and the ant poison and made a mixture of it.
>
> Then I waited, like a cat for its prey. I got as close as I could and threw the poison. He shot away like a hot rod and took cover again.

Now I was really mad. I found a board and waited. He ventured forth and I told myself, Now or never, hit him hard! I threw the board on him and stepped on it. I could hear his shell crack.

When I looked at the board, he was a brown paste. I took it down to the garbage immediately, swept the poison into the trash, and wiped it up with paper towels. Then I took a shower and dressed for dinner. I was shaken but I had won out over my fear.[2]

With all three rehearsal methods—imagined, enacted, and written—it's essential to relax before starting. It's also important to set aside enough time so you don't feel rushed and can really get into it.

As you rehearse an upcoming or past confrontation, envision two variations of the interaction: a "worst of all outcomes" and a "best of all outcomes" version. In the "worst of all outcomes" version, what you most dread occurs. The other person screams and yells, is cruel or unkind, ignores you, or slams the door in your face. Despite this, you still function at your best. It's as if you are the most assertive person on earth. You stay calm, cool, collected, confident, and clearheaded throughout the interaction, no matter what. You handle the worst with poise and dignity.

In the "best of all outcomes" version, the most desirable results come about. Those you're dealing with are pleasant, responsive, and understanding. If this seems too farfetched, they are at least civil and cooperative. Once again, you are clear, centered, composed, and self-assured. You communicate with warmth, sincerity, and heart. You even keep your sense

[2]Tristine Rainier, *The New Diary*, J. P. Tarcher. 1978, page 93.

of humor. Be sure to devote the bulk of your time and energy to this "best of all outcomes" version, and end with it so that it's the last one imprinted on your mind.

Your Mind Is a Catalyst for Change

There's nothing new about the idea of using your mind to bring about change. Visualizing yourself as you want to be is an age-old self-management technique. Research supports the notion that the mere act of holding positive mental images can produce measurable behavioral changes. The evidence demonstrates that the human brain does not distinguish between events that actually occur and those that are only imagined. For example, when psychologists ask people to imagine themselves running, there are (during the visualization process) small but measurable contractions in all the muscle groups used while running.

One famous visualization story involves three groups of students trying to improve basketball free throws. The first group practiced on the court for 20 days, the second group did not practice at all, and the third spent 20 minutes a day imagining that they were shooting free throws. If members of this third group missed a shot during their mental exercise sessions, they corrected their aim and saw themselves sinking it perfectly on the second try. All three groups were tested on both the first and last days and showed the following results: The first group improved by 24 percent; the second group showed no improvement; the third group improved by 23 percent.

Visualizations are powerful stuff. Mary Lou Retton mind-scripted every move the night before her Gold Medal performance. Greg Louganis, the only diver ever to score a perfect 10 in international competition, said he relied on mental preparation as much as he did physical training—he visualized each dive as he wanted it to be, step by step, forty times before mounting the platform.

Visualizations can produce incredible results in all areas of your life, not just sports. They can change you emotionally as well as behaviorally. They can improve the way you respond to criticism, take a stand, or confront your boss. Visualizations are the seeds from which your next emotions and behaviors burst forth. By changing the pictures that run through your mind, you can determine what emotional responses you experience and what actions you take.

Some Emotions Are False Alarms; Some Are Real Ones

Your emotional alarm system, like your mind, malfunctions at times. When it does, so, it produces false alarms—much ado about nothing. Given the close tie between mind and emotions, it should come as no surprise that such malfunctioning is the result of faulty thinking. False emotional alarms are set off by misunderstandings and irrational thinking.

When your emotional alarm system functions properly, the alarms it sets off are well-founded concerns appropriate to a given situation. These "real alarms" signal you to take notice or move into action as need be. I call these prompts gut feelings because they are one primary way in which your intuition (your "gut") makes its presence felt.

Fear, for example, can be a gut feeling that alerts you to

true danger and prevents you from doing foolish things. For example, gut fear keeps me from going into Central Park at midnight when I'm in New York City. It keeps me from driving fast in dense fog. In such situations, fear jolts us to attention and prompts us to move with caution or avoid a situation altogether.

The overwhelming majority of our fears, however, are *false alarms*—the product of faulty thinking. They result when our minds misread problems or blow them out of proportion. When such mental mistakes occur, we get worked up unnecessarily over situations that are, in reality, relatively insignificant or benign.

Guilt, anger, and sadness also function at times as gut feelings. As a real alarm, guilt informs you that you're doing something you know deep inside is wrong to do. When this is the case, feeling guilty is appropriate. The idea, however, is not to beat yourself up or wallow in worthlessness. It's to use the guilt as a signal for self-correction. It's very simple: Once you stop doing what you know is wrong to do (and make apologies and amends), you won't feel guilty anymore.

As with fear, though, most guilt is a false alarm. Needless to say, female programming creates a great deal of inappropriate guilt. We were taught to put others first so we feel guilty when we finally get around to taking care of our own needs, especially if we disappoint others in the process. We were told always to help others out, no matter what the cost to us personally, so we feel guilty if we turn others down. We were told never to put others out, no matter how pressing our need, so we feel guilty if we put anyone to extra trouble.

As a false alarm, guilt gives you a chance to uncover the faulty thinking (*"I'm a bad person because I didn't help her out"*) and faulty beliefs (*"It's selfish to turn people down"*) that lay at the root of your distress. Once you know the unreasonable thinking that is fueling your guilt, you can change how you feel by changing your thoughts and beliefs. You can tell yourself, *"Sometimes it's okay to turn others down—even when they truly need help. I am not responsible for helping all people at all times. In fact, sometimes rescuing others does them a disservice."*

How to Tell Real Alarms from False Ones

The first step in discriminating real alarms from false ones is to probe the "how come" of your upset. Let's say you find yourself feeling insulted by something a co-worker says during a staff meeting. What's causing you to get so out of shape? Ask yourself a few questions. Could you be taking what was said too personally? Are you giving this person's opinion too much power?

Use what I call the So What Test and question the true significance of an upsetting event. So what if a co-worker doesn't think your report is brilliant? So what if your husband doesn't like your idea? Does it really have to matter that much what he thinks? So what if a colleague is unfriendly to you? Does it have to be a big deal if she doesn't like you? So what if you didn't get the promotion you wanted. Do you want your peace of mind and self-confidence destroyed by one disappointment?

Another way to put an incident into perspective is to submit it to the Longevity Test. Ask yourself how much the situation is going to matter in a week. Or in a year. Or on your death bed.

I discovered the freeing power of these sorts of challenges when I was 30 years old. I had been divorced for five years, during which time I had gotten along amazingly well with

John, my ex-husband. Then, when John met the woman he eventually married, a rough period began. The two of them suddenly became very critical of me and the way I was mothering our two sons.

I was both devastated and enraged by the criticism, but mostly I was enraged. My first response was defensiveness. I thought I was a great mother, and I set about creating a list to prove it. The list was an impressive one and it convinced all my friends. Unfortunately, it did nothing to change the minds of my ex-husband and his new wife.

I was filled with indignation. The nerve of my ex! Pointing a finger at me when all he did was take the boys to the zoo on alternate weekends. This was not the age of shared custody. As a single mother working full-time, I handled all the babysitter arrangements, trips to the emergency room, parent-teacher conferences, and PTA meetings by myself. I alone slaved over sloppy joes and English muffin pizzas, read *Green Eggs and Ham* till I was green in the face, and refereed fights over Hot Wheels and GI Joes.

Endless angry dialogues spun out in my head, but they only served to solidify my anger. My rage ran me for two full months. I rekindled my fury repeatedly by rehashing all the gory details of the attacks on me. Sometimes I vented with friends who helped me fan the flames with outcries of "You're kidding—they said that?!" But mostly I did it on my own. I gnawed on every allegation like a dog on a bone. I remember one criticism in particular that galled me. It had to do with the fact that I did not bleach my wash. I couldn't believe it. My failure to use Clorox was being used as proof of maternal negligence. My blood boiled!

One night near the end of this two-month run of rage, I was alone at home working myself once again into a lather. Suddenly a little voice from inside my head piped up and asked:

"So what if they criticize you? It doesn't matter what they think. *You* know what kind of mother you are; it doesn't change that. The kids know what kind of mother you are; it doesn't change that. It doesn't matter *what* they say!"

"It doesn't matter?" The notion seemed revolutionary. *"It doesn't matter??"*

"It *doesn't* matter," the voice answered. "How much will it matter on your deathbed what they're saying about you and the underwear? Let them think whatever they want to think. Let them say whatever they want to say. It doesn't matter a hoot."

The effect was remarkable. It was as if two thousand pounds were lifted off of me in a second. I couldn't believe the power I had been giving to their opinion of me.

The experience was a turning point for me. I felt a new sense of liberation from caring so much about what others thought. I began the long road to emotional freedom. And, by way of a postscript, my ex, his wife, and I survived this difficult time, even learning from it and laughing over it. We're now, I'm happy to say, close friends.

YOU'RE THE ONE WHO'S IN CHARGE

It is never "circumstances" that determine your mood. It's what happens in your mind. If it were circumstances that caused a person to feel one way or another, then people with fabulous circumstances would never feel miserable. This is hardly the case. If you want proof that great circumstances are no guarantee of happiness, follow the supposed "happily ever after" of a lottery winner. If circumstances made us happy or unhappy, people with *horrible* circumstances would never feel happy. This isn't true either. The story of two disabled Vietnam vets illustrates:

The first man—I'll call him John—lives with truly terrible circumstances. He lost both arms and both legs in the war. Supported financially by the government, John spends his days in a dark, depressing studio apartment parked in front of a television set. He is an intensely angry man. And no wonder, right? Here he is, crippled and completely dependent on others as result of a war nobody appreciates. He isn't even a hero.

The second vet I'll call Ted. He, too, is a quadruple amputee, but that's where the similarity with John ends. With his money from the government, Ted purchased a ranch that he runs very successfully. He goes about the business of each day with good cheer—driving his tractor, taking care of the animals, managing employees, and handling administrative chores. In addition to running his business, Ted is an active member of the community. He sings in the church choir, tutors teenagers in town, and has a lively social life. What a difference from John's story of self-pity and rage.

What could account for such a huge difference between these two men? The circumstances were equally negative for both, and Ted didn't like his situation any more than John did. But, whereas John was angry and reclusive, Ted led a full, happy life. The difference was that Ted knew there were important choices to be made. He could let himself be immobilized with self-pity and rage, or he could make the most with what he still had. As Harold Russell, a paratrooper who lost his hands in World War II put it: "It's never what you have lost, but what you have left that counts."

You're Not a Victim—You Always Have Choice

Victims look at circumstances and whine:

"I feel bad because my sister hurt my feelings."
"I feel bad because my boyfriend mistreats me."
"I feel bad because my staff doesn't like me."
"I feel bad because my car broke down."
"I'm a failure because I lost money in the stock market."
"I'm a failure because I have an unimportant job."

Self-responsible individuals look *inside* themselves for the source of distress. They convert disturbed feelings into "school bells," signals that a lesson is at hand. Life provides them with on-the-job training—endless opportunities for self-awareness and growth. Self-responsible men and women tell themselves:

"I feel bad because I'm worrying too much about what other people think of me. So what if they don't like everything I do?"
"I feel bad because I'm still brooding over that fight I had last week with my mother. It's time to let that go now."
"I feel angry because I wanted Cathryn's support in the meeting and didn't get it. I need to talk with her about that."

Emotions Are Your Teachers; They Deserve Your Respect

Used as alarms, feelings warn you about abusive or unacceptable situations. They provoke you to take charge of the situation. If you expect friends to keep promises and a close friend doesn't, your upset can prompt you to talk with her about the problem. If a boyfriend hits you, your anger and your fear can motivate you to issue an ultimatum (*"If you hit me again, I'm out the door"*). Or it can spur you to end the relationship right there and then. Properly utilized, emotions serve as a healthy source of steam for setting limits. Even false alarms are useful in that they reveal faulty thinking—inappropriate personalizing, catastrophizing, or misunderstandings—that needs to be cleaned up.

Unfortunately most of us are a long way from honoring and learning from our emotions. Instead, we subject ourselves to emotional double whammies. We're impatient over feeling impatient, mad at ourselves for being angry, or embarrassed at our embarrassment. But judging your emotions only makes you feel worse. The SoftPower way is to get off your own back and cultivate an acceptance of all your feelings—the pleasurable and the painful, the logical and the off the wall. When you look upon emotions as information, you can't lose.

Feelings are self-induced temporary events. This too *shall* pass. You've been scared, guilty, depressed, and angry before, and you've made it through. You'll make it through again. In the meantime, learn all you can from the experience, make your smartest moves, then let upsetting matters go.

Here's the bottom line: You have a choice about who and what upsets you. You have a choice about how upset you become and how long you stay upset. These simple facts are your ticket to a life of greatly increased emotional freedom.

5

COURAGE TRAINING
Facing Life's Big Bears

Fear is clearly the most formidable emotional block to power and honesty. For this reason, the issue of courage—the ability to overcome fear—deserves further attention. It takes courage to tell the truth. While speaking up and setting limits are not usually life-threatening moves, they can rock the boat and perhaps land you in hot water. Having the courage to be honest in such situations does not mean all fears disappear. It means you function despite your fears. True courage is an inner state of power that enables you to act even when you're afraid, even when there's a chance of getting hurt or losing something you value.

For women, maintaining courage is a tall order, given that the messages directed at us as young girls encouraged and reinforced fearfulness. *"Be careful!" "Watch out!" "Don't talk to strangers."* We were not only taught that there were good reasons to be scared, we learned from experience that there were appealing payoffs to being a scaredy-cat. *"She's afraid—isn't that precious?" "Come here sweetie, I'll take care of you."*

Our adult fears range from spiders to loud voices to growing old alone. When it comes to relationships, we are usually most afraid of criticism, conflict, and failure—all risks of honesty. Friends can be offended if we turn them down. Bosses might get angry and fire us if we disagree with them. Lovers could walk out the door if we don't do as they ask. Given the risks involved, fears about self-expression are frequently founded on an element of true jeopardy.

Let's look at these three relationship fears more closely. In the light of awareness you can better evaluate what, if anything, there is to be afraid of. With understanding, you'll find that what frightens you is often nothing more than a molehill in disguise—a concern that is both manageable and minimal. And even when you find legitimate cause for worry, with awareness you can think more clearly and make wiser choices.

BIG BEAR #1.
DISAPPROVAL: FEARS OF CRITICISM
AND REJECTION

Fears of disapproval deserve the lion's share of our attention, because they are so dominant in most of our lives. We tend to have extremely low thresholds of tolerance for criticism and rejection. We just can't stand it when someone says no to us: *"No, I don't like your idea, it's stupid." "No, I don't want to be married to you." "No, I don't want to be your friend."*

When we count on validation from others as proof of our self-worth and what we get instead is criticism, it can feel unbearable. If your sensitivities in this area are severe, the mere prospect of criticism or rejection becomes cause for terror. You fall to pieces even when the person who might reject you is someone you yourself don't like or respect. While you yourself certainly don't approve of everyone, you want everyone to approve of you.

Not surprisingly, intolerance for criticism inhibits honesty. If you're after everyone's "Good Housekeeping Seal of Approval," the odds are you'll be less than candid and direct with them. You'll hold back out of fear that others will see you as overly sensitive, demanding, bossy, controlling, fussy, or aggressive.

An overblown need for approval tends to create problems where none need exist. You feel hurt at the slightest rebuke and insulted by the mildest of snubs. You may do nothing about these hurts and insults (because of your need to be "nice"), but you feel the pain of them acutely.

Fears of rejection and criticism make you a sitting duck for intimidation and control as well. To operate as a free agent, you need to feel assured that, even if someone turns you down, views you as a terrible person, or ends a relationship, you'll survive in good shape.

Unfortunately, most of us do not enjoy such a relaxed disposition toward disapproval. Instead we literally lose sleep when we discover that someone doesn't like us or what we've done. We obsess over the charges and plot out diabolical responses and counterattacks.

How "Addicted" Are You to Approval?

Just as you can be hooked on alcohol, pigging out, or men to dull your pain, you can be hooked on approval and acceptance

from others. Typically, of these three, we are most desperate
for approval. If we can't have that, we'll settle for acceptance.
If we can't get even that, we're willing to take plain old attention.

Addictions to approval are invariably tied to shaky self-esteem. Without a strong foundation of self-love and self-acceptance, it can be excruciatingly painful when others turn you
down or dislike you. When this is the case, you may go to
extraordinary lengths to get validation from others in order
to spare yourself misery. Catering to others can become a
lifestyle. You dress to please, do things to please, say things
to please, and keep your mouth shut to please. You live as a
performer while the real you (who might at times do or say
things that others wouldn't like) stays safely in the wings and
watches the show.

One way to free yourself from such sell-your-soul-for-ap-
proval behavior is through an age-old law of the universe: the
"give to get" principle of energy circulation. This principle
holds that to get more of something in life, you must *give
away* the very thing you desire. To get more love, you need
to give more love away. To get more money, you need to give
money away. Thus, to get more approval, acceptance, and
attention for yourself, you need to *give* more approval, acceptance, and attention.

Charity Begins at Home

Start by giving to yourself. One reason we're so starved for
the approval, acceptance, and attention of others is that we
fail to give these same things to ourselves. Instead, we
dump on ourselves, reject parts of ourselves we deem unac-

ceptable, and neglect ourselves to the point of exhaustion and disease.

Give yourself more *approval*. You deserve a lot of credit for all that is unique, admirable, and special about you. Respect even those aspects of your personality that seem to work against you. As Emerson taught, your greatest liability is your greatest asset carried too far (or at the very least, it's a trait that, while no longer functional, served you in the past).

Give yourself *acceptance* as well. You are a miracle worthy of awe and reverence, *flaws included*. You don't have to become anything or accomplish anything or get rid of anything to be worthy and acceptable. You already are. As Emmanuel says:

> Until you can accept yourself you lock the doorway to the expansion you yearn for. This expansion comes through your heart. Be kind to yourself. . . . To insist on perfection precludes growth. To accept imperfection as part of your humanness is to grow. If you can love the part of you that you think is imperfect then the act of transformation can begin. When you judge it and throw it out of your heart it becomes a hardened shell that blocks the Light.
>
> If you deny what is your nature you become deeply attached to that denial. When you accept what is there, in its truth, then you are released. One does not release through rejection. One releases through love.[1]

It bears repeating. One releases through love. You don't have to wait until you're all fixed up to accept who you are. You can do it now. Affirmations facilitate the process. Each morning as you arise, say to yourself:

[1] Pat Rodegast, *Emmanuel: A Manual for Living Comfortably in the Cosmos*, Friends' Press, 1985.

"Today I am treating myself kindly in thought, word, and deed."

"Today I am gentle with myself when I feel confused or scared."

"Today I keep a sense of humor about my less than perfect nature."

Last but not least, give yourself *attention*. The relationship you have with yourself is the most primary one in your life. Don't neglect it. We so often dedicate hours, days, and years to our relationships with others while the one with ourselves struggles on a starvation diet of stolen moments squeezed into jam-packed days. You deserve prime time, not the crumbs.

William Buckholtz, a California physician who teaches stress management to executives, suggests a "Four-Percent Rule." Allot an hour each day (four percent of your time) to yourself. Spend 20 minutes of this hour on a quiet activity like meditation or gardening. Devote a second 20 minutes to some form of aerobic activity like hiking, biking, swimming, or jogging. Spend the third 20 minutes on a flexibility activity such as stretching.

Spending prime time with yourself helps you construct a foundation of self-trust that in turn allows you to center yourself and clarify priorities.

Give to Others As Well

The second part of the "give to get" formula involves giving more approval, acceptance, and attention to others. Start by giving them increased *approval*. Actively look for what you appreciate in the people you come into contact with and compliment them in heartfelt, appropriate ways. Reinforce the growth and accomplishments of those around you with a sincere pat on the back. Don't be stingy—let your approval flow freely and generously. Approval and appreciation, when genuinely expressed, are a warm, wonderful, and enriching experience for all involved.

Unfortunately, competition sometimes blocks our celebration of a friend or colleague's victory. Our competitive spirit pits us against others and views only the first one to accomplish something as the winner. When you feel competitive in this way, instead of rejoicing when you hear someone's good news you feel the less for it. You may give a perfunctory "That's great," but privately you envy the success and walk away depressed because it didn't happen to you.

Give others *acceptance*, too. This doesn't mean you need to be buddy-buddy with everyone in your life or approve of all they do. Nor should you stop setting limits when your rights are violated or your boundaries overstepped. Greater acceptance of others is more of a "live and let live" attitude that shows you don't expect perfection in others any more than you expect it in yourself. Conduct an experiment. The next time you encounter nerve-wracking incompetence, treat the inept person lovingly anyway. You wouldn't think of being angry or impatient with a kindergartener who can't yet read. Some people are still covering the curriculum you've already mastered, but everyone is learning at exactly the rate suited to himself or herself. If you must, you can still set limits with those who are slow or bumbling. Just do it with heart. It's not necessary to be angry and upset.

Finally, give others *attention*. Even if you don't have a lot of time to offer, be present for every second you have. It's easy to live the better part of life distracted, thinking of something else as you go through the motions of small talk or habitual routines. Most of us live absent-mindedly—thinking of sex as we brush our teeth, thinking of the grocery list as we make love, thinking of tomorrow's meeting as we buy the groceries. Pay attention to what's in front of your nose. Listen intently to what others say to you, even if the interaction is only a fleeting one. As John Handley, the founder of Life-Spring, a personal growth workshop, put it, "Show up for your life!"

Get Used to Criticism and Rejection

You don't have to fall apart at the seams when someone doesn't like you. Criticism and rejection are inevitable aspects of life, so get used to them. No matter how carefully you tread or how wonderful a person you are, you're bound to encounter occasional complaints from others and get a few doors slammed in your face. Desensitize yourself to disapproval. Once you get accustomed to the idea that criticism is unavoidable, it becomes easier to hear what others have to say without it getting to you.

You might want to imagine criticism rolling off you as water rolls off a duck's back. Actor Michael Landon once told an interviewer that early in his career he adopted such an attitude to help him deal with the continuous stream of professional criticism he received as a public figure. If someone tore his acting to shreds, he told himself, "Hey, if they don't like my work, they've got lousy taste." For him, it was an issue of survival—had he let all the negative feedback in, he would have given up on himself.

Most of the time, of course, you don't need this kind of fortress mentality to protect yourself. In fact, an extreme state of being closed down to the opinions of others will usually work against you. A more balanced response lies somewhere between walled off (*"Screw him. He doesn't know what he's talking about"*) and wide open (*"He must be right, I'm no good"*). I like using an imagery of roses to foster an "open yet guarded" SoftPower state. See yourself surrounded by roses with thorns that gently deflect negative and unwanted energy yet allow you to stay open to what's happening around you.

Opinions Are Fickle and Fleeting

If a five-year-old calls you "poo-poo head," you don't brood about it for weeks or let it eat you up inside. You don't talk it over ad nauseum with your girlfriends (*"Can you believe the nerve of him calling me 'poo-poo head'!"*). You shrug, smile, say "Isn't that silly," and move on. See if you can't do the same thing with criticism that comes your way. Smile, shrug it off, and move on with your life.

Opinions—the stuff of which criticism is made—are not necessarily truthful or useful. What they are is universal. Just as *you* go around life making nonstop judgments about everyone around you, so everyone else is walking around making nonstop judgments about you and everyone else. What's the big deal?

Abraham Lincoln once wrote,

> If I were to read, much less answer, all the attacks made on me, this shop might as well be closed for business. I do the very best I know how, the very best I can, and I mean to keep doing so until the end. If the end brings me out right, what is said against me won't amount to

anything. If the end brings me out wrong, ten angels swearing I was right will make no difference.[2]

Of course, if someone's opinion of you is about to end a friendship, cost you your job, or lose you a promotion, you may not be quite so cavalier about the matter. But most situations are nowhere near this serious. Most are in the "poo-poo head" category. And even when a clash of opinions feels significant or does result in the ending of a relationship, it doesn't have to be the end of the world. Consider it instead a reflection of a deeper "misfit." Perhaps you've simply grown in different directions or outgrown the relationship.

Adopt a Posture of Curiosity When Criticized

When criticism comes your way, say to yourself, *"Isn't this interesting that somebody is reacting negatively to me. I wonder what I'll discover from this?"* Postpone feeling angry, defensive, or hurt. You can get all upset later on if you still feel the need. While maintaining a curious, emotionally neutral state may seem impossible when you're at the brink of rage or despair, it *is* doable—especially if you practice with ahead-of-time visualizations.

Be brave—find out more. Face criticism squarely even when it means recognizing rude realities. As a friend once put it, "Facts are friendly—at least you know what you're dealing with." Facts *are* friendly. And someone's opinion of you, while

---

[2] From Francis B. Carpenter's *Six Months with Lincoln in the White House*, Watkins Glen, New York, Century House, America Life Foundation.

not necessarily valid, *is* a fact. Hiding from what's unpleasant may offer you temporary relief, but, in the long run, denial dooms you. It's only by looking at yourself and others with eyes wide open that you find true power.

A good first response with criticism is to seek more information. Clearly this is a smart move when criticism is confusing, but it also works well even when you think you've fully understood what's been said. If nothing else, it's a way to stall for time before responding to the criticism itself.

As you ask questions, stay aware of your tone of voice and manner. A belligerent, challenging "What do you mean by that?" will only lead to a battle. And be careful not to fight what is said in response to your questions. Remember, your critic is responding to *something*, even if it's a figment of the imagination or a distortion of the truth. Put your ego on the back burner as you gather useful information. You don't have to agree or admit to anything. Understanding is the goal.

Consider the merit. Resist the tendency to unilaterally reject criticism directed toward you. Let it in temporarily even if it seems completely off the wall. Once you check it out to see what foundation it could have, you may be surprised to find a few grains of truth in the feedback. If nothing else, it will be invaluable information about how you're perceived by at least one individual.

Patterns of criticism (feedback you hear on a regular basis) is especially worthy of your attention. A pattern doesn't necessarily mean the criticism itself is valid, just that there is surely something to be learned from it. A close friend, for example, had heard for years that others saw her as cold, aloof and unapproachable. In reality, this couldn't have been further from the truth—my friend is warm, thoroughly approachable, and extremely loving. Obviously, though, for some reason, she *was coming across* as cold, aloof, and unapproachable. When she stopped defensively resisting the feedback (*"That's not true! I'm not cold, am I?"*) and instead asked herself, *"I wonder what this is about?"* she immediately realized that her shyness with strangers was probably looking to others like aloofness. Once she began making an effort to be outgoing when meeting new people, her image problem disappeared.

Consider the source and the motive. Ask yourself, *"Do I respect this person's opinion?" "Is this person negative about lots of things?" "Do we have radically different styles or perspectives?"*

When you and others are on completely different wavelengths, disapproval or rejection from them should come as no surprise. I remember a time at the start of my speaking career when I almost threw out a brochure that I had just spent months and a good deal of money producing, because a colleague was highly critical of it. Then I took a long look at *his* brochure and was amazed (and amused) to find it the worst brochure I'd laid my eyes on in a long time. Yet there I was ready to give up on my own style of doing things because of what he thought!

Don't dismiss feedback entirely, however, just because you don't see eye to eye with the person giving it. Such information can sometimes be the most interesting criticism of all because it gives you a slant on yourself and your ideas that you ordinarily wouldn't get to see.

As you evaluate feedback, consider your critic's motives as well. Does the feedback seem well-intentioned or manipulative and cruel? If you're unsure of the motive involved, you might want to ask the person directly about it: *"Why are you telling me this?" "What are you hoping to accomplish with this criticism?" "I'm not sure what you expect me to do with this feedback—what did you have in mind?"* Even if you don't get much response to your questions, you will probably at least get the other person thinking.

Review your options and make a decision. Depending on the source, motive, delivery, and content of what's been said, you may do little with criticism or quite a lot. Here are a few possible courses of action:

1. *You can thank the person.* If the criticism seems well-intentioned, you might want to acknowledge the person for taking the time and trouble to be honest with you (*"I appreciate your willingness to share your feelings. Thank you"*), even if you do nothing further with the information or completely disagree with what's been said.

2. *You can agree.* Used judiciously, agreement is a powerful, assertive response (*"You're right. I should have called you to tell you I'd be late"*). If there is truth to the allegations, bite the bullet and admit you were wrong. If you agree with only part of what's been said, say so (*"You're absolutely right—I didn't handle this very well, but I don't agree that what I said was a lie"*).

3. *You can say you're sorry.* Saying you're sorry is different than admitting you did anything wrong. You can express sincere regret over the fact that a misunderstanding or conflict is taking place (*"I'm sorry you took it that way. I certainly didn't intend to be abrupt. I was concerned about my time because I was very rushed"*) without assuming blame. When criticism is well-founded, however, there's nothing like a sincere apology and admission of fault (*"I'm sorry for yelling at you—that was uncalled for"*) to smooth out the situation.

4. *You can give your side*. If you disagree with criticism and want to explain your side of the situation, it's fine to do so, but in terms of timing it's usually best to hold off a bit before having your say. Otherwise, the person you're dealing with will probably only see you as defensive and won't really listen to what you say. Hear your critic out. Ask a few questions. Think about what you hear. *Then* give your perspective. The important thing is to take your time. There's no rush. You have plenty of time to respond.

When you do react, be sure to "speak for yourself." "You're wrong, that's not true" or "You're nuts!" will only inflame the situation. You'll get better results saying, "*I don't agree with you on this*." "*I see this differently*." "*I remember what happened differently*." (We'll be talking more about this important skill of "speaking for yourself" in the next chapter.)

5. *You can make amends and take preventative measures*. It can be easy to become so caught up in defensiveness that you forget to think about what could happen to make things better. If criticism is legitimate and something can be done to right a wrong (or avoid a similar conflict in the future), by all means do it. When a situation has been hashed and rehashed, continuing to talk about it is like beating a dead horse. Once you've discussed a matter to everyone's satisfaction, bring "future focus" and closure to the interaction by asking, "*What will settle this for you?*" "*What do you want me to do differently next time?*" (You'll find more information on the idea of "future focus" in the next chapter.)

6. *You can set limits on how you've been treated*. If criticism is delivered in an abusive manner, it's appropriate to set limits about the treatment you're receiving, even if the charges are valid ones ("*I don't like how you're talking to me. If you want me* *to listen to you, you need to stop the name-calling"*). When the attack is a generalized personality assault (*"You're very difficult to get along with." "You're a slob." "You never think of anyone but yourself"*), focus on the specifics of the situation and dismiss the generalizations (*"You're right—in this case I was thinking of myself. But I certainly don't agree that I never think of others"*).

Do Whatever You Do, Then Let the Whole Thing Go

It's the nonstop, never-ending, after-the-fact obsessing over criticism that invariably takes the biggest toll. You relive the charges again and again, stirring yourself up over and over by rerunning it in your mind and recounting all the gory details to friends. Reworking an upsetting situation is productive only if the goal is to better understand what happened or envision a "best you" response. Then you'll profit from the rerun. But when all you do is get yourself worked up one more time, you are just prolonging your misery.

As you desensitize yourself to disapproval, remember that it's perfectly natural to want to please. We all want approval. It's wanting approval *too much* that causes problems. Brian Tracy, on his audiotape program *Peak Performing Women*, says that peak performers tend to live their lives independent of the blame or praise of others.[3] Like everyone else, they enjoy applause when it comes their way. But, when they get boos or yawns instead, they don't see it as all that traumatic. Like Abraham Lincoln, they know that what counts is not what someone thinks of them but whether or not they're being true

[3] For information, contact Brian Tracy Learning Systems, Suite 202, 462 Stevens Ave., Solano Beach, CA 92075.

to themselves and whether or not they've given a situation their best shot.

BIG BEAR #2.
CONFLICT: THE FEAR OF ARGUING
OR FIGHTING

A second fear that commonly inhibits limit setting is the fear of a fight. We're afraid that if we tell the truth, a situation will get out of hand and there will be a scene. When you're dealing with someone with a bad temper or a tendency to break down and cry the possibility of out-in-the-open conflict becomes even more worrisome and the name of the game can become sidestepping at all costs the other person's anger or tears.

There are a number of reasons why the threat of conflict is particularly scary to women. For one thing, conflict usually involves exposure to disapproval that we otherwise might never know about. For another, we frequently don't trust ourselves to handle conflict with poise and dignity. It's not so much someone else's emotional outburst we fear, it's our own. We're scared we might blow up, say something we later regret, or —heaven forbid—break down and cry.

Sometimes your fears may center around indirect retaliation rather than an out-in-the-open fight. You're afraid you'll be made to pay for your honesty. And sometimes this *can* happen. You turn someone down and he gets even by turning you down the next time you ask for something. You bring up a problem with your boss, and she suddenly decides you're not right after all for that big promotion. You finally get the nerve to stand up to your mother and, next thing you know, you're written out of the will.

Such passive-aggressive "guerrilla warfare" tactics are understandably difficult to deal with. It's like shadowboxing an unknown entity. If you suspect covert, "get even" behavior, consider bringing your suspicions out into the open with direct questions (*Are you turning me down because I didn't help you out last month?*"). When a relationship is riddled with passive aggression, you might want to ask *yourself* a few questions as well. Do you really need this person in your life? Do you really want him or her dictating or undermining your life, and how honest you can be? I know a 35-year-old man who missed out on the chance to finally meet the father he'd never known as a child because he let himself be emotionally blackmailed by his mother, who threatened to disown him from a sizable inheritance if he were to ever see his dad. Can any amount of money or any job or relationship be worth selling out on yourself to such an extent?

Where There's Pain, There's Gain

Painful and frustrating as disputes can be, they also serve as powerful, positive forces for our learning and growth. They are a great way to develop backbone. It's been said you can learn more about yourself from two days of agony than you can from ten years of bliss and contentment. The hard times of conflict season you. They are a chance to strengthen yourself from the inside out. Periods of crisis and conflict often motivate you to turn to inner spiritual resources and force you to tap into otherwise unused creative powers.

Tough times season relationships as well. Bringing a disagreement out into the open can show you where communication tends to break down, where emotional sensitivities lie, and what needs to be done if a relationship is going to survive (at the very least) or thrive (at the very best) in spite of conflicting differences. When you take the risk of bringing differences out into the open, you discover what kind of commitment and caring a relationship is made of. If a relationship can't survive a bout of conflict, it's built on landfill and isn't much of a relationship at all.

BIG BEAR #3.
FAILURE: THE FEAR OF FALLING ON YOUR FACE AND LOOKING FOOLISH

The last of the fears that significantly interferes with power and honesty is the fear of failure (*"But what if I sound stupid?"* *"What if I get tongue-tied?"* *"What if it doesn't work and I stand there with egg on my face?"*). If the thought of failure is more than you feel you can endure, "Better safe than sorry" may become your modus operandi. You say nothing rather than risk saying something dumb. You swallow your anger rather than end up at a loss for words. You feign agreement rather than risk losing an argument.

Just as there's no escaping criticism and conflict in life, there's no avoiding failure. In fact, success and failure go hand in hand. Successful individuals who are in command over their own destinies invariably experience more than their share of wrong moves and defeats. They just refuse to let setbacks stop them. Babe Ruth is a perfect case in point. While Babe Ruth made baseball history as home-run king, the very same year he set the home-run record he also earned the title of strike-out king.

To be able to get the big ones in life, you must be willing

to strike out repeatedly and not let it stop you. As Al Siebert discovered with extensive research on "survivor personalities," those able to thrive against tough odds are those willing to "look foolish, make mistakes, and laugh at themselves."[4] We need a new definition of winning that includes trying something new even if we fail miserably. As Dennis Waitley says, "winning" should be "coming in fourth, exhausted and ecstatic because last time you came in fifth." As Ben Franklin boasted, "I have never failed. I have stumbled and learned but I have never failed. It is only failure when you quit." A good way to foster a change of heart toward failure is to drop the word itself from your vocabulary. Terms like "temporary setback," "challenge," and "learning experience" make it easier to see mistakes as opportunities—chances to discover, expand, and advance. From this healthier perspective you know that even if you royally botch things up, you at least get a chance to identify what not to do next time. With this attitude the prospect of doing something less than perfectly won't be so terrible.

There Are Ways to Reduce the Risks

With information, risks become more manageable. When there's a chance of a major blowup, keep your eyes wide open and carefully assess the risks at hand and the best ways to handle them. If you're afraid of having a fight with a significant person in your life, this is the time to review what you know works.

---

[4] You can get more information on Siebert's work by writing Al Siebert, P.O. Box 535, Portland, OR 97207.

Reread this book (the next chapter is full of strategies for reducing risks and ensuring success in difficult interactions) and other favorite self-help books. You'll get the most from such resources when you're in the middle of a mess because you'll have grist for the mill and can try out the advice in real-life situations.

Self-help tapes are another excellent way to refresh and strengthen your skills. Audio tapes have revolutionized adult learning, and with good reason. They're convenient—you can listen to them as you get dressed, do chores, or commute. They make it easy to "overlearn"—you can hear them over and over again. They have vitality—the spoken word gives you information that is impossible to communicate in print. It's like the difference between reading a written "Call Nancy a.s.a.p." message and listening to Nancy herself on your answering machine give you the full scoop on what's going on.[5]

Your Worst Fears Are Not All That Bad

In the long run, as you no doubt already know, everything has a funny way of turning out for the best. The biggest loss can (over time) bring surprise gains. Your worst nightmare come true can ultimately bring you your greatest heart's desire. Earl Nightingale, a well-known motivational speaker, once told of the coral found on the turbulent side of the great barrier reef between New Guinea and Australia. This particular coral

---

[5] Get yourself on the mailing lists of major producers of audio-tape learning programs, Nightingale-Conant (800-323-3938) and CareerTrack Publications (800-334-1018) are two of the best. There is information on ordering the *How to Speak Up, Set Limits, and Say No* audio program at the end of this book.

is especially bright, vibrant, and abundant. In contrast, the coral on the inside reef (where things are calm and quiet) is pale and lacks vigor. A guide once explained to him that the coral on the protected side dies off quickly because it doesn't have to deal with daily challenges to its growth and survival. The coral "facing the surge and power of the open sea," on the other hand, "thrives and multiplies because it is challenged and tested every day."[6]

In a similar way, each of us as a growing human being needs a certain level of healthy tension in our life. When things go too smoothly, our creativity is cramped and our discipline lost. It's not that you should invite turbulence and strife into your relationships. Just recognize that criticism, conflict, and failures are the stuff of life. With the right attitude, they serve to enliven you instead of destroying you.

One of the best techniques for preparing for a bout of expected criticism, conflict, or failure is the "best you" rehearsal described in the last chapter. In addition to helping you determine what to do to straighten out a situation, such a scenario shows you that you can handle a situation even if communication totally breaks down. You get the chance to picture even the worst occurring and imagine yourself responding at your very best.

Pave Your Way with Care

A SoftPower approach blends caution with the gamble. Thus, you take into consideration all implications of a communication, positive and negative, before deciding on a direction.

---

[6] Dennis Waitley, *The Psychology of Winning*, Berkley Books, 1979.

You know there are times when keeping your mouth shut may be the worst thing you can do and times when it may be the best.

You don't have to indiscriminately blurt out everything that you think with brutal frankness. Timing, tact, tone of voice, and choice of words all should be considered. These factors make a world of difference in increasing your odds for success. With a softer touch, an assertion becomes less jolting and is easier for others to accept.

Under certain circumstances you may want to make an extra effort to be low-keyed in your approach. Such special care might be warranted, for example, when you're dealing with someone who is elderly, from another culture, or likely to be explosive. It can be called for in high-jeopardy situations or when an interaction takes place in circumspect settings (such as a concert hall, church, or funeral home). You may also want to "come on easy" when you put someone to a lot of time and trouble with a request.

Following are examples of low-keyed ways in which to state a limit or make a request. A number of these start out by stating positive intentions or an expression of empathy. Others involve asking for a response or information. Imagine saying these statements in a neutral, pleasant tone of voice. The "generic" part of each is set in italics so you can see at a glance the phrasing to remember:

> "*Excuse me, you may not be aware of it*, but you're kicking my chair."
>
> "*Were you aware* that you missed our luncheon appointment yesterday?"
>
> "*I thought you'd want to know*—if I do this for you, I doubt if I'll be able to meet our Friday deadline for the Morgan report."

> *"Would you be kind enough* to return this dish to the kitchen. It's much too salty for me. I'd like to order something else."
>
> *"Would you be good enough* to take off your hat? It's blocking my view."
>
> *"Please don't take it personally*—I just don't feel like talking about this."
>
> *"I'm sorry to trouble you*, but we'd like to change tables— this location is too noisy."
>
> *"I don't mean to be unfriendly*. However, my schedule is so busy right now I'd rather not make any plans."
>
> *"I don't mean to be difficult*, but I need to have this invoice redone as soon as possible."
>
> *"Would it be possible* for you to loan me some money until Friday?"
>
> *"Would it be a problem* if I ask for your help on this as I need it?"

In considering ways to tread lightly, a word of caution is warranted. If you tend to be timid about setting limits, you may need bolder strategies, not softer ones. Plus, in certain situations, no matter what your usual style, it may take increased directness, not subtlety to "get through." For example, when you know you're nonnegotiable about a position, expressing yourself in a "Would you mind if . . ." manner is misleading. Or if someone is blatantly violating your rights and ignoring your attempts to deal with the matter, you may need to come on stronger to resolve the situation. I remember a time when I tried to discourage an overly friendly stranger in a bar with nonreinforcement (refusing to acknowledge his presence, much less his comments). When this didn't work, however, there came a point when I needed to make my point more directly (*"Get lost!"*).

If You Still Feel Nervous, Try the Following:

Focus on your positive intent. Before approaching potentially contentious interactions, spend a few minutes contemplating your motives. What do you want to accomplish with your communication? Are you seeking increased understanding? Or the preservation of a friendship? Do you want to clear the air or prevent a similar problem from happening in the future? Why is it important for you to tell the truth in this situation? Hold your highest intent clearly in mind and forge ahead even if you feel apprehensive. When Joanne Woodward admitted to Eleanor Roosevelt that despite a lifetime in front of the camera she was still terrified of public speaking, the First Lady assured her that she would have all the courage she needed as soon as what she had to say became "more important than the fact that your knees are knocking."

Put your mind on something else. In *Who Dies?* Stephen Levine tells of American Indians who used "power chants" as centering devices to keep their hearts open and their minds clear at times of great danger. Each Indian brave repeated a particular affirmation of courage over and over until it became so familiar it was second nature to him. That way, in a crisis he wouldn't have to think about it or try to remember the words of the chant. They would be right there at the tip of his tongue.[7]

Create a courage chant for yourself to help you steady your mind when you're feeling scared. One popular affirmation is,

[7] Stephen Levine, *Who Dies?* Anchor Books, 1982.

"I let go and let God." In Siddha Yoga, the mantra *"Om Namah Shivaya,"* (*"I honor the Self within"*) is used. Here are other possibilities:

"As sunlight fills my heart, evil leaves my life."

"I am centered and calm—ready for anything."

"I have unlimited wisdom and energy to carry me through."

"I trust in the Higher Good knowing I am taken care of."

"My heart is filled with love and I am at peace."

"I am at peace inside and out—tranquil, alert, and confident."

"I quiet turbulent emotions and calm my racing thoughts."

"I am composed and serene, able to gracefully handle all that is before me."

"I breathe in clean, fresh air and release all tightness, fear, and anger."

"I am filled with great strength, clarity, and courage."

"I feel strong, capable, and ready to enjoy life."

Pull back and regroup. In Chapter Two, I mentioned that a "time-out" period is useful for gaining greater self-awareness. It's also helpful in calming yourself down and gaining courage. If emotions are getting out of hand in an interaction, call for a time-out (*"I'm too upset to talk about this anymore—I'd like to take a break and talk some more later"*). By leaving the scene of the problem, you give yourself a chance to restore clear-headed bravery. In a state of panic or rage, you will probably not be thinking straight. Your mind will make a lot of bad guesses about what things mean. Your upset state handicaps you in another significant way as well—it makes it difficult for you to access inner sources of wisdom. Much as clouds temporarily interfere with the sun's rays on a stormy day, a stormy emotional state blocks you from your intuition.

If you take a breather from an upsetting interaction, be sure you use the time you gain to your advantage. It's not going to help if you let your mind run wild and get more worked up. Create an "eye of the storm" environment for yourself where you can settle down and cool out. This can be a real or an imagined setting that feels safe and comfortable to you. In such an atmosphere, you can more readily restore a reasonable frame of mind. You might want to use music as a backdrop for a calming ambience. Listening to Chopin or Bach can be far more tranquilizing (and certainly healthier) than popping a Valium or downing a glass of wine. While silence can be equally healing, when your mind is in a highly agitated state music may be more effective.

Another way to create an "eye of the storm" spot is to climb into Mother Nature's lap. Take a walk in the park while repeating your courage chant. Spend some quiet time sitting under the stars. Pass an hour relaxing in a meadow. Mother Nature helps us regain perspective and find answers and directions we didn't know we had.

Fill your heart with love. Last but not least, one of the best ways to quell fears is to fill yourself up instead with love. *Women Beyond the Wire* is an inspiring book on the British women who spent World War II in Japanese concentration camps in Indonesia. In it, there is a description of the "unshakable serenity" some of these women maintained, even in the face of angry, raving Japanese prison camp officers. Loving compassion for the enemy deflected the worst of the outbursts and helped the women sustain spirit and stamina through unbelievable adversity.[8]

[8]Lavinia Warner and John Sandilands, *Women Beyond the Wire*, London: Joseph, 1982.

Another story demonstrating the power of love is told in *Return from Tomorrow*, a book by psychiatrist George Ritchie. It describes a man called Wild Bill, also a concentration camp survivor from the war:

> He was one of the inmates of the concentration camp, but obviously he hadn't been there long: His posture was erect, his eyes bright, his energy indefatigable. Since he was fluent in English, French, German, and Russian, as well as Polish, he became a kind of unofficial camp translator . . .
>
> Though Wild Bill worked fifteen and sixteen hours a day, he showed no signs of weariness. While the rest of us were drooping with fatigue, he seemed to gain strength . . .
>
> I was astonished to learn when Wild Bill's own papers came before us one day, that he had been in Wuppertal since 1939! For six years he had lived in the same airless and disease-ridden barracks as everyone else, but without the least physical or mental deterioration . . .
>
> Wild Bill was our greatest asset, reasoning with the different groups, counseling forgiveness.
>
> "It's not easy for some of them to forgive," I commented to him one day . . . "So many of them have lost members of their families."
>
> "We lived in the Jewish section of Warsaw," he began slowly, the first words I had heard him speak about himself, "my wife, our two daughters, and our three little boys. When the Germans reached our street they lined everyone against a wall and opened up with machine guns. I begged to be allowed to die with my family, but because I spoke German they put me in a work group.
>
> "I had to decide right then," he continued, "whether

to let myself hate the soldiers who had done this. It was
an easy decision, really. I was a lawyer. In my practice I
had seen too often what hate could do to people's minds
and bodies. Hate had just killed the six people who mat-
tered most to me in the world. I decided then that I would
spend the rest of my life—whether it was a few days or
many years—loving every person I came in contact with."

This was the power that had kept a man well in the face
of every privation.[9]

Love and fear are incompatible states. There's no way to
experience them simultaneously. I know it's a tall order to feel
love when you're dealing with an arrogant bully who is treating
you like dirt. I know it's a challenge to open up your heart
when your feelings have been crushed or your hopes dashed.
But at moments like that when it seems impossible to do, think
of Wild Bill. If he could do it, so can you.

[9]George G. Ritchie, with Elizabeth Sherrill, *Return from Tomorrow*, Zondervan,
Grand Rapids, MI, 1978.

6

STANDING YOUR GROUND

When Push Comes to Shove

Standing your ground" implies strength, not violence. Pam McAllister in an essay called "A Little Bit of Ghandhi with a Touch of Ethel Merman," uses the image of two hands to symbolize the nonviolent response. One hand stops an assault from others in much the manner of a cop halting traffic. The other simultaneously reaches out to calm an attacker with a soothing gesture of conciliation. McAllister tells of a group of women who used a nonviolent display of power during the course of a peace march when they encountered an angry, out-of-control mob:

> People jabbed the pointed tips of their little American flags like tiny spears at the peace camp women and screamed, "Commie dykes, go back to Russia!" and "All you girls need is a little rape."
>
> I saw that a number of women had sat down, then

formed a circle together . . . I can remember the reassurance I immediately felt at the sight of those quietly seated figures. Without words they made the statement it was essential that we make. This statement was that we posed no threat—had no intention of trying to thrust our way through the mob. But the statement was also that we had no intention of retreating either. We knew our Constitutional rights. We had a right to walk here. This is the two-fold message that gives nonviolent response its leverage: We won't be bullied; but you needn't fear us. You needn't fear us; but we won't be bullied.[1]

The courage these women demonstrated is admirable indeed. Unfortunately most of us would not be so brave were we to find ourselves in similar circumstances. When push comes to shove, we may manage an initial act of bravery, but if this assertion is met with anger, scorn, or dismissal, we are usually quick to back down (*"I tried—it didn't do any good!"*) or stand there at a loss for words (*"Now what am I supposed to do?"*). Or we shift to a battle posture and fight it out (*"All right, I tried being reasonable. If she wants to be nasty, I'll be nasty, too"*). The challenge, therefore, is not just how to make a first move, but how to make a second, third, and perhaps even fourth move—all the while maintaining integrity, composure, dignity, and power.

[1]Pam McAllister, *You Can't Kill the Spirit*, New Society Publishers, 1988.

USE YOUR "MUSCLE"

Standing strong when you're up against opposition requires "muscle." The concept of muscle level was developed by Dr. Pam Butler, a writer and psychologist in Mill Valley, California who counsels individuals and conducts assertiveness workshops.[2] Using muscle level helps you preserve a position of power by moving gradually from words alone to action-backed consequences. This spirit of strength has nothing to do with strong-arming others to your will. It's a campaign of self-respect that communicates needs, desires, and limits to others in a nonabusive fashion.

The idea of "muscle" is based on the wisdom of starting out at a low level and escalating as need be. The premise is that in most circumstances you're better off bringing problems out into the open at an early stage. When you sit on resentments to keep the peace, all you usually end up keeping is tension. Not only that, by waiting until you've "had it," you frequently overreact and only make matters worse. If you're not the type to blow up, you worry yourself sick about an upcoming confrontation, then end up scared silly, unable to speak the simple truth. Confronting problems early on makes it easier to set limits with a minimum of fuss and bother. There are four levels of muscle to use in standing your ground. Let's look closely at each and see what is involved.

[2]Pam Butler, *Self-Assertion for Women*, Harper & Row, 1981, and P. Jakubowski and A. Lange, *The Assertive Option*, Research Press, 1978, remain my two favorite books on assertion.

Muscle Level One

At Muscle Level One, you state your position as clearly as you can. This may involve expressing an emotion (*"Allison, I'm angry that you wore my earrings without asking me"*), making a request (*"In the future, I want you to check with me before you borrow anything of mine"*), putting forth an opinion (*"To me, the Calloway report still needs work—it has some weak areas that need more data"*), or drawing the line on something you find unacceptable (*"If we submit the report in its current state, I'd rather not have my name on it"*).

Part of the success of Muscle Level One depends on using a civil, "grown-up" tone of voice as you express yourself. It's best to make direct eye contact with the person to whom you're speaking and to use easygoing, open body language (no clenched fists or furrowed brows).

Muscle Level Two

At Level Two, you persist in your efforts if your first attempts to straighten things out didn't produce the results you were after. You are still using words alone, but your delivery is amped up—like an industrial-strength version of Level One. Sometimes all you do is restate what you said at Level One. At other times, you might expand on what you said the first time or shift to a bolder tone. (*"I'm serious, Jim. Cut out the sarcasm"*). Muscle Level Two can also involve responding to what was said in reaction to your initial assertion or asking questions to clarify your understanding of what was said.

There are a number of ways to increase the power of your

delivery at this level. You can do it by speaking louder, by dropping your volume, or by slowing down. When not over-done, such changes create effective emphasis. Other tactics include making compelling eye contact, leaning forward, moving in closer, or lightly touching the person you're talking with, if that's appropriate. The underlying goal of Level Two is to use words and body language to convey clearly that you mean what you say and are intent on resolving the situation.

Luckily the majority of problems can be successfully handled at Level One or Level Two. Sometimes, however, words alone will not be enough and you'll need to move to Level Three.

Muscle Level Three

At Level Three, you announce what actions you plan to take if your limits are not respected ("*If you continue being sarcastic, I'm hanging up*"). The goal is not to threaten but to let those you're dealing with know ahead of time what you'll do if your limits are not respected. Once told what to expect, they can then make an informed decision about what they want to do in light of the potential consequences.

Here are examples of Level Three assertions. If these seem extreme, remember that most situations will not require this kind of "move to action" mode. Imagine the following statements expressed in a clear, strong, centered tone of voice:

"If you keep calling me names, I'm leaving the room."
"If I'm not going to receive credit for my contribution, I'd rather not be involved."
"If you're late again, I don't want to continue carpooling together."

"If I can't get satisfaction on this repair job, I'll take my car somewhere else in the future."

"If you don't stop talking, I'm going to get the theater manager."

"If you're unwilling to go with me to counseling, I want a divorce."

When you have some kind of legitimate authority relevant to the problem at hand, this is the time to mention it:

"If you continue turning in unacceptable work, Bill, I'm going to have to fire you."

"If you don't stop bothering me, I'm filing harassment charges."

This is also the time to mention natural consequences— direct and indirect repercussions that might influence the person you're dealing with to accept or cooperate with your position:

"If I do this for you Brian, I won't be able to meet our other deadlines."

"If you break that toy, Joshua, I'm not buying you another one."

In some situations, there will be nothing you can do to affect the other person. But, even then, it can still make sense to speak up about a problem. Many people will honor a request —especially if you communicate it in a civilized, low-keyed way (*Excuse me, I've been waiting in line for a long time. The end of the line is around the corner*").

Muscle Level Four

The fourth level of muscle involves follow-through on what you said you'd do at Level Three. Here is where you "walk your talk" and teach people to take you seriously. Which means it's an essential step in building credibility with others. Every time you fail to carry out your word, you show others that you don't mean what you say. Establishing credibility in this way will be especially important if you have a history of giving in when bullied, seduced, or ignored.

For obvious reasons, it's smart to announce only consequences you're willing to execute. If you're leaving for a two-week family vacation and the kids are beating each other up in the back seat, don't say, *"If you guys don't stop fighting, we're not going anywhere!"* unless you're ready to abandon the trip. Better to give a warning you can follow through on (*"If you don't stop fighting, I'm pulling over to the curb and we'll wait there until you settle down"*).

Of course, there will be occasional times when for any of a variety of reasons it makes sense to back down or reconsider your position. Just be careful not to make this a habit. If you change your mind routinely, however, the word will spread fast (*"You know her, she won't do it"*) and others will—not surprisingly—stop believing you. The following story illustrates:

Nancy was a secretary/receptionist at a printed circuit board company where I conducted team-building sessions a number of years ago. During my interviews with her, she complained to me about the time she wasted every day with countless interruptions from employees asking her for help in filling out medical and dental insurance claim forms. At my suggestion, at the next weekly staff meeting she set limits. After handing out information sheets (with specific instructions on how to complete the various forms), she announced that she'd be available for questions for one more week, then everyone was on their own.

Several weeks later, I returned to the office. Nancy shook her head in despair when she saw me.

"What did I tell you?" she groaned. "I knew it wouldn't work."

"What happened?" I asked.

"Nobody takes me seriously around here. They're still coming in with those damn questions morning, noon, and night."

"And what do you do when they ask for help?" I inquired pleasantly.

She looked at me surprised and, after a moment's hesitation, said with a red face, "I answer them, of course."

We both laughed! Nancy was right. Nobody was taking her seriously, including herself. And if she wasn't taking herself seriously, how could she possibly expect anyone else to?

Only one person has to take your limits seriously and luckily it turns out to be someone you have complete control over—yourself. By using appropriate muscle, you show others through your words and your behavior that you take yourself seriously.

You Won't Always Go 1–2–3–4 to Action

The concept of muscle level is not a carved-in-stone set of rules to be adhered to under all conditions. In the complexity of real life, you may exercise the different levels in a number of ways. Sometimes you'll assert once or twice, then "hang out" for an extended time at Level Two (where you use words alone). At other times, when a problem is serious, you may decide to *start* a confrontation at Level Three (*"You lay a hand on me again and I'm out of this relationship"*). Or you might skip words entirely, move directly to Level Four, and let your feet do the talking.

There are even times when you start out with verbal attempts to resolve a situation, then skip over Level Three and proceed straight to action because letting others know what you plan to do is not prudent or feasible. For example, if, despite numerous interactions with your boss about a serious problem, you see no improvement, you may want to wait until you find a new job before announcing your decision to quit.

Then there are times when, after asserting once or twice, you let a matter go because you realize that nothing you say or do is likely to make a difference. An experience I had a number of years ago while tent camping with my two sons is a perfect example:

It was close to midnight on the first evening of a two-week trip through Oregon and Washington. My kids were snoozing in their sleeping bags, but I lay wide awake unable to sleep because of the noise from a nearby party in the campground. For an hour, I tossed and turned, stuffed earplugs into my ears, and crammed pillows over my head, all to no avail. At one o'clock, I was still bug-eyed. Finally, in frustration, I pulled on some clothes and trooped down the trail to find the festivities and handle the problem directly.

I followed the noise to a large tent site surrounded by Harley-Davidsons. Inside the wagon train of motorcycles, six tough-looking men were having a rip-roaring time and feeling no pain. Calling on all the composure I could muster, I said in a friendly tone, "I can see you guys are having a great party. You may not have realized it, but the noise is traveling in the campground. Would you be good enough to turn off the radio now and keep your voices down?"

I felt quite pleased with myself—the delivery seemed just right—pleasant yet powerful. Unfortunately, the group was not impressed. One of the guys on the sidelines hollered, "Blow it out your ear, lady," and let out a belch to the amusement of his buddies. Another looked ready to throw a whiskey bottle at me. These were a bunch of angry drunks who were hardly about to let an uppity woman spoil all their fun.

Standing there, I made a quick decision not to go to Muscle Level Two. I doubted that even an industrial-strength response would do much good in this case. I quickly scanned my options but couldn't think of many. The only one that seemed halfway feasible was finding a ranger, and that didn't seem realistic. What was I going to do, walk around in the dark knocking on tents in search of one? The most sensible choice seemed to be to keep my mouth shut and head back to my tent. It was clear to me that the finest assertion in the world wasn't going to do a bit of good.

I turned and walked back to my tent with all the dignity I could muster. There was, I told myself, no need to feel humiliated or cowardly. In fact, what I needed to do was give myself a good pat on the back for trying. It takes guts to be assertive, and the world does not always reward us for the effort. We need to reward ourselves. Otherwise, when we don't accomplish what we're after, we end up discouraged and reluctant to try another time. Assertion *does* work. It just doesn't work all the time. As you practice the skills of SoftPower, your batting average will improve, but, no matter how skilled or courageous you become, you'll still suffer occasional defeats and disappointments. When this turns out to be the case, it's important to appreciate yourself for having had the courage to try. So as I returned to my tent, I mentally congratulated myself for giving the problem my best shot.

Once back in my tent, I faced a number of choices. One was to fight the situation. I could have stomped around, cursing about what a bunch of inconsiderate jerks those guys were (which would have been easy to do given that they had become even noisier). But such a response would have only made the situation harder on me. It would have pumped up my adrenalin and guaranteed more sleeplessness.

A somewhat smarter choice was to tolerate the situation. I could have accepted the fact that I hadn't been successful, crawled into my sleeping bag and tried my best to get some sleep. The problem was I knew I was too wired up by this point to settle down.

A third option, however, was the smartest choice of all. This involved seeing beyond "bearable" to "fruitful." It meant taking advantage of the situation. To exercise this choice, I needed to ask myself how I could benefit from the fact that I was wide awake in the middle of the night with no sleep in sight. With a little creativity, there are always ways to turn lemons into lemonade. In this case, I lit my Coleman lantern and did some reading and writing. Far better to be productive than to fight sleeplessness.

SOFTPOWER "STAND YOUR GROUND" STRATEGIES

There are a number of SoftPower attitudes and actions that can help you execute all four muscle levels with greater levels of success. Keep the following sixteen ideas in mind as you practice standing your ground.

1. Give Others the Benefit of the Doubt

As a rule, assumptions (whether positive or negative, accurate or inaccurate) tend to make themselves happen. When you hold positive assumptions, you increase your chances for success. When you hold negative ones, you set yourself up for failure. With a negative mind-set (*"I have to battle for everything I want"*), you convince yourself that the odds are against you (*"I can tell—he wants a fight"*). You expect arguments (*"He's not going to give an inch"*) and you remember only the times things don't work out (*"So what else is new—he never agrees with me"*).

With an optimistic frame of mind, on the other hand, you meet people with a comfortable aura of positive expectancy. When a problem arises, you're confident the matter will be worked out to everyone's satisfaction, and your upbeat manner shows it. Because of this positive personal atmosphere, you frequently get cooperation from others and, more often than not, end up straightening out problems with ease.

The phenomenon of the four-minute mile barrier is a good demonstration of the self-fulfilling nature of assumptions:

For years, in the field of running, there was a widely accepted belief that it was impossible to run a mile in faster than four minutes. Runners everywhere tried in vain to break the famous four-minute mile speed barrier. Finally, in 1956, Roger Bannister, a British medical student, did the "impossible" and made sports headlines around the globe. Shortly after Bannister broke the record, an amazing thing happened—a number of other runners quickly followed suit and accomplished the same feat.

The fact that these athletes suddenly succeeded at something that had so long eluded them was not mere coincidence. It was a function of beliefs fulfilling themselves. Here's how it works: When you believe something is impossible, one of two outcomes is likely. You either give up without ever trying because you're convinced you'll fail (*"Why subject myself to the misery of defeat?"*). Or, if you do try, you make a halfhearted attempt that dooms you to disappointment. Then, when you fall short of the mark, your failure becomes proof that you were "right" and you end up twice as certain you'll never succeed in the future (*"I knew it was impossible"*).

There's nothing new to the notion of self-fulfilling beliefs. Henry Ford told those who worked for him, "If you think you can or think you can't, you're absolutely right." In *Illusions*, Richard Bach said: "Argue for your limitations and you get to keep them." Some call it karma, others call it cause and effect, but by whatever name, the notion that "what goes around comes around" has been a respected principle of world-class philosophies and religions for thousands of years.

The philosophy of SoftPower rests on this same important concept—ultimately, you get back what you put out and you put out according to what you believe. You may not get back your beliefs immediately (or in any predictable form), but in one way or another, dependable as a boomerang, a predictable circle of cause and effect eventually gets completed.

During limit setting, this cause-effect cycle means that as a rule people will "play back" to what you play to. When you treat people combatively, you're likely to get a fight; when you treat them rudely, they're usually rude right back; and when you treat them with optimism and kindness, you have a better chance of being treated well in return.

It's Hard to Stay Positive When You're Dealing with a Jerk

It's easy to assume the best and act your best when you deal with people who are themselves being cordial and reasonable. It's the others—the individuals who could care less about your needs or who seem intent on making your life miserable— who present the challenge. How do you stay positive with them?

Following are two assumptions that can help you deal positively with difficult people. If the first one doesn't apply, hopefully the second one will. While neither promises smooth sailing, they definitely improve your chances of getting a decent response from others.

Assumption #1: Others may not realize that there's a problem. Even if you think others should know something is bothering you (*"Anyone with half a brain would know calling this early is rude!"*), they may not. The friend who calls at the crack of dawn may be unaware you don't get up until 8. The man at the next table who lights up a cigar may not realize that the smell of it will make you want to throw up your dinner. A boss who dumps a huge project on your desk when you already have too much to do may have forgotten all the other assignments you're handling.

Assume innocence at least for starters and maintain the optimistic view that once you communicate about the problem the two of you will be able to straighten everything out just fine.

Assumption #2: You're dealing with a good, decent person who is out of sorts. When someone seems aware but unconcerned that you're upset, try this second assumption. View the person (no matter how obnoxious or unacceptable the behavior) as a good, decent individual going through some sort of hard time. Perhaps the rude waitress is snippy because she was up all night with a sick baby. Maybe the impatient clerk in the shipping department is suffering a migraine or got a flat on the way to work. Perhaps your impossible boss was abused as a child. You never know what causes are at the root of someone else's attitude or actions. Don't take how they are personally. Instead, consider what's happening a reflection of unfortunate behind-the-scenes circumstances.

The intent of this assumption is not to make excuses for someone's unpleasant or unacceptable behavior. It's merely a reminder that underneath all unacceptable behavior there is someone like yourself who is a mixed bag of good and bad. If you play to a person's good, decent side—however poorly developed or hidden it may be—it's more likely you'll be able to turn the situation around and get a decent response in the process.

2. Make Your Delivery Congruent

All parts of your expression, including the nonverbal, need to support your communication. To ensure congruency, stay aware of your tone of voice, voice volume, eye contact, gesturing, and posture. When you tell someone you're angry with a smile on your face, you send a confusing message. If your eyes are nervously averted as you say, "I don't want you to do this!", you appear timid and tentative. If you slouch, slump, or hang your head as you declare, "I mean it!", your words lose their punch.

Few of us as youngsters saw models of strong, self-assured women who were able to stand up for their rights and manage conflict effectively. If, because of this, you have trouble imagining how you'd look were you to communicate with courage and confidence, watch for women around you who seem to operate from a position of inner strength, then use their behavior as a blueprint for your own. Or simply make it up as you go along. Gradually, as you stretch your imagination you'll find your own style.

Monitor your tone of voice. The tone of your voice is a critical dimension in a SoftPower delivery. If your voice conveys inappropriate apology, seduction, sarcasm, anger, fear, or impatience, it can undermine the most perfectly worded assertion. People will believe your tone of voice before they'll believe your words. And with good reason. When you are telling a lie, your tone of voice often leaks out the truth. If you swear you're not angry but there's ice in your voice, you're probably angry. If you insist you're not upset but your voice sounds wounded, your feelings are probably hurt.

Using a neutral tone of voice will help you calm down. It's a way to act as if you feel a certain way before you actually feel it. Expressing yourself in an "It's not a big deal" way makes it much more likely that you'll get what you ask for. On the other hand, a challenging "You'd better or else" approach usually provokes "Oh, yeah, says who?" resistance. In his book *Prescriptions for Happiness*, Ken Keyes suggests making all requests (no matter how urgent or important) with the same tone of voice you'd use to ask someone to pass the salt and pepper.[3] Remember that people play back to what you play to. Don't set up a fight unless you want one.

If a "salt and pepper" tone of voice seems out of the question because you're livid with rage, try to at least use what I call a grown-up tone of voice. Even when your blood is boiling, it's possible to speak in a calm, serious, no-nonsense manner.

The pitch of your voice is another vocal characteristic to monitor. Pitch is an important indicator of power. Authority and strength are associated with a low-pitched voice, while a high pitch is associated with children and empty-headed females. People with high-pitched voices come across as lightweights. Luckily, with breath control and the help of a speech consultant, you can learn to modulate your pitch.

If you have a medium- or low-pitched voice, there are several habits you'll still want to avoid. One is ending statements with an upward inflection. This implies uncertainty and makes you sound as if you're asking a question. It leaves your listeners hanging. Make your point declaratively by coming down in pitch at the end of what you say.

Raising your pitch to stress a word and raising your pitch when you're upset are other habits that diminish the power of your communication. Both make you sound shrill and out of control. It's better to drop your pitch when you're feeling emotional or want to emphasize something. This accomplishes two things—you come across as more grounded and you *feel* more grounded as well.

Monitor your eye contact. Eye contact communicates courage. It shows others that you're not scared and it helps you feel courage even when you're shaking in your boots. Your

---

[3] Ken Keyes, *Prescriptions For Happiness*, Living Love Publications, Coos Bay, OR. If you don't know of a speech consultant, ask local hospitals, universities and colleges, or public school systems for referrals.

ability to look someone in the eye can make or break an interaction, especially when you're dealing with a bully. In fact, if you can't look an aggressive person in the eye as you set limits, you might as well save your breath. It's highly unlikely you'll be taken seriously if you're staring at your shoes or the ceiling as you speak. This doesn't mean you have to make unremitting or piercing eye contact to communicate effectively. In fact, a stare-down will work against you. It's perfectly okay to look away from time to time to collect your thoughts and give everyone a break from the intensity of the contact.

Unfortunately, women are frequently uncomfortable making eye contact because of early training that taught such directness was dangerous and brazen, something hussies did. In certain situations, of course, direct eye contact *can* suggest seduction or be risky. Obviously, you don't want to make eye contact with a man on the street who's giving you the once-over. But if you need to set limits with this man, looking him in the eye is essential. It lets him know you mean what you say and will not be intimidated.

Monitor your voice volume. Speaking too softly can ruin the impact of an otherwise fine delivery. Even in the animal world, the animals with the least power (rabbits and giraffes) make the least noise. Mumbling and murmuring are low-powered, withholding ways to interact with others.

When you speak softly, one thing comes across loud and clear—you don't think what you have to say is worth hearing. In a matter of seconds, you broadcast low energy, low enthusiasm, low self-esteem, and high anxiety. Once again early programming is a part of the problem. If you were instructed as a young girl to keep your voice down ("*Little ladies speak softly.*" "*It's not nice to shout*"), it's easy to end up uncomfortable with the sound of your own voice.

Breaking a deeply entrenched habit of soft-spokenness usually takes time. Practice speaking with more volume while you're driving alone in your car or taking a shower. Ask friends for their help. Have them signal you when your volume drops. Although it will take a while to change, it will be worth all the time and trouble it takes. If you have something to say, it deserves to be said with a voice volume that shows self-respect.

Monitor your body language. Body and facial language are two last dimensions of congruency that need your attention. Accusing gestures, a combative stance, physical retreat, slouched shoulders, lowered head, nervous mannerisms, a stiff smile, a glare, a wince—all weaken your attempt to communicate with power.

A full-length mirror is an ideal self-awareness tool for developing assertive body language. Most women, contrary to popular opinion, spend very little time actually looking at their mirror image. Buy a high-quality mirror and use it for more than counting wrinkles, putting on mascara, and checking your hem. Observe how you walk, how you hold your body, how various gestures look. Experiment with yourself. Smile. Look happy. Look preoccupied. Look "neutral." Now frown at yourself. Pout. See what other people have to put up with when you're wearing a "long face" or "dirty look." Place a small mirror in front of you when you're talking on the phone so you can see your expressions as you converse with others.

The most effective tool for heightened awareness of body language is a video camera. You'll learn more from five minutes of studying yourself on video than you will from years of feedback from friends. The camera is a very unforgiving teacher. If you have no access to video equipment, inquire about workshops in your area that use video feedback. Or call a local

Toastmaster club and see if they videotape their meetings.[4] If you have a friend who owns a camera, arrange to have him or her film a meeting (or party) that you attend. It's fascinating to see yourself moving about informally in a group. How do you look? What impressions might a stranger have watching you? Do you notice any of these power-deflating tendencies:

Excessive or inappropriate smiling
Biting your lips
Shuffling your feet
Tilting your head to the side
Swaying back and forth
Crossing your legs while standing
Putting your hand over your mouth
Fidgeting with a pencil, jewelry, or clothing

Ideally you want a self-assured look where you stand tall with open body posture. You take full, deep, easy breaths and wear a facial expression that is in keeping with your intent. You reach out to others with a confident handshake and use gestures that support rather than detract from what you're saying.

State Your Positive Intentions

I mentioned in the last chapter that remembering your positive intent can help you overcome nervousness. If you express pos-

---

[4]There are Toastmaster clubs in most large cities. They meet on a regular basis and offer members a chance to practice public speaking skills in front of a supportive group.

itive intentions, you take this a step further and create a climate of good will. One reason people sometimes resist another's assertiveness is that they see the action as a challenge or rejection. When you let others know explicitly what your motives are, they can stop worrying about whether or not you're up to no good and be more relaxed and open to what you have to say.

Here are examples of how you can assure others that you mean well:

"I'd like to clear up any bad feelings either of us may have."

"I want to understand what happened so we can prevent this from happening again."

"I'd like to tell you my side of this situation and I'd like to hear about yours."

"I want to settle this so we both get what we want."

4. State What You're *Not* Intending

It can also help to express what you are *not* intending—especially if you anticipate a negative response to what you're going to say. This lessens the chances that your motives will be misunderstood:

"It's not that I'm trying to be uncooperative. I'm simply not at liberty to share this information with anyone."

"I don't want to tell you how to live your life, but I need you to know I'm not willing to cover for you anymore when you come in late."

"I don't mean to cut you off, but I have to get off the phone and handle a problem with the computer."

"I'm not trying to change your mind. I just want to share another point of view."

"I don't want to hurt your feelings, but I'm not interested in a dating relationship."

"I don't mean to be unfriendly, but I prefer lunching alone—it's the only chance I have to be by myself."

5. Forecast the Worst

This may seem like a contradiction to my earlier suggestion to assume the best, but in certain situations mentioning your worst fears paradoxically reduces the chances that what you dread will occur. Therapists call this "prescribing the symptom." Here are examples:

"I was afraid you'd blow up over this. That's why I've been reluctant to talk with you. Please hear me out without losing your temper."

"I've been concerned you'd take this the wrong way so I want to be very clear with you. This refusal is not personal. I just don't have time right now to go with you."

"Initially you may think this idea is off the wall, but please give it a chance. Let me fully explain it before you say yes or no."

"I've been hesitant to talk with you because I wasn't sure I'd be able to make myself clear. Hang in there if this is confusing to you."

6. Separate Intent from Effect

When others mean no harm, it can be difficult setting limits with them. Because those you're dealing with are well-intentioned, frankness and directness may seem unkind or inappropriate. For example, if a friend is trying to help you out, you may not want to hurt her feelings by saying you'd rather do a job alone. Or if a boyfriend says something insulting to you as a joke, you may not want to be a spoil-sport (or deal with his defensiveness) by expressing your feelings about the tease.

Unfortunately, even the best of intentions from a well-meaning person can backfire and create distress for you on the receiving end. When this occurs, it's easier to speak up if you differentiate between the person's positive intent and your negative response:

"I appreciate that you want to help, Helen. Thanks for your thoughtfulness. This is a job, however, that I prefer doing on my own."

"I know you're just joking, Ken. But I really don't like that kind of remark even as a joke."

7. Express Your Empathy

Another way to soften the blow when you need to turn others down and feel badly doing so is to express empathy with their side of the situation. Explain that while you're not personally able (or willing) to help them out, you do feel compassion for their plight. The tone of voice used for this sort of communication makes the difference between a heartfelt expression of caring and a hollow excuse:

> "I know you need this loan badly, Bill. I'm really sorry to have to turn you down, but it just doesn't work for me to loan you money."
>
> "I appreciate the bind you're in without a car, Sally. However, I'm not comfortable loaning mine out, even to friends."
>
> "I can see your need for help is urgent. I wish I could help you out. Unfortunately, I've got a pile of deadlines myself, so I can't take this on."

8. Be "Future-Focused"

As I suggested in Chapter Five in the discussion on criticism, a "from now on" perspective can frequently help bring matters to a peaceful close. Endless arguing about a problem goes nowhere, and all it accomplishes is an increase in defensiveness on both sides of the fence and a further polarization of opposing positions. When you've analyzed a problem sufficiently, shift the interaction to a problem-prevention mode. If a member of your staff makes a mistake, express your feelings, determine what went wrong, then turn your attention to strategies for avoiding a repeat performance (*"What do you feel needs to happen to prevent this from happening again?"*).

9. Speak for Yourself and Invite Others to Do the Same

There are three styles of communication that can be used when setting limits. The first two produce more problems than they solve:

Style #1. Speaking for nobody. Speaking for nobody is a weak, indirect, and evasive way to express yourself. It demonstrates an unwillingness to take a stand and leaves the ownership of what you say up in the air.

"That's not the right way to do it."
"One would think you didn't care."
"It's healthy to get things out in the open."
"Going through another person's desk is rude."

Who thinks it's the right way? *Who* thinks this person doesn't care? *Who* wants things out in the open or thinks something is rude? In ordinary interactions, this kind of vagueness may not be a problem. But when you set limits, a speaking-for-nobody style will lack backbone and invite "Says who?" arguments.

Style #2. Speaking for others. "Speaking for others" is a presumptuous, controlling style that does little to further your cause in touchy interactions. Using the editorial "we" or telling others what they're doing (or should be doing) will only provoke a defensive response.

"We need to get things out in the open."
"Here's what you should do."

"Let's not do that now."
"You don't care how I feel."
"You have a lot of nerve going through my desk."
"You aren't listening to me."

Most people resent being spoken for even if you're right (perhaps especially when you're right). They'll fight you tooth and nail ("*I am so listening!*") or come back with a counterattack ("*You're not listening to me either!*").

Style #3. Speaking for yourself. Speaking for yourself is the direct, responsible way to state your position. This is the style of communication to use when you want clarity and power. It demonstrates self-respect and shows a willingness to go public with your feelings, opinions, and desires:

"I'd like to get things out in the open."
"In my opinion this is the best way to do it."
"I don't want to do that now."
"I'm not comfortable that you went through my desk while I was away. Please don't do that again."
"It's hard for me to tell if you're listening when you keep writing while we're talking."

Speaking for yourself tags what you say as one of many perspectives, not necessarily the truth. This encourages others to speak for themselves and arouses less resistance to your ideas. As you look over the following pairs of statements, notice the difference between the various styles:

Speaking for others: "You're wrong."
Speaking for yourself: "I remember it differently."

Speaking for others: "Stop crowding me."
Speaking for yourself: "I'd like more room."

Speaking for others: "You never intended to talk with him about it."
Speaking for yourself: "I don't believe you ever intended to talk with him about it."

Speaking for nobody: "It's rude to interrupt people."
Speaking for yourself: "I don't want to be interrupted."

Speaking for nobody: "That movie was terrible."
Speaking for yourself: "I didn't like the movie."

10. Be As Specific As You Can Be

In general, the more explicit you are about your limits, the better. Specificity requires self-awareness. If you're annoyed by a co-worker's gripe sessions about her husband, you need to first identify what is bothering you before you can clear the problem up. Is it the length of the interactions—does she go on forever? Is it the frequency—does she bad-mouth her partner every time she sees you? Is it the timing—does she greet you with her woes first thing in the morning as you walk through the door? Is it what she tells you—are you uncomfortable hearing the intimate bedroom details of her marriage? Or is it all of the above? The more specifically you understand what lies behind your own reactions, the better you'll be able to communicate (*"Marianne, I enjoy having coffee together in the morning, but I wanted you to know I'm not comfortable hearing the details of your sexual problems with Dick"*).

One reason why it's essential to use specifics is that words are such imperfect vehicles for conveying complex thoughts and feelings. Even when you try to transmit a simple idea, a word or phrase can mean completely different things to different individuals. For example if you and two co-workers agree a project is top priority, one colleague may drop everything and go full force on that one project alone. The other may work on several projects simultaneously while giving the top-priority job the lion's share of time and energy. And you may see completion as the critical issue— the top-priority project needs to be *done* first, no matter what that takes.

Specifics are especially important when crossed wires could spell disaster. Then you need to spell out what you mean with precision. *"I want this done right away—please have it on my desk no later than 3 this afternoon."* Specifics are also useful when you are seeking group agreement. They help you reach out-loud, explicit consensus: *"Do we all agree that this top-priority project must be done by Friday at 5, even if it means suspending everything else to make this happen?"*

Be especially careful about the use of nonspecific pronouns like "it," "that," or "this." Such statements as, "It doesn't matter," "That's what I don't like," or "I'm upset over this" can foster a good deal of confusion. When there's any chance of a misunderstanding, avoid ambiguous pronouns and say exactly what you mean (*"I'm upset over the fact that you told me you'd call yesterday and you didn't." "I don't like it when you correct my grammar in front of friends"*).

Being specific helps you broach problems without condemning or scolding. Contrast the following pairs of statements. The first of each is a nonspecific, global attack. The second is a factual description of the same problem:

"You're unbelievably rude!"
"I'm angry that you cancelled on me at the last minute."

"You have a nerve doing that!"
"If you're going to make decisions about our pension
    fund, I want to be involved."

"Your sloppiness is driving me nuts."
"I don't want you to leave your clothes all over the living
    room."

Specifics are also a way to elaborate on how strongly you
feel about something and why you feel the way you do:

"I prefer driving, but it's no big deal if we walk."
"I know for sure that I don't want to take on this re-
    sponsibility."
"I'm *extremely* upset over the fact that you lied to me
    about this."
"I resent it when you're late because it makes me late too."
"I'm annoyed that you're late because I rushed to be ready
    for nothing."

11. Consider Setting Partial Limits

Limit-setting situations are not necessarily "yes/no" affairs.
Sometimes you want to say "*yes, if,*" "*yes, but,*" or "*yes, and.*"
Partial limits allow you to define under which circumstances
you feel okay about something or under which you do not.
It's one more way to use specifics to pinpoint your position
with precision:

"I'm fine about going to your mother's if we can be home by nine."

"I'm willing to hear what I've done that's made you angry, but I don't want you yelling at me."

"I'd love to go to the movies, but I won't be able to go out afterward."

"I'm happy going out for dinner so long as I don't have to dress up."

"I'd like to buy this if I can return it for a refund, not a store credit."

"I'm willing to stay another ten minutes, then I want to leave."

"I'll chair the committee if I have approval over the budget."

"I'd love to get together on Saturday, but it will have to be afternoon. I need to get chores done in the morning."

12. Ask All the Questions You Want

Asking pointed questions can buy you time, fill in missing gaps, and clarify ambiguities. It also gives others a chance to tell their side of the story (which can lead you to all sorts of revelations you would otherwise never discover).

Here are examples of "inquiry" questions that could elicit interesting, useful information. Imagine asking them in a sincerely curious tone of voice:

"How did you come to that conclusion?"

"Were you aware that this is due tomorrow?"

"How come you say that?"

"What are you expecting from me right now?"

"How do you feel about this?"
"How would you feel if I turned you down?"
"What's *your* opinion?"
"What do you want from me?"
"How firm is this deadline?"
"What specifically do you mean when you call me diffi-
    cult?"
"I'm wondering why you didn't keep your promise."

When others express themselves in nonspecific pronouns,
ask for clarification. If someone says, *"That bothers me,"* ask,
"What bothers you?" If they say, *"It doesn't matter,"* ask, *"What
doesn't matter?"* You'll be surprised at the responses you'll
get—even when you were certain you knew exactly what the
person meant.

In a similar fashion, questions let you check out other kinds
of ambiguous communication:

"I noticed you hesitated—do you have a problem with
    this?"
"It sounds like you're uncertain. Are you?"
"Are you saying that if I refuse this project, my job is in
    jeopardy?"
"Do you mean that as a threat?"

Questions are also a good way to encourage openness and
honesty. When someone stares at you blankly, looks away,
changes the subject, or starts to walk away without a response,
it's appropriate to take the initiative and ask for a reaction:

"Pete, before you leave, would you please give me your
    response to what I've said?"

"You haven't said much, Lisa. How do you feel about this?"

"I don't know what you mean by your shrug. Does that mean you don't agree?"

And by inquiring if there's a problem with a request you're making, you invite the person you're dealing with to be frank with you. This makes it easier for people to set limits with *you*:

"Are you being completely honest with me? I really want to know your true feelings."

"Arc you okay with changing our plans for dinner?"

"Will this work for you? If not, please say so and I'd be happy to figure out another solution."

"Do you have a problem with this idea? I'd be glad to discuss it if you do."

"Do you mind taking on this extra assignment?"

13. Be Ready to Change the Topic

Occasionally a secondary problem crops up as you discuss a primary one. For example, you may feel frustrated because a conversation seems to be going nowhere or you're being mistreated during a confrontation. Suddenly there are two issues that need attention—the "presenting" problem (the issue you were talking about in the first place) and a secondary one (the frustration you're experiencing as you talk about the presenting problem).

When this happens, you can drop issue number one and address the more immediate concern—what's happening at the moment. By doing this, you move from *content* (the original problem) to *process* (the current interaction). For this reason, such a maneuver is sometimes called a content-process shift. Here are examples:

"You seem distracted, Tom. Do I have your attention?"
"I feel we're going in circles. It seems as if we're both trying to convince each other and neither of us is succeeding."
"Hal, stop shaking your fist at me. I don't want to be bullied."
"That sounds like a threat. Is it?"
"I'm not sure why you're laughing, but I'd like you to stop. I'm serious about this."

14. Play a "Broken Record"

Back in the '70s, when the first of the assertiveness books hit the stands, many of them recommended a technique called the broken record. The reader was told that one way to get through to others was to repeat a point over and over and over and over. While most situations are far too complex for this kind of simplistic strategy, occasionally parrotlike repetition works beautifully. For example, if you're dealing with someone who's ranting and raving, repeating a limit over and over in a strong, clear voice can be very effective:

"I do not want to be yelled at."
The other person keeps yelling.
"I do not want to be yelled at."

He or she keeps yelling.
"I do not want to be yelled at."

You just keep repeating yourself until the person quiets down.

15. Use "Verbal Aikido"

Locking horns with someone in a disagreement or conflict typically gets you nowhere fast. Aikido, a martial art from Japan, teaches students to deal with opposing force by refusing to engage with it. Instead of fighting an obstacle, students of aikido learn to sidestep it, thus disempowering its force. This principle works equally well in limit setting.

"Fogging" is one form of verbal aikido that involves acknowledgment of another person's position without agreement or disagreement.[5] It's a "maybe yes, maybe no" response. For example, if you're dealing with a know-it-all, you could say *"Perhaps you think this is the best way to do it. I see it differently."* Or if your kids resist a curfew you might say, *"Maybe it doesn't seem fair to you. I still want you home by midnight."* You refuse to be sidetracked by futile, frustrating debates about the fairness of the curfew, which is not even the relevant issue. Instead, you let them think whatever they want (they're entitled to an opinion), all the while maintaining your limit.

The power of fogging comes from the fact that while you don't agree with others you also don't disagree. You simply do not get into it with them.

[5]The concept of fogging was developed by Manuel Smith, author of *When I Say No I Feel Guilty*, Bantam, 1985.

Fogging is a practical skill useful in many situations. It's a good response to use when others label you negatively:

"You're being ridiculous!"
"Maybe it seems ridiculous to you. To me, it's not. I don't want to go."

"You're being too sensitive."
"Perhaps to you I seem overly sensitive. However, that is how I feel."

"Don't be so uptight—it's not that big a deal."
"Maybe it's no big deal to you. To me, it matters a lot."

A second form of verbal aikido goes beyond fogging. Here, you get in step with others by first agreeing with them, then restating your limit:

"You have a good argument for continuing the old way, Linda. However, I'd still like to try this new approach and see what happens."
"I agree with you, Ken. It doesn't make sense. Nevertheless, I want to go anyway."

16. Stand Up to Bullies

Bullies are frequently deprived of honest feedback because the people they deal with are too intimidated to say anything. What bullies usually get instead is passive-aggression—indirect behavior designed to get even or punish. Those they push around undermine, sabotage, and withhold as revenge. Thus, bullies "get theirs" in the end, but they usually don't know where it came from or what it's related to. Consequently they fail to learn from experience.

Dealing with a bully out in the open by standing your ground can work miracles. The following story illustrates the amazing results you can achieve when you use SoftPower directness to deal with a bully:

Harry Stone was a senior bank vice-president with a notoriously nasty temper. He was especially abusive with his secretaries and, as a result, lost most of the women he hired within a matter of months. When Harry's latest secretary quit after one of his tirades, a woman from another department in the bank took the job. Harriet knew about Harry's reputation but wanted the increase in salary and responsibility that the job offered. She also felt confident she could handle his bully tactics.

For the first few weeks, there was a honeymoon period when all went smoothly and Harry was on his best behavior. Then one afternoon about a month after Harriet started the job, all hell broke loose. Harry roared out of his office and read Harriet the riot act over a mistake she had made.

Harriet had been expecting the outbreak and had carefully planned how she was going to respond. For starters, she did nothing. She simply let him explode. She knew it would be unwise to confront him while he was enraged. Besides, doing nothing bought her time to steady herself and figure out exactly what she wanted to say in response.

After Harry finished his tirade and stormed back into his office, Harriet calmed herself down (telling herself she'd handle the problem the next day) and continued as best she could with her work. Later, she scheduled herself into Harry's appointment book for the following day. Because she knew he was generally more approachable after the bank closed, she set up the meeting for late afternoon.

To prepare herself for the confrontation Harriet asked a friend for help. That night they practiced together what she would say to Harry and how she would say it. Instead of escalating her anxiety by spending the night in worried anticipation, she used the time productively. With "best you" role-plays, she created a behavioral groove in which to move when face to face with Harry.

The next day, she began by stating her positive intentions: "Harry, I want our relationship to be successful. That's why I asked for this time with you. I'd like to talk with you about what happened yesterday."

Then she expressed how she felt and what she wanted:

"First of all, I want to apologize for the mistakes I made. I've corrected them and will do my best to see they don't happen again. But I can't guarantee that I'll never make another mistake. And, when I do, of course I want you to point it out to me. I do have a problem, however, with being yelled at and called names. In fact, I know I'm not willing to work in a situation where that happens. But I *want* to work with you. I know I have the skills you want in an assistant, and I know there's a lot for me to learn in this job. So I'd like to have an agreement with you. Can we agree that when I make a mistake, we can discuss it privately in your office without any yelling?"

She said no more. At first Harry was speechless. No secretary had ever talked to him like this before. Then without looking at her, he grunted, "Fine, no problem," and went back to the work on his desk. Harriet didn't press the point.

Harriet and Harry became a legend in the bank. While he didn't change his personality with others, he treated Harriet with the highest respect. And all it took was one gutsy interaction.

Of course, things don't always work out with such storybook endings. Another ending might have seen Harry screaming and yelling like a lunatic (*"Who the hell do you think you are telling me what I can and can't do?! I run this office, not you! If you don't like my temper, leave!"*). But had that happened, Harriet would at least have found out where things stood. She could then have made an informed choice: Stay and accept the outbursts as part of the bargain or find another job and leave.

By the way, a decision to stay under such circumstances isn't necessarily a bad one. You have a perfect right to stay in less than perfect relationships. The important question is whether you're staying as a free agent or as a scared victim. When there are compelling reasons to stay despite serious problems that aren't going to go away, by all means stay if you want. Just don't whine and complain about the situation if you do. Instead of grumbling, figure out a way to use the situation to your advantage. But please don't misunderstand me. I'm not suggesting you subject yourself to mistreatment or intimidation. However, if for whatever reasons you find yourself staying in a relationship with a bully, there *are* useful lessons that can be learned. Perhaps the most valuable one is how to stop giving bully behavior so much power over you that it has you scared stiff. Each outburst from the bully can be a chance to practice emotional detachment. See if you can ride out the worst tirade with the same level of emotional engagement that you would have watching a show on television. Feel compassion if you can (*"My, isn't it a shame what he puts himself through!"*), but other than that don't bite the bait.

Bullies deserve your compassion. They suffer a great deal

of wear and tear as they storm through life with a hot temper, clenched fist, and short fuse. They deserve your compassion for another reason as well. Ultimately bullies get back what they put out. The abuse they heap on others eventually comes back to haunt them—somehow, somewhere, sometime. But perhaps the biggest reason they deserve compassion is that bully behavior is rooted in pain and fear. The anger and hatred before you is all self-protection. Bullies are invariably hurt, scared individuals. So instead of fortifying yourself in response, see if you can't open up your heart and send them some much-needed love even as you draw the line with them.

Putting It All Together

We've covered a lot of ground in exploring the topic of standing your ground. Let's review the attitudes and behaviors that help you to have power with heart:

Use "muscle" to back up your limits. Start at a low level and escalate gradually to action-based consequences as need be. Muscle gives you a way to gently confront and apply greater intensity when you fail to get satisfactory results from your initial efforts.

In addition to using appropriate muscle, keep in mind the following:

1. Give others the benefit of the doubt. Assume the most optimistic assumptions feasible in a given situation. A state of positive expectancy sets up self-fulfilling prophecies.

2. Make your delivery congruent. Monitor your tone of voice, pitch, and voice volume. Use a mirror and/or video technology to help you develop posture, bearing, and body language that communicate your power, confidence, and self-respect.

3. State your positive intentions. Don't leave people guessing about your motives. Spell them out explicitly to avoid misunderstandings.

4. State what you're *not* intending. If you suspect someone may misinterpret what you say or do, explain what you *aren't* trying to do as well as what you are.

5. Forecast the worst. When there is reason to expect a difficult interaction, defuse the situation by prescribing the symptom. To do so, state out loud what you're afraid may occur.

6. Separate intent from effect. If you are reluctant to set limits because others are well-intentioned, acknowledge that they mean well. You can still set limits even when another person intends no harm.

7. Express your empathy. When it's difficult to turn someone down, let the person know that you appreciate his or her side of the situation, despite the fact that you've decided to say no.

8. Be "future-focused." After processing a problem to the satisfaction of all, shift your attention to solutions and preventions. Make agreements on what will be done "from now on" to prevent the same conflict from occurring down the line.

9. Speak for yourself. Label what you say as strictly your own opinion and experience, not some universal truth. Invite others to speak for themselves as well.

10. Be as specific as you can be. Be exact about what you say. Expressing yourself precisely saves time and grief for everyone.

11. Consider setting partial limits. Push your thinking beyond the obvious and consider all possibilities. There are usually creative, "outside the nine dots" ways to work out a situation so all parties get their needs met.

12. Ask all the questions you want. Use questions to bring information to the surface, clear up ambiguities, and buy time.

13. Be ready to change the topic. If an interaction is going badly, shift your focus from the problem being discussed to the process at hand—what's happening as you talk.

14. Play a "broken record." When all else fails but you're not ready to walk away, state your limit over and over until you get through.

15. Use "verbal aikido." Defuse opposition to your position with either acknowledgment or agreement. Don't waste energy and escalate confrontations by meeting force with force.

16. Stand up to bullies. Remember Harriet and Harry. Bullies need feedback badly. Give them the gift of honesty.

The following two vivid examples show how SoftPower can work miracles in daily life. The first was sent to me by a woman from Astoria, New York. She wanted to share her success in setting limits under the most challenging of circumstances— a mobbed New York subway in the suffocating heat of July:

"I put one of your techniques into practice and even got a compliment from a total stranger in the process. I was trying to get into a crowded subway car but one woman wouldn't move an inch. I guess she wanted to lean on the door. I tried to edge in. The woman became very angry and said, 'Come on, lady, give me a break.' Rather than get into an argument, I said calmly, 'I'm sorry but I have to get home. I'd be more than happy to change places with you once I'm in.' With a huff she let me in and we proceeded on our way without unduly upsetting ourselves.

"This was an extraordinary accomplishment for me because I am very hot tempered. After the woman got off the train at her station and the train emptied out, I finally got a seat. The woman sitting next to me remarked, 'I can't get over how you handled that situation so calmly, especially at the end of the day and on the subway.' I was happy that someone had noticed. I couldn't help but tell her I was just learning about setting limits and it was great to have it work so well!"

The second story is coincidentally another subway story. It takes place in Japan and is an extraordinary example of the beauty, simplicity, and power of a true aikido response:

The train clanked and rattled through the suburbs of Tokyo on a drowsy spring afternoon. Our car was comparatively empty—a few housewives with their kids in tow, some old folks going shopping. I gazed absently at the drab houses and dusty hedgerows.

At one station the doors opened, and suddenly the afternoon quiet was shattered by a man bellowing violent, incomprehensible curses. The man staggered into our car.

He wore laborer's clothing, and he was big, drunk, and dirty. Screaming, he swung at a woman holding a baby. The blow sent her spinning into the laps of an elderly couple. It was a miracle that the baby was unharmed.

Terrified, the couple jumped up and scrambled toward the other end of the car. The laborer aimed a kick at the retreating back of the old woman but missed as she scuttled to safety. This so enraged the drunk that he grabbed the metal pole in the center of the car and tried to wrench it out of its stanchion. I could see that one of his hands was cut and bleeding. The train lurched ahead, the passengers frozen with fear. I stood up.

I was young then, some twenty years ago, and in pretty good shape. I'd been putting in a solid eight hours of Aikido training nearly every day for the past three years. I liked to throw and grapple. I thought I was tough. The trouble was, my martial skill was untested in actual combat. As students of Aikido, we were not allowed to fight.

"Aikido," my teacher said again and again, "is the art of reconciliation. Whoever has the mind to fight has broken his connection with the universe. If you try to dominate people, you are already defeated. We study how to resolve conflict, not how to start it."

I listened to his words. I tried hard. I even went so far as to cross the street to avoid the chimpira, the pinball punks who lounged around the train stations. My forbearance exalted me. I felt both tough and holy. In my heart, however, I wanted to save the innocent by destroying the guilty.

"This is it!" I said to myself as I got to my feet. "People are in danger. If I don't do something fast, somebody will probably get hurt."

Seeing me stand up, the drunk recognized a chance to

focus his rage. "Aha!" he roared. "A foreigner! You need a lesson in Japanese manners!"

I held on lightly to the commuter strap overhead and gave him a slow look of disgust and dismissal. I planned to take this turkey apart, but he had to make the first move. I wanted him mad, so I pursed my lips and blew him an insolent kiss.

"All right!" he hollered. "You're gonna get a lesson." He gathered himself for a rush at me.

A fraction of a second before he could move, someone shouted, "Hey!" It was earsplitting. I remember the strangely joyous, lilting quality of it—as though you and a friend had been searching diligently for something, and he had suddenly stumbled upon it. "Hey!"

I wheeled to my left; the drunk spun to his right. We both stared down at a little, old Japanese man. He must have been well into his seventies, this tiny gentleman, sitting there immaculate in his kimono. He took no notice of me, but beamed delightedly at the laborer, as though he had a most important, most welcome secret to share.

"C'mere," the old man said in an easy vernacular, beckoning to the drunk. "C'mere and talk with me." He waved his hand lightly.

The big man followed as if on a string. He planted his feet belligerently in front of the old gentleman, and roared above the clacking wheels, "Why the hell should I talk to you?" The drunk now had his back to me. If his elbow moved so much as a millimeter, I'd drop him in his socks.

The old man continued to beam at the laborer. "What'cha been drinking?" he asked, his eyes sparkling with interest. "I been drinking sake," the laborer bellowed back, "and it's none of your business!" Flecks of spittle spattered the old man.

"Oh, that's wonderful," the old man said, "absolutely wonderful! You see, I love sake too. Every night, me and my wife (she's seventy-six, you know), we warm up a little bottle of sake and take it out into the garden, and we sit on an old wooden bench. We watch the sun go down, and we look to see how our persimmon tree is doing. My great-grandfather planted that tree, and we worry about whether it will recover from those ice storms we had last winter. Our tree has done better than I expected, though, especially when you consider the poor quality of the soil. It's gratifying to watch when we take our sake and go out to enjoy the evening—even when it rains!" He looked up at the laborer, eyes twinkling.

As he struggled to follow the old man's conversation, the drunk's face began to soften. His fists slowly un-clenched. "Yeah," he said. "I love persimmons, too . . ." His voice trailed off.

"Yes," said the old man, smiling, "and I'm sure you have a wonderful wife."

"No," replied the laborer. "My wife died." Very gently, swaying with the motion of the train, the big man began to sob. "I don't got no wife, I don't got no job. I'm so ashamed of myself." Tears rolled down his cheeks; a spasm of despair rippled through his body.

Now it was my turn. Standing there in my well-scrubbed youthful innocence, my make-this-world-safe-for-democ-racy righteousness, I suddenly felt dirtier than he was.

Then the train arrived at my stop. As the doors opened, I heard the old man cluck sympathetically. "My, my," he said, "that is a difficult problem, indeed. Sit down here and tell me about it."

I turned my head for one last look. The laborer was

sprawled on the seat, his head in the old man's lap. The old man was softly stroking the filthy, matted hair.

As the train pulled away, I sat down on a bench. What I had wanted to do with muscle had been accomplished with kind words. I had just seen Aikido tried in combat, and the essence of it was love. I would have to practice the art with an entirely different spirit. It would be a long time before I could speak about the resolution of conflict.[6]

There are other choices beside fight, flight, and guerilla warfare. With your heart open and your mind clear, you can stand your ground in a dignified and caring way. You don't have to take others on and create bigger battles. Neither do you have to limp off bruised and battered. In the middle zone of SoftPower, you can communicate with clarity and strength: *"I will not be bullied, but you needn't fear me. You needn't fear me, but I will not be bullied."*

[6] Ram Dass and Paul Gorman, *How Can I Help*, Alfred A. Knopf, 1985. Copyright by Terry Dobson.

7
PLAYING WITH YOUR FULL DECK

A Balanced Blend of the Best of All

Everyone at birth is dealt a full deck. Unfortunately, most of us don't play with all our cards. Instead, we limit ourselves by overdeveloping and overplaying certain aspects of ourselves as we correspondingly neglect and underutilize others. To develop SoftPower, you need to open up to *all* of who you are. This brings you the advantage of a balance and versatility that include the entire spectrum of human capacities—from sincere compassion to no-nonsense action, from nonnegotiable firmness to openhearted flexibility, from analytic thinking to illogical intuitiveness, from benevolent self-interest to consideration of others. Luckily, because by nature you are an androgynous being, you already have what it takes to operate with this kind of SoftPower adaptability.

Androgyny, an ancient philosophy from the East, holds that all individuals, male and female, arrive on earth equipped with both a feminine (yin) and masculine (yang) side to themselves.

These "sides" are actually complementary aspects of a single unity, not opposites. To operate with all of your power, you need a rich mix of yin and yang. Yin without the backbone of yang is too weak—a spineless way to operate. Yang without the temperance of yin is so forceful it can backfire or blow up. But when you play with the entire repertoire—with all your cards—you can face challenges with just the right combination of firmness (yang) and flex (yin), emotion (yin) and reason (yang), self-interest (yang) and consideration for others (yin). Used together, innate yin and yang resources offer you tremendous strength and a wealth of options. This, then, is a primary goal of SoftPower: to be equally at ease and competent with all facets of yourself, both the yin and the yang.

While there is no set-in-stone agreement on how the many diverse human aptitudes should be assigned to the yin and yang stacks of an androgynous deck, here's one way to place them:

The Yin Cards

Flexibility
Awareness of responsibility
Focus on relationships
Dependence
Passivity, receptivity
Satisfaction with the status quo
Empathy, understanding
Emotion
Intuition, inner knowing
Patience
Imagination
Synthesis

The Yang Cards

Firmness
Awareness of rights
Focus on self
Independence, self-reliance
Activity, initiation
Striving for more

Objectivity
Reason
Thinking
Intolerance
Realism
Analysis

Ability to see the bigger picture	Ability to deal with details
Ability to handle a lot at once	Ability to sequence/ organize
Vulnerability	Strength
Gentleness, tenderness	Forcefulness
Caution	Courage
Playfulness	Seriousness
Ambiguity, subtlety	Clarity, directness
Expansiveness	Groundedness
Listening	Expressing
Being	Doing

Don't Confuse Androgyny with "Unisex"

Some people resist the idea of androgyny because they think it implies that there are no differences between men and women. Of course there are differences between the sexes. An androgynous viewpoint recognizes that women and men are paradoxically both precisely the same and not the same at all. Underlying all the obvious differences, we are all, independent of gender, bestowed with common capacities that make us very much like one another.

This "completely the same yet totally different" contradiction is played out *within* each gender group as well as between them. All women are alike in some ways and unique from each another in others. In fact this "unity within diversity" theme exists everywhere in the universe. Way down where the electronic microscope goes, everything—from a tree to a rock to a baby—is composed of the same building blocks of pulsating electrical energy. Yet in some miraculous way this underlying sameness ends up in the outer world as a complex tapestry of unending variation and change.

In Real Life Things Are Never Simple

For simplicity's sake, I'll be referring to certain acts (or states of being) as exclusively yin or yang. In real life, yin and yang forces always occur together. Even when there is a clear preponderance of one or the other, there is always at least the seed of its complement at work as well. Asking for help, for example, is frequently seen as an expression of the feminine (because it originates from a vulnerable, receptive state). But the "asking" part of such a gesture is active and therefore could be properly considered yang. Likewise, any creative process (often labelled yin) involves both modalities—intuition (yin) receives inspiration; the rational mind (yang) plans and executes the idea. The artist gets her vision, then buys supplies, goes to the studio, and paints.

How much yin or yang is called for in a given limit-setting situation depends on a host of circumstantial factors. Sometimes the best card to play is a high-yang "I won't budge" one. At other times, the same tough, nonnegotiable stand will land you in big trouble. Dysfunctional styles of setting limits are almost always rooted in an excess of either yin or yang. Three of the types described in Chapter Two, for example, (setting limits too little, too late, and too meekly) reflect an overdose of yin and insufficient yang. These are associated with non-assertion and the feminine mystique. The other three (setting limits too much, too soon, and too forcefully) indicate runaway yang and not enough yin. These are associated with aggression and the macho mystique.

Most of us have a primary operating style that favors either the yin or the yang in tone. For example, one of my friends is, as a rule, extremely spontaneous (high yin). She loves living life by the seat of her pants. She loathes plans and resists being boxed in by a schedule. This freewheeling style works perfectly for her but would be too free for me. I like more predictability and order in my life. Neither of us is right or wrong. We're each doing what suits us personally. Flexibility is the issue. A stubborn adherence to one style or the other is almost always a handicap. If, on a busy Friday night, my friend heads out to a popular restaurant, she needs to be able to ditch spontaneity in favor of a reservation (if she wants to eat before midnight, anyway). I, on the other hand, need to be willing to toss plans out when need be or hang loose without any plans at all if they put me at a disadvantage or restrict me unnecessarily.

A SoftPower style has this kind of flexibility. You may still maintain a bias for yin or yang, but you're ready and able to switch modes when it's appropriate to do so. Thus you are equally comfortable acting impromptu *or* doing things by the clock. But playing with your full deck in this way means more than either/or choices. It means opening up to a vast range of *both/and* options as well. This allows you to make plans and stay open to something better coming along at the last minute. It lets you take a nonnegotiable stand yet remain willing to get off your position if changed circumstances demand it. This is what a true balanced blend is all about.

Going to Extremes Doesn't Work

As I've indicated, yin and yang capacities on their own are neither good nor bad. They're neutrals. Whether they serve you as assets or work against you as liabilities depends on how you use them and how much you use them. As a rule, when you drastically overplay either side of the spectrum (and by implication underplay its complementary component) you end up with problems. By confining yourself to one half of your nature, you not only shortchange yourself, you run the risk that over time those neglected parts of yourself will wither and atrophy from lack of use.

The charts on the next few pages show what happens to limit-setting behavior when you overplay various yin and yang cards:

Healthy Yin

Healthy Concern for Relationship:

You are considerate of others in appropriate ways. Because you care about relationships, you're willing to engage in "give and take." If someone else's need is especially urgent or you've had your way a lot, you are able to gracefully yield on what you want and defer to another person.

Yin Trait Carried Too Far

Concern for Relationships Carried to Extremes:

You pander to everyone's desires and demands, losing sight of what's important to you. Obsessed about relationships, you worry incessantly about the feelings of those you deal with (*"I wonder if he's upset." "I hope I didn't hurt her feelings"*).

Unfortunately, you fail

to show yourself the same level of respect, care, and attention that you so generously dole out to friends and strangers.

Healthy Flexibility:

You are able to go with the flow and change your mind, priorities, or behavior as situations demand. This adaptability prevents you from getting stubbornly hung up on one "right" way.

Flexibility Carried to Extremes:

You're spineless and wishy-washy. Because you're unable to take a solid stand or stay strong in the face of opposition, the minute someone expresses disagreement or displeasure, you cave in and relinquish your position (*"Okay, let's do it your way"*).

Healthy Sense of Responsibility:

You are willing to look at your role in the problems you face. You take responsibility for verbalizing your own needs, feelings, and desires. When you do so, however, you communicate in a responsible fashion without pointing a finger of blame

Sense of Responsibility Carried to Extremes:

You carry the world on your shoulders and assume inappropriate responsibility for everything and everyone around you. You blame yourself for matters that had nothing to do with you. When others have problems, you rush in to rescue them, foregoing or abusing the rights of others.

your own feelings and needs in the process. When others are upset with you, you bear responsibility for their feelings, even when you did nothing wrong.

Healthy Passivity and Receptivity:

You wait for the opportune moment to speak up about problems instead of rushing headlong into action without forethought. You know some things are better left unsaid and that nonaction, in certain circumstances, can be a powerful choice.

In terms of receptivity, you graciously accept what others have to give, whether it's help, a change of heart, a willingness to do you a favor, or a compliment.

Passivity and Receptivity Carried to Extremes:

Doing nothing is a way of life. You'd rather wait and see than face the risk of failure or conflict. Taking action and taking charge make you very uncomfortable.

You are overly receptive. You take in criticism, discouragement, and abuse like an undiscriminating sponge. You don't know how to appropriately protect yourself by setting limits (*"I don't want to be insulted. If this doesn't stop, I'm leaving"*).

Healthy Dependency:

You seek help when you need it. You're not afraid

Dependency Carried to Extremes:

You're a clinging vine and are convinced you can't

to let others know that you need assistance or answers.

When others earn your respect and trust, you are comfortable counting on them. You surround yourself with people who complement you in terms of personal strengths.

take care of yourself. As a result you look to others to do what you could properly be doing on your own. With little sense of self-reliance, you think that, without others, you'd be lost. When there's a job to do, you're afraid to make a move or a decision unless you have the go-ahead from an "expert." Left to your own devices or judgment call, you are anxious and insecure.

Healthy Acceptance and Satisfaction with the Status Quo:

You accept "what's so" instead of fighting it. Because you recognize that life is a mixed bag of good and bad, you don't expect people or situations to be perfect.

You are equally accepting of your own shortcomings. This relaxed self-acceptance makes it easy for you to try new

Acceptance and Satisfaction with the Status Quo Carried to Extremes:

You are accepting to a fault and, as a result, allow others to abuse, mistreat, and shortchange you. You accept whatever is given to you, even when it falls drastically short of what is fair or appropriate.

You get stuck in ruts because you're unwilling to take the trouble to grow and make changes in your things, make mistakes, and occasionally look foolish.

While you have goals for the future, you notice and appreciate what's in front of your nose. You are easily satisfied and content to rest in the moment. Consequently, you take time to smell the roses.

life. Your general attitude is, *"I'm fine the way I am,"* *"It's fine the way it is."* In this way, you dog-paddle through life, content to stagnate and just keep your head above water.

When you overplay the yang side of the deck, it doesn't work any better:

Healthy Yang

Healthy Concern for Self:

You are your own best advocate. You speak up when your rights are violated and ask for what you want when your needs are unmet. This "benevolent self-interest" demonstrates to others your commitment to give to yourself the same respect and consideration you give to them.

Because you are good to

Yang Trait Carried Too Far

Concern for Self Carried to Extremes:

You are self-centered and egotistical, concerned about only your own opinions, desires, and feelings. You're oblivious to or couldn't care less about the rights and needs of others.

You're so worried about your own comfort and needs that you put others to unreasonable lengths to please yourself. The only thing that matters in your yourself, you treat yourself to regular rest and recreation instead of working yourself to the bone. You know that when you take care of yourself, everyone in your life stands to gain.

mind is that you get what you want.

Healthy Firmness:

You have enough backbone to stand on your own two feet, take charge when you need to, and maintain a strong stand if it's important to do so. Your style of communication reflects this inner strength.

As a result of personal fortitude, you can hold your own even when others try to sway you off your position.

Firmness Carried to Extremes:

You are stubborn and bullheaded, unwilling to yield an inch. You have a macho attitude about giving in. To you, surrender represents selling out and is, therefore, totally unacceptable.

Closed-minded and opposed to compromise, you consistently make insistent demands upon others.

Healthy Initiation:

You are fully capable of taking charge and making things happen. Instead of being a bystander in life who merely waits and watches, you are a player.

When a problem needs

Initiation Carried to Extremes:

You are overcontrolling, bossy with others, and unable to leave well enough alone. You always have to have a say about what's happening.

You speak up about

addressing, you speak up. When you have needs that are frustrated, you say so and do what you can to get what you're after.

Healthy Independence:

You have enough self-assurance to know you can count on yourself to handle whatever happens in your life. While you are comfortable relying on others, first and foremost you rely on yourself.

You take care of your own needs and have well-developed survival skills to help you along the way.

Healthy Striving and Ambition:

You have exciting dreams and aspirations, visions of how you ideally want to be. You do what it takes to move yourself forward toward these goals. You

petty issues when you'd be better off holding your tongue. You take action when it would be better to sit still and do nothing.

Independence Carried to Extremes:

Your modus operandi is "I'd rather do it myself!" You feel nervous and vulnerable depending on others. Your unwillingness to ask for or accept help, even when you could clearly use a hand, puts unnecessary burdens on you and isolates you from others. Because of a Lone Ranger attitude, your ability to function as a cooperative member of a team is limited.

Striving and Ambition Carried to Extremes:

You never feel satisfied with your own progress. Even when you finally accomplish a major goal, you feel compelled to keep your shoulder to the wheel know that once you stop growing, you might as well be dead. Consequently, you are continually learning, developing, deepening, expanding yourself. and your nose to the grindstone. It's hard for you to take well-deserved time off to enjoy the fruits of your labor. In your mind, things are never done, never good enough. There's always more to be done.

As you see, on both sides of the yin-yang spectrum any one trait can be either properly utilized or carried to extremes. When well used, an inherent capacity serves you as a strength. When overdone, the same strength becomes a liability.

The SoftPower solution is balance—a balanced blend of the full range of your inner resources. When you play with your full deck, inborn capacities temper and complement each other. Your style becomes a rich mix of all of who you are.

THE SEESAW STAGES OF MALE AND FEMALE

To fully understand this concept of personal yin-yang balance, it's helpful to look at how yin-yang extremes have played themselves out with men and women as social gender groups. Over the last few decades we have passed through three distinct stages. While Stages One and Two are fading social realities, they are hardly over and gone. Some of what is described for these stages is still very much with us today. And while any one individual does not necessarily experience all three stages, most of us who are over forty can personally relate to at least the extremes of Stages One and Two. Certainly, most of us, no matter what our age, continue to struggle and search for suitable ways to operate as balanced human beings.

Stage One:
When Men Were Men (Overyang) and
Women Were Women (Overyin)

Betty Friedan wrote *The Feminine Mystique* in the 1964. Before that landmark book blew the whistle on female programming, the majority of women lived lives enslaved by the feminine. Most of our mothers and most of their mothers before them were reared to be excessively dependent, selfless, nonassertive and long-suffering—the Edith Bunkers of the world.

There are still women today who operate from this overyin framework. They follow Tammy Wynette's advice and stand by their men through thick and thin, even when it means putting up with abuse and neglect. All their energy is devoted to nurturing others and searching for love and approval via feminine wiles. Some of these women are quite happy with this arrangement, but probably most feel powerless to change.

Men with Stage One mentality valiantly try to live up to the tough, hard, unfeeling overly yang ideal of Gary Cooper, John Wayne, and the gang. The majority fall pitifully short of hero status, but that doesn't keep the macho mystique from running their lives. Here are the Archie Bunkers to go with all those Ediths. The Rambo craze is proof that the Stage One ideal is still alive and kicking. A benign version of Stage One masculinity is the "Father Knows Best" Good Provider who joins the daily bumper-to-bumper rat race to take care of the little woman and the kids. With the advent of the two-income family, he is a rapidly vanishing breed. Behind the scenes both the Rambos and the Good Providers feel isolated, empty, and scared.

In the last decade there have been a number of "back to the good old days" backlashes directing us to return to the simplistic he-man, total woman gender roles of Stage One. Fundamentalist religions preach this to their followers. This message is also found in mainstream circles. For example Toni Grant, a radio talk show hostess and psychologist from Los Angeles, recently wrote a book called *Being a Woman* in which she seems to be telling her reader that, to be loved by a man, one must return to being passive, submissive, and devotional. The same message is espoused by California trainer Justin Sterling in his workshops called *Women, Sex, and Power* and *Men, Sex, and Power*. Both Grant and Sterling claim the key to having a successful relationship with a man rests on making him "right" 100 percent of the time, even when he's flat-out wrong. As Grant puts it, "Men need to be right even when they are wrong, and smart women know this and let them."[1]

Stage Two:
The Seesaw Swings the Other Way

Stage Two began in the late '60s and continues to this day. While this era ironically reflected a search for balance, what it in fact accomplished was the replacement of one extreme with the other. In trying to overcome the feminine mystique, many women unfortunately go too far and replace overyin with overyang. They feel compelled to prove (and insist) that they can do it on their own without any help from anyone, thank you very much. "How dare you open the door for me? What do you think I am, helpless?" is the etiquette of Stage Two.

During this stage, women grow suspicious of their own feminine nature. What they learned about nurturing, softness,

[1]Toni Grant, *Being a Woman*, Avon, 1988. p. 175.

and sensitivity was taught only in the context of white-gloved, ladylike feebleness, so they throw out the baby with the bath water. They disown a vital part of their nature because they erroneously associate it with weakness.

Stage Two men have their own version of this see-saw act. They become what Robert Bly calls New Age Soft Men. These men bend over backward to prove their vulnerability and sensitivity. Their worst fear is that others will see them as chauvinists or sexist pigs. God forbid they should open a door for a woman or be attracted to her for sex alone.

The seesawing from one extreme to another that occurs when you graduate to Stage Two demonstrates an important principle. Fighting a stereotype is just as inhibiting as buying into it. When you rebel against something, you are still being run by it. None of these women is a free agent:

The Stage One "Stand By Your Man" Woman who is content to be the power behind the throne and make her man right even if he's a cad or a bore.

The Stage One Seductress who uses "feminine" manipulation to get what she wants without anyone (especially him) being the wiser.

The Stage Two "Man Hater" who blames men for everything from her own miserable lot in life to the state of the planet.

The Stage Two "Man Imitator" who figures if you can't beat 'em, join 'em, and ends up like the throngs of lifeless men devoting their lives to the pursuit of a forty-year watch.

These caricatures of Stage One and Stage Two women, so different from one another on the outside, are all alike in an important way. All forfeit the power and freedom of full choice.

Stage Three:
The Middle Ground Between Machismo and the
Feminine Mystique

Stage Three is, of course, the arena of SoftPower. As a Stage Three woman, you no longer resist or disown one half of your nature. You are a fully developed woman who is neither enslaved by nor fighting against your feminine nature. Instead, you embrace and enjoy all aspects of yourself—your power and your vulnerability, your intellect and your spirit, your independence and your deep desire for relationships, your ambition and your desire to stay at home and build a nest. In the words of John Welwood, you ". . . accept and express both the yin qualities of yielding and devotion and the yang qualities of clarity and independence garnered from the revolt . . . of always pleasing men."[2]

The Stage Three man is equally balanced and at home with himself. He is neither apologetic about nor run by his male energy. He expresses and relishes his tenderness and his might, his ability to be passive and his desire to take charge, his connection with others and his need to be alone.

Together as a couple, Stage Three individuals create relationships based on respect rather than subservience of one partner to the other. They share the responsibility for maintaining a home and parenting children. The careers of both are acknowledged as equally meaningful and important.

While a description of such an egalitarian relationship may seem pie in the sky, there is evidence such partnerships once existed as a norm in human society. In *The Chalice and the*

[2] John Welwood, ed., *Challenge of the Heart*, Shambala, 1985.

Blade, Raine Eisler tells of discoveries in archaeology and anthropology that point to a long era in human history when male-female relationships were founded on equality and mutual respect.[3] In ancient Crete, for example, everyone—male and female alike—honored the feminine life-giving, life-sustaining forces of the universe. This was not, however, a matriarchy where women ruled men. It was a time when men and women stood shoulder to shoulder, side by side, as partners and peers.

According to Eisler, around 1500 B.C. there was a "cataclysmic turning point," an "evolutionary crossroads" when societies shifted from "partnership" values to "dominator" ones. This change came about as a result of invading Kurgan tribes from the East. These conquerors brought with them a new mode of organizing relationships based on domination and control. They saw the destructive power of the blade, not the creative power of the chalice, as the ruling force of society. Unfortunately these dominator values slowly entrenched themselves and, over a period of several centuries, became the new norm. Aside from a few brief resurgences of life-oriented values (as occurred during the Renaissance), they have stayed the norm ever since.

One of Eisler's central points is that the way in which a society organizes its male-female relationships determines all else that happens within it. Thus in a dominator society, technologies are geared toward destruction, nature is seen as a force to be tamed and conquered, and women are viewed as reproduction machines who, as the property of men, are subject to control and exploitation.

We now stand at another critical evolutionary crossroads.

[3] Riane Eisler, *The Chalice and the Blade*, Harper and Row, 1987.

We are gradually realizing the necessity for moving away from dominator values that destroy and abuse and returning to partnership values that protect life and promote peace. As threats of nuclear annihilation and environmental destruction loom on the horizon, our very survival as a species depends on such a shift. This is what Stage Three seeks to accomplish.

What's Keeping Us from Stage Three?

Given the appeal and importance of Stage Three, you'd think we'd all be rushing headlong in this direction. There are, however, a number of significant hurdles to overcome in order to make this change—some societal, others personal. Fear of the unknown, the absence of role models to emulate, resistance from existing social systems with an investment in the status quo—all play a role.

The kind of changes needed to create a new social order are not simple ones. It's not as if all women need more yang and all men need more yin. Perhaps in earlier times this was the case. As someone back in 1850 supposedly said, *"The woman who needs liberating the most is the woman in every man, and the man who needs liberating the most is the man in every woman."* Nowadays, however, things are not so cut and dry. Each of us has our own individual pattern of excess to contend with. There are plenty of women who could use more yin and plenty of men who could use more yang. This is in part due to the rebellion of Stage Two, when some women become so disenchanted with "femininity" they disavow themselves of their natural feminine strengths. Consequently our inner woman is often just as much in need of respect and liberation as our inner man.

ARE YOU A "PERPETUAL MOTION MACHINE"?

One of the ways in which modern women tend to "overyang" it is by overdoing it. As busy professionals with active personal lives to tend to as well, our days are crammed with nonstop activity, our nights and weekends are packed with meetings, social obligations, and chores. For those juggling multiple roles as wife, mother, student, and/or career woman, overdoing it becomes a way of life. I remember the craziness I experienced as a 25-year-old. I was the single mother of two small sons, a full-time graduate student, a half-time intern psychologist at Letterman Army Hospital, and a newly divorced woman meeting and dating men. It was a schizophrenic existence packed with term papers, finals, lunch boxes, Halloween costumes, miniskirts, boyfriends, clinical reports, and project deadlines.

Even if the life you lead is not so complex and crowded, it's easy to end up in perpetual motion because, as women, we are trying to both catch up and keep up with men. If we're not careful, our newly found ambitions can land us in the same rat race men have been complaining about for years.

A perpetual motion machine lifestyle reflects not only external imbalance but inner overload as well. A mind spilling over with facts, figures, and "to do" lists leads to a life of running yourself ragged. Besides being a drain on your health and your spirit, living as a perpetual motion machine strongly affects your personal relationships and personal power. When you're running around in circles, guess who and what gets crowded out of your busy schedule? Gone goes time with those most important to you—time with your honey, time with your friends, time with your kids. And, of course, gone goes time with yourself. This, in fact, is usually the first to go.

Unhealthy, overloaded lifestyles are unfortunately strongly reinforced by our society. The media regularly reminds us that the woman who has it all is doing it all and incidentally never knows when to stop. Take, for example, Martha Stewart, who was featured by *Savvy* magazine in an article called "In Search of Stamina." Bear in mind, Martha is someone we're supposed to want to emulate. She is offered up to us as a model of success. The message is: If she can do it, so can we:

Here Martha describes a typical day: "Yesterday I got up at 4:30 A.M. and finished two columns. I caught the 7:30 A.M. train into New York and dropped them off at King Features. I worked straight through till an 11:00 A.M. meeting with Sterling Vineyards to discuss funding for a TV special. Then I raced out to the airport and got the noon shuttle to Boston for a 1:30 P.M. meeting with WGBH, which is producing the show. I got back to the airport in time to catch the 3:00 P.M. shuttle to New York where I worked the rest of the day and then went to a Perrier-Jouët dinner at Maxim's. A driver took me back out to Westport and when I got home, I cleaned closets all night."

Martha goes on to tell of an eight-day period during which time she flew to six cities, conducted numerous seminars, lectures, and interviews, catered a dinner for 450, wrote three columns, spent one entire day writing copy for a new book, sorted through 25,000 photographs for another book, and planned a publicity party. In her spare time, she spent an evening with her daughter, gave a small dinner party for friends, and did her "normal round of household chores, which included feeding 120 exotic chickens, assorted dogs and cats, and one parrot."[4]

Had enough? I don't know about you, but if I were Martha I'd be ready for the intensive care unit. It's no wonder we're catching up to men in heart attacks. And not only heart attacks—the ratio of male to female ulcer patients in 1966 was 20 to 1. Today it is 2 to 1.[5]

But don't get me wrong. If Martha's nonstop schedule is what you want, fine. And maybe it is. There *are* periods in life when you might freely choose to live as a perpetual motion machine. The key word here is "freely." I remember that during the first few years of establishing my speaking and consulting business I worked round the clock, eight days a week, and loved every minute of it. My kids were grown, the work I was involved in was fascinating, and I was delighted to be consumed by it all. After a certain point, however, I realized that, no matter how exciting the work, I needed to slow down and build into my life time for picnics, time with family and friends, do-nothing time for renewing my spirit.

A SoftPower approach to life requires the balance of breathing room. Without it, you risk being swept up in a frenetic schedule that burns you out both physically and emotionally. You need "down" time alongside bustling activity, time to sit still and take stock. Otherwise, you'll end up carried along by a tidal wave of activity that ultimately crashes you, bruised and battered on the shore. A friend's story is an example:

For over ten years, Michelle lived a high-powered life selling residential real estate in Manhattan. For five of these years, she loved her busy regimen. Every morning she happily dove

---

[4]Courtney Beinhorn, "In Search of Stamina," *Savvy*, September 1986.
[5]"Harper's Index", National Institute of Health, *Harper* magazine, 1987.

into mountains of phone calls to return, leads to follow up, appointments with clients, and activities for networking.

One day she realized that the whole thing had stopped being fun. She tried to slow down but found it impossible. As Michelle put it, "You can't just say, 'Excuse me, I'm stepping off the tidal wave for a rest.' It doesn't work because the wave goes on without you so there's no climbing back. You're left behind. You either continue at the mad, inhuman pace or you don't play the game."

For her, the answer was to leave the game. She sold her condo, packed her bags, said good-by to the Big Apple, and flew west to a Colorado tempo that better suited her deprived spirit. She now lives in Aspen and is happily creating for herself a different kind of success story.

Of course, Michelle's answer may not be "your" answer any more than Martha's was. There is no one answer for everyone. If Martha is happy and healthy feeding 120 exotic chickens and cleaning closets all night after working all day, more power to her. And if Michelle knows she no longer wants to live life on the fast track and what she wants is to move to the mountain top, more power to *her*.

True power is feeling free choice and courage enough to march to your own drummer. And it does take courage. It's scary to realize that you've been dancing to the wrong tune for years. It's upsetting to face the fact that, if you are to respect deeply felt needs and adjust to your own rhythm, you'll need to make big changes. At the age of 50, Linda's changes were anything but easy to pull off. Yet it had become clear that the cost of living against her own grain and violating her spirit was much too high to pay.

HOW ABOUT *YOUR* LIFESTYLE?

It's time to look honestly at your life. Is it the way you want it to be or does it reflect chronic workaholism or an unhealthy "misfit" of some sort? How much do you gripe about how things are? How much is it the same old gripe? I have friends who have been complaining about working too hard and being too busy for literally years. Yet nothing ever changes. The nonstop pressures continue. The never-ending deadlines still loom. Day after day, year after year, they relentlessly sustain the same exhausting pace.

As you assess your own situation, be sure to read your body to see if it may be telling you things your mind doesn't want to face. How do you feel physically? Are you filled with aches and pains? Are you tired much of the time?

Check your feelings as well. What are your emotional patterns? Is your life mostly satisfying and fulfilling or mostly a grind? Do you suffer on a regular basis from bouts of depression or low levels of motivation?

When lifestyle changes need to be made, you'll need to overcome not only your own fears and reservations but societal resistance as well. Cultural chauvinism and double standards may make it hard for you to slow down and achieve better balance in your life. As Kati Marton lamented in that *New York Times* article I mentioned in Chapter One, men are "praised to the skies" for family involvement and concern for their kids. Women aren't. The woman who seeks better home-work balance is "written off as someone not interested in her job." The underlying feeling in corporate America seems to be that a woman's value to business declines when she is a responsible, involved mother and private person. There remains a widely accepted implication that by definition high-powered corporate positions demand the sacrifice of friends and family.

Thank heavens there are also signs of positive social changes afoot. Many organizations are now more receptive to innovative work arrangements like job sharing, flex-time, and electronic cottages. Childcare is finally gaining long-overdue attention and even prominence as the political issue of the '90s. Another promising sign of the times is that, as mentioned earlier, women are becoming entrepreneurs in unprecedented numbers. As business owners, we can maintain more flexibility and control over our own schedule. We may still work our buns off, but we can bring the baby to the office or have the office at home.

Achieving and maintaining balance—both inside of you and externally in your life—is a key principle of SoftPower. To develop a balanced style of power, you need a well-crafted combination of yin and yang—thinking and feeling, firmness and flexibility, concern for self and concern for others, ambition and satisfaction, doing and being.

The first step is to recognize the vast array of inner capacities with which you are naturally endowed. Next, you must develop these talents and proclivities to their fullest. Finally, you need to exercise them, as needed, in your day-to-day life. By using all of who you are and all of what you've got, you play at last with your full deck. This is what SoftPower is all about.

8

TRUSTING YOUR INSTINCTS

Use Your Head,
Then Follow Your Heart

Self-trust is as vital a prerequisite to developing SoftPower as balance. To feel powerful under trying circumstances, you need to know that you can handle whatever comes down the pike. You need to be able to count on your own instincts even when you feel unsure of your moves. With faith in yourself, you can be comfortable in the most challenging of situations.

Most of us fall far short of this kind of self-confidence. We were told as little girls to search for a man to take care of us and count on. A knight in shining armor was going to one day appear and be the "provider." He would bring us what we could not possibly be expected, as mere female of the species, to provide for ourselves. History books in school reinforced the message. Men, we read, have always been the movers and shakers of the world, the heroes who surmount difficulties and solve problems. Women were the ones who stood by and cheered them on.

Overcoming such programming and building greater self-trust is a long-term project. It doesn't happen overnight. The building process usually proceeds gradually as you weather and even profit from hard times. Self-trust also springs from the discovery that you have within you an amazing private well of wisdom called intuition. As Philip Goldberg puts it, intuition is "a subtle guide to daily living, the greatest therapist of all, the one who lives within."[1]

Intuition, as an interior realm of knowing, is described by writers and thinkers in a variety of terms. It has been called our sixth sense, gut, heart, instincts, inner voice, voice of God, and Higher Self. What you call it is unimportant. The important thing is remembering that it's there and using it on a regular basis.

It *is* there. At all times, under all sets of circumstances, an all-knowing force exists within you. This source of wisdom offers you a never-ending fund of answers, directions, and perspectives. It is with you right this minute, at your beck and call, waiting to be used. With SoftPower, your intuitive guidance system functions as an inner compass that points you in the right direction when you're feeling scared or confused.

EVERYONE HAS AN INTUITIVE GUIDANCE SYSTEM, BUT NOT EVERYONE USES IT

Despite our legendary "woman's instinct" and female "sixth sense," many of us have lost touch with (and lost trust in) our

---

[1] Philip Goldberg, *The Intuitive Edge*, J. P. Tarcher, 1983.

intuitive powers. Reestablishing and expanding the relationship you hold with intuition is, therefore, a primary goal of SoftPower.

Women are not the only ones out of touch with intuition. In contemporary Western societies, intuition is a pathetically underutilized force for male and female alike. From grade school to graduate school to the adult world of work, we are taught to discredit inner knowing and imitate instead an idealized model of the scientific process. The way to be smart, we're told, is through the use of rational, analytic, step-by-step, left-brained thinking. Small wonder that we end up relying exclusively on our heads for answers, that we are always laboriously trying to "think things through" and "figure things out."

Excessive reliance on left-brained problem solving is a severe handicap because, as Goldberg points out, the left-brained bias of the scientific method held on a pedestal for most of the twentieth century bares little resemblance to life. It misses out on key aspects of reality. As sheet music compares to live music, a strictly analytic approach offers a framework for study but can never substitute for the real event. We need more than logic, facts, and figures to live our lives successfully. We need wisdom mixed in with the smarts. A SoftPower style of power provides the right mix of wisdom and smarts. By reclaiming intuitive awareness and elevating it to a rightful role of leadership in your life, intuition becomes a key player on the SoftPower Team.

The SoftPower Team has three performers: intuition, mind, and actions. While all three are essential to the game, intuition plays the command role. It tells you where to go, how to best get to where you're headed, and how quickly or slowly to proceed. Your mind and behavior occupy support positions on the team. They function as servants to your intuition. Your mind gathers information, checks things out, and analyzes situations. Your behavior carries out intuitive directives through words and actions. Steve Jobs, a founder of Apple Computer, described a similar team concept with his advice to, "Follow your heart, but do it with your head." I prefer putting it the other way around: "Use your head, then follow your heart." Think things through, but at a certain point stop thinking so much and turn matters over to a wiser part of yourself. Give intuition the final say on what you're going to do about a situation.

With regular reference to your intuitive guidance system, difficult limit-setting interactions can become virtually effortless. In tune with intuition, you can know in an instant what needs to be done to clear up a problem. You can "feel in your bones" the right way or right time to approach a difficult person you're dealing with. You can realize instinctively that letting go of a hassle is smarter than confronting. For this reason, an increased ability to read and follow intuitive signals is one of the most powerful and special aspects of a SoftPower limit-setting style.

It's a "Grandma Knows Best" Family Affair

Another way to think of the SoftPower Team is to envision a happy family living inside of yourself. The female members of this inner family represent your sensitive, emotional, intuitive self. The male members reflect your think-it-through, action-oriented self. Everyone gets along beautifully. They appreciate, respect, and rely on each other. This is a "Grandma Knows Best" family where the unique wisdom of Grandma Intuition is honored above all. What she says goes. Her word is backed up by the entire family.

This image of the older woman as a wise and valued member of the clan is much needed in today's world. In fact we lack both male and female cultural archetypes of the wise elder. Instead we have the bag lady, the street bum, the senile, "useless" inmate of the nursing home, and the aging parent who brings financial and emotional burden to grown kids. In the SoftPower family, wise ol' Gramma finally gets the respect she deserves. She represents our lost roots with ancient, timeless knowledge. She is our connection to all that has come before and all that is yet to come.

When all dimensions of your being are regarded as powerful, valuable members of the whole, you gain great inner strength and confidence. Much as structural beams give a house "holding power" against wind and rain, your inner family provides internal support that enables you to handle the most intimidating bully in a poised, self-assured way.

Of course, charming as this notion of a powerful family residing happily within may be, it hardly jibes with most people's actual inner reality. Most of us live with our male and female sides bickering like jealous siblings or repressive parents. Our mind puts down our feelings as a bother and liability and discounts intuition as sheer nonsense. Our emotional self, on the other hand, looks down on reason as overcontrolling and a bore, and frets that taking action might get us into trouble. With SoftPower, all that changes. Your male and female sides wake up to the realization that they are on the same team. They kiss and make up.

SoftPower Teamwork in Real Life

In the complexity of day-to-day life, SoftPower teamwork might go something like this: Your actions gather information (you make a phone call and ask some questions). Your mind analyzes whatever data comes in, then turns its conclusions over to your gut. Your intuition considers all the information at its disposal (some of which the mind is not privy to), reaches a decision, and then communicates back to the mind via a variety of physical and emotional signals. Your mind interprets the signals (hopefully correctly), then tackles the logistics of the intuitive instructions. Your behavior kicks in once again to carry it all out.

In *Where's My Happy Ending*, Lee Morical tells a story that beautifully exemplifies the back-and-forth process of Soft-Power teamwork. She describes a crisis she lived through in her mid-forties, a time in her life when she seemed, by most standards, to "have it all." At the time of this episode, Lee had a successful career, a loving, long-term marriage, three beloved grown children, and friends galore. She had seen her share of life's ups and downs, had grown from her experiences, and was feeling on top of it all. She continues:

> So what if my calendar had no free spaces on it for the next six months, that a spontaneous lunch with a friend was a dim memory, that clients could rarely get an appointment, that I hadn't read a book for fun in years, that the canoe hadn't been in the water all summer, that sometimes I didn't have the time to unwrap the clothes I'd bought with the money I was working so hard to earn? What difference did it make that work consumed most of

my waking hours and that I was tired most of the time? I had it all!

I was, in fact, so busy that it was only grudgingly that, on a brilliant day in May, I squeezed in my annual physical between a consultation in St. Louis and another in Columbus. A biopsy followed the physical, a diagnosis of breast cancer followed the biopsy, a mastectomy followed the diagnosis.

Lee went to the hospital the evening before her biopsy with the usual "I'll hand the problem over to the expert doctors" mentality so deeply ingrained in us from earliest childhood. At one point during the evening, a nurse came into her room and asked her to sign a surgical permission from which gave the surgeon, as she put it, "carte blanche" on her chest the next morning:

> As I looked out my hospital window at the midnight pines, I knew sleeping pills could not blot out the fact that tomorrow was going to be a day which would call upon all the courage I could muster and which needed, tonight, my input into the preparation for it.
>
> The decision to refuse to sign the permission for the one step procedure (mastectomy to be performed immediately after the biopsy if cancer were found) was a hard one for me to make, given a belief in law, order, peace, and quiet in hospital settings. The nurse had told me hours earlier that my surgeon had left and could not be disturbed. I was alone. It was dark and it was late, and there was no "expert" with whom I could discuss my feelings of not wanting to do this thing in one step because of the need I felt for more time to think things through if the outcome

was what I feared. I was frightened and angry and confused, but as I began to relax and to pray, I was gradually
moved to a certainty that I had never felt before: I knew
that if there had been one hundred "experts" at my bed-
side, it would still have to be my decision to make there
in the dark. I knew I needed my rest, I knew that the
surgeon would not be pleased with my decision and worse,
I knew that this was neither his nor the hospital's treatment
of choice. But I also knew it was a decision I had to make.
I rang for the nurse.

Numerous aspects of Lee's experience reflect SoftPower
teamwork in action. For starters during the early part of the
evening when she had to make her decision on the surgery
consent, she realized instinctively that she needed solitude and
quiet in order to make up her mind. She knew that had she
been surrounded by friends and family spouting well-intentioned advice, it would have been very difficult to figure out
what she truly wanted to do independent from everyone else's
opinions. She therefore set limits by telling the nursing staff
that she did not want visitors. Assertive action thus helped her
intuition do its work.

In the decision-making process, Lee used her head as well
as her gut. She wasn't intuitive in a vacuum. She knew making
such a critical decision without considering all the facts would
be foolhardy. She did what fact-finding she could regarding
the pros and cons of undergoing a second round of surgery.
In this way, her mind and actions served her intuitive process.

After the first surgery, once she had heard her diagnosis,
Lee knew in her gut that she wanted the friendlier environment
of her hometown hospital for the second operation. Her head
insisted, however, that she obtain opinions from specialists at
a nearby teaching hospital on the treatment she was receiving.

There were other ways as well in which she backed up deep, intuitive yin desires through yang planning and initiative. Deep down she knew that she would need lots of tender, loving care during this difficult time. She asked for hand-holding, back rubs, hugging, the comfort of physical touch. She even had her husband bring a favorite stuffed teddy bear from home to be at her side at all times. She wasn't ashamed of her own needs or feelings. And, finally, she knew she would need to recover from the surgery at her own pace with plenty of rest and relaxation. Because of this, she made a decision to sit out some of the usual holiday hoopla that first year after the surgery. Instead, she spent a quiet time at home with her immediate family.[2]

Living by Your Gut Takes Guts

As Lee's story shows, it takes great courage to live intuitively. This is especially true when, as is occasionally the case, an intuitive directive defies reason or the advice of experts. When you turn to intuition for guidance, you need to be prepared for unconventional counsel. Sometimes your gut will tell you to move you out of your comfort zone into new territory where the risk of disapproval, rejection, and failure is considerable. At other times, your hunches and urges may not make any sense or seem socially appropriate. When you're stressed out from work pressures, for example, your gut may tell you it's time to take a "mental health" day off even though your mind thinks the last thing in the world you can afford is time off, given the fact that you're already rushing to meet deadlines.

[2]Lee Morical, *Where's My Happy Ending?*, Addison-Wesley, 1984.

Thank goodness, following intuitive instincts doesn't have to mean throwing responsibility or consideration for others out the window. Nor does it mean spending your life in bed reading novels and eating chocolates because you can't face the demands of work. It simply means opening up to *all* options, not just obvious or socially mandated ones. Who knows what innovations your imaginative intuition will concoct. How about spending all day in bed eating chocolates *while* you finish your report?

In a nutshell, living intuitively means choosing options that both have integrity for you and match your personal values, needs and priorities. As Shakti Gawain describes it, "Trusting your intuition means tuning in as deeply as you can to the energy you feel, following that energy moment to moment, trusting that it will lead you wherever you want to go and bring you everything you desire. It means being yourself, being real and authentic in your communications, being willing to try new things because they feel right, doing what turns you on."[3] Ultimately, the payoff for living in this way is more than worth the risks involved.

Women Are More Intuitive Than Men, Right?

Despite the fact that intuition has been long considered a natural feminine strength, it's still a matter of debate whether or not women truly have more intuition than men. The "nature-nurture" question of womanly intuition is a part of this yet-to-be-decided issue.[4] There is, however, considerable

---

[3] Shakti Gawain, *Living in the Light*, Whatever Publishing, 1986.
[4] The nature-nurture argument asks: If women *are* more intuitive, is it because of cultural programming or inherent physiological gender differences?

evidence and agreement that women generally seem to have easier access to intuition and that they certainly have had (in most societies) greater cultural permission to express it aloud.

Part of contemporary reasoning behind the "women are more intuitive than men" argument has to do with a companion belief that women are more "right-brained" than men. This implies that intuition is a right-brained affair. Yet neither the Nobel Prize–winning split-brain research by Roger Sperry nor subsequent studies have supported the hypothesis that women are more right-brained (or that intuition is predominantly a right-brained affair). Brain research has, however, demonstrated a few indisputable differences between men and women. For one thing, women tend to be more sensitive to context and peripheral information than men. Women also tend to process information faster. We are quicker and more capable of interpreting nonverbal data (including facial expressions). We are better at noticing subtle variations in sound and odor. Men, on the other hand, tend to have more aptitude with spatial visualization (dealing with maps, mazes, 3-D objects). They also seem to excel when it comes to mathematical reasoning—particularly when, as in geometry, it involves spatial organization.

One especially interesting neurological distinction between the sexes is that, while both men and women display the usual differences in hemispheric specialization, women seem to have a better capability to communicate between the hemispheres —a fact that could explain our apparently easier access to the intuitive. This crossover advantage seems partly (if not entirely) due to the fact that female brains have significantly more corpus callosum connective tissue linking the two halves of the brain. The corpus callosum binds the cortical hemispheres with over 200 million fibers, each of which, according to psychologist Bernard Baars, can fire up to a thousand times a second.[5]

But even established gender differences are relatively small and show up only on the average. In other words, the range of difference between individual men and women *within* each gender group is always greater than any difference existing *between* the sexes.

What Exactly Is Intuition and How Does It Work?

To use intuition as a source of power it helps to know what the intuitive experience is like and how it works in conjunction with (and distinctive from) your thinking mind. The more aware you are of the varied aspects of intuition, the better you'll be able to decode its subtle, sometimes confusing signals.

As with all yin and yang phenomena, your mind (yang) and intuition (yin) are always to some degree working together. Under ideal circumstances, they function as a complementary relationship, not a rivalry. To ignore either your mind or your intuition is to impoverish yourself. As Philip Goldberg puts it, it's like "tuning in mono to a stereo world."

What constitutes a proper mix of the two channels depends on the situation at hand. When you're driving in bumper-to-bumper traffic, you need to be tuned in primarily to the "object control" left-brained channel of your mind. In this mode, your primary objectives are to maintain control and operate logically. With matters of the heart, on the other hand, logic usually recedes into the background as a more intuitive, receptive state comes forward and takes the lead. In this mode,

[5]Philip Goldberg, *The Intuitive Edge*, J. P. Tarcher, 1983.

what counts is letting things happen and feeling your emotions.

With limit setting, you need both channels—the feel *and* the facts of the situation at hand. If you lose your sense of reason, you can be overwhelmed by emotions. If you lose emotional and intuitive sensitivity, you can end up doing what is right by the books but feels wrong in your heart.

Your Body Knows More Than You Think

Your intuition often uses your body as a conduit for expressing itself. This is why so many descriptions of intuition refer to physical experiences (*"I feel it in my bones." "I got chills when the idea came to me." "My stomach wrenched at the thought of it"*). Therapists frequently rely on such bodily signals for knowing when more is going on during a session than meets the eye. But you don't need to be a therapist to use intuition in this way. You can use bodily responses in day-to-day life to alert you that something "is rotten in Denmark" or doesn't jibe. A sudden body tension, according to Goldberg, can be like a telegram warning you: *"Don't believe a word this guy says"* or *"Get out of here immediately!"*

Of course, intuition doesn't concern itself only with what's wrong. It can just as easily tell you what's right, what rings true, or just "clicks." It both offers guidance regarding what to steer toward and warns you what to steer away from.

Use Your Intuition As a Pacing Device

If you're rushing and racing through life as a perpetual motion machine, intuition can help you slow down. There's an old story that tells of a man named Nasruddin who rides his horse through town one day. As he passes a grocery store, the horse gets sidetracked by open sacks of chickpeas in front of the store. The shopkeeper, seeing the horse eating his goods, hits the animal angrily with a stick. The horse rears up and runs off. As it gallops wildly down the street with Nasruddin frantically clutching at the mane, a man on the street shouts, "Hey, Nasruddin, where are you going in such a hurry?" Nasruddin hollers back, "I don't know. Ask the horse!"[6]

Many of us live like Nasruddin, charging about madly without knowing where we're going. We plunge into life's bottomless pile of things to do with no consultation whatsoever with our inner self or higher goals. Because of this, our time and energy end up consumed by what's trivial, off purpose, and against our true priorities.

By using intuition as a "pacing device," you spare yourself considerable wear and tear. Plus, you increase the odds that what motion you do engage in takes you in the right direction. In fact, with the help of intuition, you, like my friend who moved to the Rockies, can create an entirely new success story for yourself that truly suits you and your needs.

To use intuition in this way, as a pacing device, you need to periodically stop the action in your life and take an intuitive reading. At these pause points, you turn to your gut to find out what feels right for an upcoming time span. In this way,

[6] Nasruddin stories are a collection of tales from the Muslim Sufi tradition that are used to illustrate basic life truths. There are several excellent collections edited by Idries Shah if you are interested in reading more of these teaching parables.

you learn to step back from the hustle-bustle of day-to-day life and "gut plan" before making or firming up your schedule. Do you want an action-packed day or a contemplative one? Do you want an evening at home with quiet music and a good novel? Or a high-energy night out on the town? Do you want a weekend getting chores done around the house or would you like to spend Saturday and Sunday out of town with your sweetie at a B&B? Once you determine in your gut what you want to do, you can plan accordingly.

Sometimes checking with your gut will not be enough. Even having done so, you may still feel confused about how to best schedule your time. When this happens, try envisioning a variety of options to see which one feels the best. For instance, at the start of the day, you might imagine one version where you plug away all day long at work, another where you play hookey and go hiking by the ocean, and a third where you work hard all morning, then kick back in the afternoon with a leisurely drive (during which you perhaps mull over next week's project). In this way, your imagination collaborates with your intuition to create innovative alternatives for you to pick from.

When an obligation that you supposedly "must" do feels wrong in your gut, challenge all assumptions you're holding and examine all choices you have regarding the matter. Do you really have to do it? Must it be done right now? Is there a way to delegate some of the responsibility or negotiate on the deadline? If you find numerous "must dos" in your life that your gut resists, perhaps it's time to take stock of your situation in a more global way. How is it that you've filled your time with obligations and demands you aren't happy with? How can you clear your calendar and prevent more of the same from being heaped on you in the future?

The process of gut planning is more a function of feeling than facts. While you take into consideration your to-do list, the final decision is not necessarily a pragmatic one. This is why it takes guts to live by your gut. If you honor what you know, deep down, you should be doing, others might be angry or disappointed.

Gut planning is but one of many practical applications of intuitive awareness. It's a great way to stay in touch on a daily basis with your deeper self, higher goals, and free spirit. Even if you aren't sure you're ready to break with convention to follow your own inner rhythm, try it out for awhile and see what happens. Who knows? Little by little and day by day, you may find the courage to be more and more true to yourself.

Reading Your Intuition Can Be a Challenge

Intuition, of course, can only be useful to the extent that you are aware of it. Like oil, it's an "underground" resource that must first be accessed and brought to the surface to be utilized. But you need more than just awareness. You also need understanding. Once you're aware of intuitive signals, you then have to decode them before you can follow them. Reading intuition accurately is a sizeable stumbling block to an intuitive style of power. Intuitive signals can be subtle, even obtuse. Thus while by definition intuition is never wrong, you can certainly make mistakes in your attempts to decipher it. And you will make mistakes.

The subject of interpreting intuition is complex and beyond the scope of this book. To further your awareness and abilities in this area, I recommend you read a few of the following books: *Awakening Intuition, Journey of Awakening, Dream Power, Creative Dreaming* and *The Intuitive Edge.*[7]

THE MAGIC INGREDIENT: BREATHING ROOM

Just as you must clear land before drilling for oil, you have to clear space in your life in order to connect with your inner voice. You need to have breathing room. There are three characteristics that qualify time as breathing room as I'm referring to it: silence, sitting still, and solitude. Such time is rare for most of us. While we'd all probably agree that spending quiet, restful time alone on a regular basis is a great idea, it's not something we in fact do. Instead, the perpetual motion lifestyles spin on relentlessly. For some working mothers, the only way to find quiet alone time is to slip into a coma. There's got to be a better way! Let's look at each ingredient of breathing room—silence, stillness, and solitude—and consider how we can build more of each of these daily qualities into our lives without resorting to such drastic measures.

1) Silence

Find a little peace and quiet. It's entirely possible to have intuitive breakthroughs in the midst of chaos, clutter, and

[7]Frances Vaughn, *Awakening Intuition*, Doubleday, 1979; Ram Dass, *Journey of Awakening*, Bantam, 1978; Ann Faraday, *Dream Power*, Berkley Books, 1972; Patricia Garfield, *Creative Dreaming*, Ballantine, 1974; Philip Goldberg, *The Intuitive Edge*, J. P. Tarcher, 1983.

cacophony, but intuition is much more likely to make its presence felt in quiet, peaceful environments. The small faint voice of intuition gets lost easily in the commotion of modern living. To live more intuitively, it therefore makes sense to periodically quiet things down.

Silence can be hard to find in today's noisy world. Most of us live and work in a three-ring circus of commotion. Phones ring, radios and televisions blare, horns honk, kids fight, mouths yap, doors slam, and computers beep. With all the ruckus, it's no wonder we're ready for the looney bin by bedtime. The problem of too much noise is not just a personal issue. It's a societal one as well. In modern life, we receive more stimulation in a day than our ancestors received in a month. Experts warn that as a result we are becoming "adrenalin junkies." Raised on megadosages of stimulation, we are always after a bigger hit. Generations ago, life may not have been easier, but it was certainly quieter. People worked in the field all day long with only the birds and the bees keeping them company. Women stayed in the kitchen for long hours on end. They kneaded bread, tended the fire, and mended socks without a constant backdrop of daytime soaps and game shows.

There are basically two ways to respond to the dilemma of overstimulation. One is to go for more, amping up until you roast your brain but good. The other—the SoftPower way—is to go for less. You learn to wean yourself from the constant excitement with periodic shutdowns of stimulation. In practical terms, this means that on a regular basis you turn off the noise in your life. You turn off the music. You turn off the television. You turn off the computer. You turn off the telephone. You turn off the car. You let yourself float for a while on a sea of silence.

Quieting down the outside noise is only half of the story. Turning off the outside noise of your life is by itself insufficient. You must also quiet down inside noise. You need to shut up that overactive, dominant, verbal thinking mind of yours that blabs away nonstop virtually every minute of every waking hour. Every day you need to take a well-deserved "mental vacation."

Countless meditative disciplines promote quieting down the mind. The process almost always begins by limiting external stimulation. Next, you still your mind by giving it an "assignment"—a focus point upon which to place its attention. This resting place acts as an anchor that steadies and slows down your thinking. When your mind "trips out" in its usual way (as it will), all you need to do is to gently self-correct. You simply bring attention back to the anchor.

It works best to use a mental focus point that is boring and repetitive. This lulls your mind into a trance. It's as if your mind takes a little nap. The breathing process is ideal to focus on. It's repetitive—you breathe in, you breathe out, you breathe in, you breathe out. And it's boring—you breathe in, you breathe out, you breathe in, you breathe out. It's also portable. You take it with you everywhere you go.

Some people like to concentrate on a visual focus point— a candle flame or a flickering fire. Others prefer using a word or a phrase. When this word or phrase is designed to promote spiritual awareness it's called a mantra.

Find a special spot and make it sacred. No matter what your living situation, if you're creative and persistent, you should be able to find a private sanctuary somewhere to serve you as an eye of the storm for undisturbed retreats of solitude. In *The Book of Uncommon Sense*, Kim Williams describes how her large family (including her mother, grandmother, aunt,

father, various siblings, cousins, and an assortment of pets)
got along beautifully despite a tiny, crowded household and
very little money.[8] She was convinced the secret was that "people could get away from each other. Everyone had a hideaway,
a secret little nook to be alone in." Her sister took over a
corner of the attic where she kept fresh flowers and her journal
so she could write undisturbed whenever she pleased. When
Froni was up in the attic writing, everyone knew to leave her
alone. Her mother's hideaway was her bedroom, nothing big
or fancy, but it was her private, not-to-be-entered-without-
knocking room. Her brother's hideaway was a lean-to shed
attached to the garage. He even put a small grill there so he
could barbecue meals for himself when he needed space from
the family. The song "Up on the Roof" told of a similar asylum
that an enterprising young man created for himself in the
middle of a ghetto.

If people can create refuge for themselves in tenements and
overcrowded households, you too can stake out a retreat area,
no matter what your circumstances. If you're lucky, it can be
an entire room. If you're desperate, it can be a bathroom with
a double lock and "Do not disturb!" sign on the door.

Locate one or two "eye-of-the-storm" spots somewhere outside of your home as well, including one near your place of
work so you can get away from office pressures for quiet
respites during the day. A break in the middle of an otherwise
packed afternoon can work wonders for a tired body and neglected spirit. Churches, synagogues, and libraries are ideal
places for quiet contemplation. In his book *Psychology of Consciousness*, Robert Ornstein says the mere act of sitting in a
building that has nonrectilinear architecture (like the curved
and arched spaces found in most churches and synagogues)

---

[8] Kim Williams, *Book of Uncommon Sense*, Fawcett Crest, 1986.

slows down brain waves and facilitates an altered, more intuitive state of being.[9] In modern life, most of our time is spent in squared-off, rectilinear spaces that box us in both mentally and physically. Get out of your boxes and spend quiet time in a chapel or temple. Give your spirit room to expand.

Once you've found (or created) a couple of private havens, head to one of them every day. Settle down, sit quietly, and steady your mind with a focus point. Imagine yourself going from the surface of a wind-torn sea to a protected place of great dark stillness deep beneath the frenetic surface of your mind. Over time, in the safety and tranquillity of this inner sanctuary, you'll find that guilt, fear, confusion, and anger are temporary, transient states and nothing to be afraid of.

Climb in Mother Nature's lap. Spend some of your breathing-room time out of doors and soak up the healing power of nature. For some of us, the only contact we have with the outdoors is the walk between our front door and the car or the parking lot and the office. When you hang out with Mother Nature, you become realigned with what George Leonard calls the "silent pulse," an inner rhythm easily lost in the midst of urban stimulation.[10] Mother Nature also helps you keep things in perspective. There's nothing like the grandeur of the ocean, the expanse of a star-filled sky, the spaciousness of wide open fields, the majesty of the Redwoods, or the magnificence of the mountains to make troubles less overwhelming and remind you that your drama is not the only thing going on.

If your schedule doesn't permit much time outdoors during the week, use weekends to ensure that you receive an adequate

[9] Robert Ornstein, *The Psychology of Consciousness*, W. H. Freeman & Co., 1972.
[10] George Leonard, *The Silent Pulse*, Bantam, 1978.

dose. Set aside a part of each Saturday or Sunday for relaxing outside. Sit by the ocean and feel the rhythm and flow of the sea. Lie on the grass and watch the clouds. Rest against a favorite tree and enjoy a sunset. Rock on your front porch under a skyload of stars. Walk in the rain. Hike a few hours by yourself or with a friend who respects silence and space. The idea is to build into your schedule regular periods of time away from the planning, fretting, and nonstop activity of your life, time dedicated to such truly important endeavors as smelling the roses, listening to the birds sing, and hearing the crickets chirp.

2) Stillness

Park your body as you quiet your mind. To qualify a break as breathing room, you need to reduce motion as well as noise. At first, you may become quite antsy doing absolutely nothing at all, but sit still anyway. Just notice your restlessness and let it be there—it's a normal part of the quieting-down process. As you resist the urge to get up, you'll find it disappears on its own without any effort from you.

The problem is that for those who live in the fast lane it can actually be painful to sit still. It's like stripping the gears of your car by shifting from fourth gear to neutral. Consequently, even the thought of doing nothing can make you nervous.

If sitting still feels unbearable, gear down gradually with a mindless activity. Needlepoint, knitting, jigsaw puzzles, exercising, drawing, grooming your cat, gardening, long drives —any of these will slow you down. So will housework. Household chores such as vacuuming, ironing, or folding clothes are mindless and, therefore, potentially meditative. In fact, I believe that one reason women have been historically considered more intuitive than men is that we've been traditionally assigned the most monotonous routines of society. If nothing else, this has given us more opportunity for quiet introspection.

The goal of a meditation break is to rest your mind and stop thinking so much. The form of the break is not all that important:

> As meditation, almost anything will do: music, a quiet walk, an excellent meal, firelight, candlelight, holding the hands of a loved one, whatever causes you to center into the joy of your beingness and disregard the clamoring of your intellect . . . Everyone needs to go into their own inner silence, their own inner truth, in whatever way they can. This inner illumination is your birthright. It is the key to the essence of your being, to your soul's wisdom.[11]

In addition to taking 20-minute breathing room breaks, schedule extended breaks as well. Enjoy the luxury of spending an entire evening at home baking or doing laundry. Indulge in a lazy afternoon wading in a stream or relaxing in the park. Once or twice a year take the kind of solo retreat I described in Chapter Two, where you go to a country inn by yourself for a weekend.

I know—it's easier said than done. We are all familiar with the excuses (*"I'm too busy to take a break." "I can't stop now—maybe tomorrow"*). Take the time anyway. The benefits will be more than worth it. A breathing-room break, whether for a few minutes or a full day, is ultimately a great time-saver and

[11] Pat Rodegast, *Emmanuel's Book*, Some Friends of Emmanuel, 1985.

stress-reducer. It will allow you to reenter your fast-paced world centered and rejuvenated. You'll see things more clearly and be focused instead of fragmented and drained. You'll find it easier to laugh at life's little dramas. You'll feel calmer and more patient, and at ease with both yourself and those around you.

3) Solitude

Despite the many benefits of alone time, many of us detest solitude. Left to our own devices we get bored and jittery. The prospect of missing out on something or losing our connection with others can even send us into a state of panic. In extreme cases, a woman may spend her entire life in an unhappy or destructive relationship just to avoid being alone. Or she may become a workaholic and toil around the clock seven days a week to escape having to face herself in solitude.

Solitude takes getting used to. It also takes self-discipline and an ability to set limits. If you're like most, you'll need to schedule alone time as an important appointment with yourself. Then it will be much more likely to happen. I guess writing it down in your calendar book makes it official. Once you book this appointment, consider it sacred and protect the time by setting limits when others make demands on you. As the bottom line, you must be occasionally willing to say no to children, friends, and family if you are going to say yes to yourself.

Once alone time has become a regular part of your routine, you'll wonder how you ever managed without it. In *Gift from the Sea*, Anne Morrow Lindbergh is eloquent in describing the value of solitude:

> It is a difficult lesson to learn these days—to leave your friends and family and deliberately practice the art of solitude for an hour or day or week. Yet, once done, I find there is a quality to being alone that is incredibly precious. Ironically, I feel closer to others, even in my solitude. For it is not physical solitude that actually separates you from others, not physical isolation, but spiritual isolation. When you are a stranger to yourself then you are estranged from others too. Only when you are connected to your own core are you connected to others, I am beginning to discover. And, for me, the core, the inner spring, can best be refound through solitude.[12]

To exercise power, you need to trust your instincts. Intuition is the SoftPower key to self-trust, and intuitive awareness is, therefore, a central factor in the SoftPower formula. All too often, in our crowded, noisy, chaotic world, intuition gets lost in the shuffle. Consequently, to establish a better connection with gut instincts, you need to build *breathing room* into your life—daily breaks when you can unwind in an atmosphere of space, solitude, silence, and stillness. With regular spells of breathing room, you'll be better able to quiet down fearful and confused thinking. You'll also discover answers you didn't know you had, and find the courage of your convictions.

[12] Anne Morrow Lindbergh, *Gift from the Sea*, Pantheon Books, 1955.

9

LETTING GO

Cutting Your Losses
to Move On

Nothing creates more misery or undermines power faster than an inability to let go. Whether the clinging is to ancient gripes and resentments, yesterday's failures and mistakes, outdated guilt and shame, crushed hopes and dreams, or relationships that are over and gone, you pay a steep price for holding on too long. Failure to let go produces and prolongs emotional pain. It consumes physical energy. And it crowds out what's next.

An ability and willingness to let go are both complement and catalyst to setting limits. They impact on your limit setting in the following ways:

1. As an auxiliary skill, letting go reduces your need to set limits in the first place. When you're able to let go of things instead of being bothered by them, you won't have as many limits to set because, once you let go of minor irritants, there won't be as many situations that provoke you to speak up. For example, when you let go of perfectionistic standards, you won't get hot and bothered over an occasional blooper by your secretary and you'll feel no need to mention it. You'll just let it pass.

2. In other circumstances, letting go facilitates limit setting because it diminishes emotional blocks to being truthful. By releasing fear, you finally find the nerve to speak up to your father-in-law about smoking in your home. By letting go of guilt, it suddenly feels okay to turn down a friend's request for a favor that you don't want to grant.

3. If you do decide to speak up about a problem, letting go can either mellow your style or, if it's already too mellow to start with, beef it up. For example, when you let go of having to prove yourself right during a disagreement, you'll be better able to state your position without engaging in a fight. If you let go of caring so much what others think, you'll have the guts to take an unpopular position at a staff meeting even if it means potential censure from colleagues.

4. During a limit-setting confrontation, letting go helps you give and take. It increases your flexibility. Successful negotiating requires this sort of adaptability. The line you draw or the stand you take will occasionally call for an adjustment because of circumstances. You may need to drop certain demands in favor of others. You may want to shuffle your priorities when given new information.

5. After unsuccessful attempts to handle problems, letting go saves you both time and grief. When you're able to forget about an upsetting situation, you won't pollute today (or tomorrow) with yesterday's defeats. After successful interactions, letting go means you don't dwell needlessly on what is over and gone. For example, a friend of mine has finally learned to say no to her boss but when she does so she worries and suffers guilt for days afterward. She needs to learn to let it go.

To facilitate the letting-go process, it helps to remember that letting go invariably brings increased freedom in its wake, even as you suffer a loss. One of the reasons we so often find letting go excruciating is that we focus on the loss of the experience rather than the gain. To plug in to the latter does not mean you deny the reality that something is over and gone. Nor does it mean you avoid the sometimes painful grieving process associated with true loss. It merely means you open up as well to the other side of the coin. You know that loss implies gain, surrender implies liberation, and release implies replenishment. Letting go from this posture, you know that good things are in store for you if you unblock yourself as you venture forth into the future.

Recently, during a meditation, I stumbled upon an imagery that brought home to me the close link between letting go and freedom. Here's what happened:

To steady my mind I used a mental image as a focus point. I imagined on the left side of my body a pair of French doors opened inward (toward me). Outside the doors, I envisioned a beautiful expanse of ocean, complete with crashing surf and a stunning sunset on the horizon. During each inhale, it was as if a fresh breeze blew in from the ocean and washed over me. On every exhale, I pictured the breeze exiting through a second pair of French doors situated on my right, opened outward toward the world. To further anchor my mind, I repeated silently, "*I take in*" with the intake part of each breath and "*I let go*" with each exhale. The effect was instantaneously calming and healing.

Soon I found my mind spontaneously shifting to a variety of phrases on the in-out beat of each breath. First came: "*I receive, I release.*" Then came: "*I accept, I give out.*" And finally: "*I hold on, I set free.*"

The last of these startled my attention. "*Of course,*" I thought as I let a thought momentarily intrude on my experience, "*letting go is nothing more than 'setting free.'*"

HOW CAN LETTING GO HELP YOU?

We all have our own specific needs regarding when and where in our lives we need to let go. If your style of limit setting is excessive or forceful, you probably need to learn to let go of picayune issues instead of battling over them. To do so, it might help if you conduct the following little experiment. Whenever you can honestly say to yourself, "*This doesn't matter that much*" or "*Something else matters to me more*" (like your time, health, or peace of mind), simply drop the matter just to see how it feels.

On the other hand, if you're a person who is always trying to dodge trouble rather than handle it, you probably *overdo* on talk-yourself-out-of-it tactics. Nonassertive folks tend to let go excessively in this way. They are always telling themselves, "*It's not worth it,*" "*It's not that important,*" "*It doesn't matter,*" even when it is and when it does. This doesn't mean that if you're meek about setting limits learning to let go won't be of value to you. It will still be important but for other reasons. For example, you may need to release old beliefs of unworthiness so you can imbed in their place new ones that encourage you to stand up for your rights.

Letting Go Can Make a Huge Difference

A personal example illustrates how letting go can significantly improve a relationship:

My mother was an advice-giver. For years, I argued with whatever advice she gave me, just on principle. Even if I secretly agreed with her suggestions (which I rarely did) I still argued. I did not want her running my life. But rather than set appropriate limits (*"Mom, I know you mean well but I would rather not hear all the advice"*) or let go (*"So what if she gives me advice—she's entitled to her opinion"*), I quarreled with her incessantly. Neither of us was ever able to drop an argument. Like stubborn 10-year-olds, both of us would try to get the last word in.

Somewhere along the line it dawned on me how silly and inappropriate this constant bickering was. There was no longer any need to be concerned about my mother controlling me— I was not 10 years old anymore. It was time to let go of my struggle with her. Determined to create a truce, I made a personal vow that our next visit together would be different.

Several months later, she flew from New York for a week-long visit. On the second day of her stay, while we were in the kitchen getting things ready for dinner, she started in. "You know, your silverware drawers are full of crumbs—you're going to get bugs in the house."

Ordinarily, this would have set me off but good. I would have told her in no uncertain terms to mind her own business—my housekeeping was fine just the way it was and

I didn't have bugs in my house, thank you very much. But, instead, because of my new resolve, I replied pleasantly, "I never noticed that before, Mom. You're right. Those drawers are disgusting." I was amazed she didn't faint from shock.

"Would you like me to clean them out?" she asked rather sweetly.

"That would be great," I answered. "Thanks a lot."

She proceeded to clean out not only the drawers but all the other drawers and cupboards as well. My kitchen has never been so spotless before or since.

What a time-saver. What an energy-saver. What a relationship-saver. What a great way to get my kitchen cleaned!

While in this situation I switched sides and agreed with my mother, it's not always necessary or appropriate to do so in order to let go. Had I truly disagreed with her criticism or advice, I could have remained privately convinced that I was right and still let the whole thing go. A simple "Thanks for the suggestion, Mom" would have sufficed.

It's amazing how easy letting go can be once you get the swing of it. At times you'll find it almost effortless to let go of things you previously would have argued over ad nauseam.

Letting Go Is a Profound and All-encompassing Life Issue

From the moment you are born you begin a letting-go process that continues until the moment you die. You need to let go of the womb to enter the world. You need to let go of dependency on mother to grow up. You need to let go of childish innocence to move into adulthood. You need to let go of fingernails when they break. You need to let go of youthful looks as you age. You need to let go of gripes and resentments unless you want life to eat you up alive. On and on it goes— a life of nonstop letting go is part and parcel of a life of nonstop change.

This sometimes painful release aspect of life spins into daily living in many varied forms. It's there when you get divorced, get fired, or get turned down for something you want. It's there when you lose a game of tennis, a lover, an important client, an argument, or a favorite possession. It's there when you end a friendship, break a habit, take a deep breath, or relax physically. It's there when you accept a death, break down and sob, or forgive the unforgivable.

The experience of letting go also has a great deal to do with every choice you make in your life. Whenever you say yes, by implication you let go of incompatible options. If you agree to go out to the movies with friends, you won't be able to help the kids with homework. If you accept a mammoth new project, you forego sleep and free time on weekends. Whenever you say no, you let go, too. If you turn down a date, you relinquish the chance to spend time with the person asking you out. If you reject a job offer, you lose the benefits and opportunities it offered to you. If you decide not to go on vacation, you miss out on fun, adventure, and relaxation.

Letting go is related to choice in another important way as well. If every choice you make implies letting go, then every letting-go experience implies more choice coming your way. When you release something, you create space for new options that would otherwise never come your way. You will not meet Mr. Right if you stay stuck in a relationship with Mr. Wrong. Letting go, you relax, unclench, and live with palms open, ready to both receive and create.

Given the fact that we have so many opportunities to prac- tice the process, you'd think we'd all be experts at letting go.

Unfortunately, this is hardly the case. Because we're scared
and don't trust ourselves, most of us go to our graves fighting
the process. We frantically hold on, grasping and clutching
for dear life.

Being Flexible Is What Letting Go Is All About

Flexibility is at the core of the letting-go experience. This
ability to bend and yield when need be is a central component
of strength. It's the capacity to be flexible that enables a fragile
willow to outlast a mighty oak. It's the capacity to yield that
enables a skyscraper to withstand the massive power of an
earthquake. And it's the ability to be personally adaptable that
enables *you* to handle situations gracefully by shifting or altering your position.

Because traditional feminine programming presented flexibility at its extreme, you may at first be turned off by the
notion of giving in. According to Stage One mentality, it was
the woman's place to continuously defer to others and sacrifice
her own needs and desires for the happiness of friends, family,
and even strangers. Consequently when female consciousness
was raised in the late '60s, many of us felt we had had our fill
of flexibility. What we wanted was firmness. "I'll be damned
if I'll budge!" became proof that we finally had power. But
flexibility is not the enemy. The enemy is inappropriate and
extreme flexibility. As we saw in Chapter Six, flexibility becomes a liability only when it is untempered by a complementary, commensurate yang ability to stand your ground.
When you're appropriately flexible you are all the stronger
because you have a broader repertoire of perspectives and responses to call upon. You're still able to draw the line, but, if

this doesn't produce the results you're after, you're able to gracefully let go and try something else.

Surrender Can Be a Smart Choice

Letting go becomes easier when seen as inner surrender out of intelligent choice. In this light, it becomes a smart move that makes the difference between a tortured state and peace of mind, a way to cut your losses and move on. Remember my camping experience when I walked away after trying to set limits with the rowdy, drunken bikers? Letting go in that instance was a wise strategy, not a humiliating failure. The risks were too high and the chances for success too slim to warrant additional effort. A world apart from defeat, letting go in such situations is one of the biggest lessons of SoftPower.

There are at least five ways in which you can experience letting go. You do it *mentally* when you let go of beliefs, opinions, expectations, obsessive thinking, etc. You let go *physically* when you relax. You let go *emotionally* when you free yourself from fear, anger, or guilt. You let go at the level of *motives and desires* when you stop wanting something (or stop wanting it so much). You let go *behaviorally* when you change your actions (you stop complaining or walk away from an argument).

While letting go behaviorally is not strictly speaking an inner surrender, it frequently springs from an internal release or paves the way for one if it has not yet occurred. But for true peace of mind, some internal component of letting go is a must. For example, in the campground by walking back to my tent with no further ado about the noise, I let go behaviorally.

This was a good start, but to spare myself suffering I also needed to to let go emotionally. Otherwise anger and frustration could have kept me awake long after the noise from the party subsided.

Here's how the various aspects of letting go would look if, during an argument, you let go of the need to prove yourself right:

At the physical level, you would release tightened muscles and breathe more easily.

At the mental level, you would change your opinion about the importance of the argument. You'd say to yourself, *"It's no big deal if he disagrees with me. He has a right to his opinion."*

At the emotional level, your frustration and annoyance over the squabble would lift. You'd no longer feel upset by what was happening.

At the level of desire, you'd stop feeling a need to convince anyone of anything. Instead you'd feel fine letting the other person think whatever he or she wanted to think.

At the behavioral level, you'd simply stop arguing. You would change the topic or shut your mouth and listen to what was being said.

The different dimensions of letting go are interdependent because they are both cause and effect for each other. Thus when you're able to let go at any one level, you facilitate a corresponding experience at the others. If you start the process mentally (by talking to yourself differently about a situation), this clears the way for emotional release, a shift in desire, and/or behavioral change. On the other hand, if you begin at the behavioral level (by bowing out of the argument), it becomes easier for you to let go in every other way as well.

Be Patient with the Process

While I'm making it sound easy as 1-2-3 and while sometimes it *is* that easy, in certain cases it will take considerable time and sustained effort before you feel the mental or emotional shift of surrender. The process may ensue in bits and pieces. For example, after an upsetting experience you may make yourself miserable for a while, then experience the relief of release, only to proceed an hour later to make yourself miserable once again. At a certain point, you say to yourself, "Enough is enough." You then set limits, with *yourself*, on mental obsession and let the whole thing go once and for all.

When you find yourself holding on despite sincere attempts to let go, be gentle with yourself. You may not be quite ready yet to let go. Sure it would be nice if you could shrug every upset off with a "C'est la vie" attitude, but that's not always going to happen. In fact, with significant disappointments or losses, trying too soon to let a matter go can work against you because denied feelings only get stuck in your body as tension. Before feeling better, you may need first to feel worse. You may have to pound a few pillows to get rage or despair out of your system. Healing takes time. So rant, rave, and properly grieve over what has happened if that seems appropriate and necessary. Just be sure to do your pillow-pounding and hollering where they'll do no damage to you or anyone else.

It's ideal to let go at all levels, but this is not always required in order to feel relief. For example, it may be enough to let go *mentally* even if you don't let go *emotionally*. This might be the case if you continue to feel disappointment over a rejection yet are able to let go of obsessing about it.

Or you can let go behaviorally without letting go emotionally. You can stay irritated with your kids for forgetting their chores but drop the matter once you've had your say.

You can also let go emotionally without letting go mentally. You can forgive someone while maintaining an opinion that what the person did was wrong. While you don't condone what happened, your hatred and anger over the incident dissipate.

You can let go behaviorally without letting go of desires. You can still want to be in a relationship but, because it's become obvious that it's not going to work out, you quit trying. You stop calling, writing letters, and making approaches.

You can even let go emotionally and mentally yet persist at the behavioral level. With those guys at the campground, although I let go of my anger and did not dwell on the problem after returning to my tent, the next morning I took action by reporting the incident to a ranger and requesting a new tent site far from the noise.

WHERE IS IT HARD TO LET GO?

Look around and you'll see countless examples of individuals holding on too long. A pig-headed colleague has a hard time letting go of his position. The woman in your office "who loves too much" can't let go of a dysfunctional relationship she's been trying in vain to "fix" for years. An insecure friend is unable to let go of childhood programming that has her convinced she's not smart enough or lovable enough. A workaholic partner is unable to let go of doing it all.

There are six letting-go trouble spots that deserve special

attention when it comes to setting limits. Let's take a look at what they are:

Trouble Spot #1:
Letting Go of the Need to Be Right

Endless arguments over who's right and wrong are hardly unique to my mother and me. Of course, not all arguments are negative experiences. Conducted in the right spirit, an argument can be provocative, tension-reducing, and even fruitful in that you succeed at changing someone's mind. But most quarrels are neither successful nor fun. Most are a giant waste of your time and energy. They produce nothing but anger, frustration, and polarization of positions.

You, like everyone else, probably have a number of people in your life with whom you tend to squabble. The list may include both those you love the most (your kids, your partner, or a dear friend) and those you can't stand (an annoying co-worker, a least-favorite relative, an arrogant friend of your husband's).

Luckily, as my experience with my mom shows, bowing out of arguments, be they with your boss or your in-laws, need not be difficult. All it takes is for one person to let go and the game is over. It can be as simple as saying, "*It looks as if we see this differently, doesn't it*" or "*I guess we don't see eye to eye—how about if we agree to disagree?*"

Or sometimes a change in strategy is what's needed. You don't necessarily have to change someone's *mind* to get what you want. When you can't convince others of your viewpoint, perhaps you can persuade them to at least change their *behavior*. I know of an affirmative-action program, for example, that tells its male managers, "*You don't have to change your opinions, you just have to change what you do.*" The company doesn't expect "chauvinist men" to change colors overnight. But it does expect them to cut out locker room talk and stop unfair, condescending treatment toward women. In much the same way, you may want to drop a fruitless argument over who's right and establish instead what behaviors need to change.

But, you may be asking yourself, what if you back out of an argument and the other person doesn't stop? Fortunately, as soon as one player (you) steps out of the ring, the fight is over. Some activities by definition require two people, and arguing is one of them. If someone keeps at it, mention a second time that you're not interested in arguing. If that doesn't do the job, consider switching to a listening mode and watch the person slug it out alone or excuse yourself and leave.

One of the things that blocks us from letting go in an argument is our intolerance for disagreement. We want everyone to agree with us and expect that they will. The reality is that they don't and they won't. It's delightful to see eye to eye with someone, but wanting this to be the norm is naive. Expect occasional clashes of opinion and lighten up when you encounter them. Differing points of view don't have to be insufferable. Instead see them as the spice of life.

An excellent alternative response to a disagreement is a posture of curiosity. With a "Let me find out more" perspective, you can transform an argument into a chance to enlarge your outlook and sharpen your thinking. Instead of the dispute being a contest of judgments ("*What a stupid opinion. I can't believe she thinks that*"), it becomes a provocative puzzle ("*Hmm, I wonder why she sees it that way*").

Sometimes, of course, there is good reason to try to "win" an argument or change someone's mind. When this is the case (and circumstances allow for it), go ahead and give it your best shot. Just be sure to speak for yourself (*"I see this differ-ently"* instead of launching into a right-wrong battle (*"That's crazy. You don't know what you're talking about"*). And remember, while you can influence others to change the way they see things, you cannot control their thinking. You can't force your views on anyone—not on your partner, your kids, or the grouch at the office. Prison camps aside, everyone in this world gets to make up his or her own mind.

Ideally, when you announce you're no longer interested in arguing, you want to do so in a tone of voice that reflects an easygoing acceptance of the difference of opinion. If you don't feel easygoing about the matter but still want to end the dispute, try "acting as if" you feel more relaxed than you do. "Acting as if," a time-honored way to change yourself from the outside in, is based on a psychological concept called "cognitive dissonance." It works as follows:

When you do something behaviorally that does not match what you feel or believe (in other words, if you act in a confident manner even though you don't feel confident), a discrepancy is created between your actions and your inner experience. This contradiction produces an internal state of dissonance. If you keep up the act, one of two things will eventually occur to break the tension. You'll either stop doing what you're doing or you'll start to feel (or believe) in a way that matches your actions. In other words, your insides shift to match your outside. "Acting as if" is the principle behind brainwashing techniques used on political prisoners. POWs are forced to repeat political rhetoric they don't believe in. After enough repetitions, they start to believe what they're saying. Even though the "act" is simpleminded and the prisoners themselves don't want to change, by simple repetition a change takes place.

In a similar way, you can use positive, present-tensed, affirmative sentences to change your mind and your feelings about a situation. To do this, repeatedly state (or write or think) statements that declare you feel the way you want to feel ("*I am calm and relaxed about this." "I am letting go of this easily*"). Sooner or later, the feeling will catch. In this way, you harness your mind as a powerful change agent.[1]

Going through actual motions and emotions is even more effective than stating or thinking affirmations. To do this, ask yourself what it would feel like inside of your body if you truly felt easygoing about a situation. In this way, like a method actress who feels the feelings of a role instead of merely saying the lines, you try the experience on for size. Don't worry that the change is only a superficial one. It may be just surface at first but, if you keep at it, ultimately your insides will catch up with your behavior and the experience will become fully authentic.

Trouble Spot #2:
Letting Go of the Need to Understand

Usually when we communicate about a problem, we seek better understanding of what transpired as well as resolution. We want to clear up any misunderstandings that may be occurring and comprehend what happened even if we fail to get what we want. Sometimes, however, for any of a number of reasons, understanding will escape you. This may happen because others withhold information from you intentionally. It can happen

[1] For in-depth information on using affirmations and visualizations to change your mind (and your life), read *Creative Visualization*, by Shakti Gawain (Whatever Publishing), 1978.

because those you're dealing with don't know *themselves* what's happening, so how can they tell you? There are even times when it happens despite the fact that others have explained themselves fully. With all the information in the world, you may still be at a loss to understand what's up. You may never fully understand why management passed you up for a promotion or a lover left you for someone else. There will inevitably be times in life when you are left scratching your head in befuddlement, despite sincere attempts to figure it all out.

Letting go when understanding eludes us can be hard to do. Because our culture places such emphasis on finding answers, most of us have a strong compulsion to know. We have little tolerance for mysteries and confusion. But having answers isn't everything. It doesn't have to be so terrible when you don't understand why someone did or didn't do something. To help yourself let go at such times, try saying to yourself, *"I'm perfectly comfortable not understanding what has happened. I'm letting go of this matter now."* Turn your attention to generating new questions (*"What can I do now to ease my mind and let this go?" "Where can I better place my energy?"*). You may find that concocting questions is as rewarding as uncovering answers.

There's another marvelous benefit to letting go of the need to understand everything. Not only do you save yourself a lot of time, energy, and frustration, but you also shift yourself to a receptive, spacious state of not knowing, in which it's more likely insights and answers will start to come *to* you instead of *from* you. You clear the deck for intuitive breakthroughs.

The flip side of the problem is the need to be understood. A related problem to the need to understand is the need to *be understood*. In this case, you try again and again to present your side of a situation in the hope that, if you say it a little differently or if you repeat yourself one more time, you may finally get through and others will at last understand you.

There's nothing wrong, of course, with a little persistence when you're trying to communicate with someone. However, if no matter how carefully (or forcefully) you speak, you continue to come up against the proverbial brick wall, you'll need to let go to make peace with the situation. The first step is recognizing that an interaction is going nowhere. The second step is dropping the matter. The world's not going to end if others fail to understand what you tell them. Say to yourself, *"I wish he understood my side, but he doesn't. I accept that and let go. Maybe he'll understand what I'm saying later when he's had a chance to think about it."* This last can be more than an empty reassurance to yourself. Sometimes, when your attempts to communicate seem futile, you find out later that what you said *did* sink in and the person has changed as a result. This, for example, is what frequently happens between a friend of mine and her husband. She has learned to make her pitch to him, then quit. She knows from experience that even when he seems totally closed during a confrontation, he does listen and is affected by what she says. In fact, her influence with him increases when she doesn't overstate her case.

Trouble Spot #3:
Letting Go of Insisting and Demanding

Insisting and demanding may work for dictators who can impose their will on others, but, for those uninterested in holding people at gunpoint, forcing is not a suitable option. Beyond the ethics issue of coercion, bully tactics are no guarantee of success anyway. No matter how much you insist and demand, there will always be those who resist and do what they want anyway. No matter how much you plead, beg, or order, there will still be unreasonable clerks who refuse to bend policies for you, loved ones who continue to defy your wishes, and bosses who stubbornly deny your requests.

To let go when you don't get what you want, you need to put an end to "must have" thinking. Recognize that when your mind tells you that you must have things a certain way or else, you paint yourself into a corner of very restricted choice. In reality there are few things you or I must have. Air and water are two of them. Everything else, if you so decide, can be held at the level of preference. You're far better off and much more powerful when you operate out of preference instead of insisting and demanding.

In his book *How to Enjoy Your Life in Spite of It All*, Ken Keyes builds an entire approach to life around what he calls "preferential programming."[2] Whereas many philosophies say you must end all desire to have peace of mind, Keyes argues that loose attachment can be as freeing as total nonattachment. In Western cultures, this position seems more practical and appealing than a recommendation for total detachment from desires. I, for one, like my desires, just as I like my opinions and emotions. They're a part of my human experience. The question, as usual, is whether or not they are functional. Desires become dysfunctional when they are rigid, excessive, negative, or unrealistic. When you change your thinking to a preferential mode, you stop telling yourself, "*I must have this in order to be happy*," and say instead, "*I prefer that this happen. If it doesn't happen I'll be fine anyway*." From this looser position

---

[2] Ken Keyes, *How to Enjoy Your Life in Spite of It All*, Living Love Publications, Coos Bay, OR, 97420.

of preference it becomes infinitely easier to let go when things don't go your way.

As you lighten up on desires and change them to preferences, you might want to examine your standards as well to see how much they are part of your problems. High standards can be a mixed blessing. Obviously, when you have Rolls Royce taste, you'll be more difficult to please than if you are content with a Ford or Chevrolet. With a preferential attitude, you can maintain high standards without falling victim to them. You may appreciate the finer things in life and prefer to dine at Chez Panisse rather than at a Doggy Diner but, if you're forced to slum it, you're able to drop your high-fallutin' standards and enjoy what's on your plate.

If you can't let go of your standards when situations call for it, you'll only end up angry, disappointed, and miserable over what's available to you. As someone once put it: To enjoy life for what it is, you must be continuously willing to let it go for what it is not. A six-week trip I took a few years ago with my older son to Thailand and Nepal brought this lesson home to me in no uncertain terms. I had given David his round-trip air tickets for the trip, but he paid his own expenses once we got there. Consequently, in Bangkok we stayed at a cheap hotel, not the famed Oriental, and ate at down-home restaurants, not five-star ones. In Nepal, there was no other choice but to travel budget-style. Our room at the Kathmandu Tibetan Guest House was a sixth-floor walk-up that cost $10 a day. From day one of the trip, it was clear that, to enjoy the vacation, I would need to let go of my usual high standards. Traveling in Asia on a budget means relinquishing control over matters of hygiene, privacy, comfort, noise, and diet. In Nepal, I learned a local expression, "Kay garne," that helped me with the letting-go process. The phrase roughly translates into, "Que sera, sera" or "What will be, will be." It's a cultural shoulder shrug that helps you accept circumstances outside your control with grace and humor. Throughout the trip and especially on our nine-day trek in the Himalayas, my son and I used the phrase frequently to remind ourselves that, when there was nothing more to be done about a situation, it was time to release resistance to "what's so" and let go.

Perfectionism means having impossible standards. When you're a perfectionist, your standards allow for zero error or fault. Expecting perfection is almost always a sorry setup for disappointment, resentment, and frustration. Because invariably everything and everyone falls short of the mark, you end up perpetually dissatisfied.

In addition to causing you untold grief, perfectionistic standards can keep you from trying new things. For example, if you feel compelled to do a perfect dive the first time off the board, you'll probably end up one of three ways—mortified as you belly flop into the pool, paralyzed at the end of the board (afraid to jump and make a fool of yourself), or seated on the sidelines, too chicken to risk bombing.

Perfectionism also interferes with your ability to continue a performance when you make a mistake during the course of it. The perfectionist who obsessively holds on to mistakes messes up the rest of her effort. The perfect illustration of this self-sabotage is the figure skater who suffers a fall at the start of her performance. To skate out the rest of the routine without further mishap, she must (at least temporarily) dismiss the mistake from her mind. If she's unable to do this, she'll no doubt be back on her rump within a matter of minutes. The first fall will hang over her head like a cloud and trip her up repeatedly during the rest of the performance.

Dropping your standards, by the way, doesn't mean you

put up with any old slop from staff, friends, family, or yourself. It merely means you learn from mistakes and failures, then let them go instead of torturing yourself over what is over and gone. In this way, you exercise damage-control on unfortunate incidents that cannot be undone.

You're bound to make mistakes. Why beat yourself up about them? You and I (and everyone else) are imperfect, flesh and blood human beings. At times we say things we regret. At times we blow opportunities by coming on too strong or not strong enough. At times we stumble and bumble and fall on our face.

When you have the authority and control, you can be as picky and perfectionistic as you choose. But when you have little or no control, easygoing and flexible standards become a tremendous advantage. They enable you to accept the fact that you are not perfect, others are not perfect, and the world is not perfect.

In fact, in most matters you don't have all the control. This means you are not always going to end up with everything the way you want it. The good news is that you control virtually everything in life that really matters, including the quality of your beliefs, the integrity of your desires, the purity of your motives, and the wholeheartedness of your efforts.

Hopelessness and despair grow from trying to control forces that are beyond your reach. The Serenity Prayer says it beautifully: "God grant me the courage to change the things I can, the serenity to accept the things I cannot change, and the wisdom to know the difference."

Stop telling yourself: *"I must have this or I'll be miserable,"* *"I must have this or I'll be furious,"* *"I must have this or I'll go crazy."*

Ask yourself instead: *"What can I realistically do about this?"*

"What am I willing to do about this?" "What am I going to do about this?" "If there's nothing to do, how would a change in my attitude help me lay this to rest?"

If there's more to be done and trying seems a wise and ethical option, go for it. Give it your best shot. Then if you don't get your way after giving it your all, consider the incident a blessing in disguise because it's a perfect change to practice letting go.

Trouble Spot #4:
Letting Go of Trying to Change Others

For some of us, trying to change others is tantamount to a full-time job. We work round the clock trying to shape and mold our kids, our men, our parents, our co-workers, our boss, our sisters, our brothers, our ex-husbands, and our friends. We bicker endlessly with loved ones about how they are, how they should be, how they shouldn't be, and how we wish they would be. The results are almost always dismal. Not only do we fail to get what we're after, we often ruin relationships in the process.

It is futile to try to change others against their will. When others have no interest in changing (or worse, are dead opposed to changing), you can scream and yell and rant and rave and pull your hair out all you want, but it will only be a waste of priceless energy. While you may be able to influence someone to do things differently, many people are never going to change to suit you.

When someone disappoints you by refusing to change, direct your energy instead to what you can do to get your own needs met independent of this person doing what you want.

Luckily, the possibilities are endless when it comes to changing yourself. This is where the real work always lies—in changing your own habits, attitudes, and inclinations.

I read once about a woman who nagged at her husband for years to go out with her on weeknights to the movies or restaurants. At the end of a long day at work, she wanted to break loose and have a little fun. But all he wanted was to veg out in front of the television with a beer and the paper. Finally, at the suggestion of her therapist, the woman gave up the battle and turned her energy instead to how she could satisfy her desires even if he stayed the same. The solutions were obvious. Soon she was going to the movies alone during the week and (to her surprise) enjoying herself immensely. She tried new restaurants with friends and had a great time. And, as frosting on the cake, as soon as she got off her husband's back, suddenly he started wanting to join her more often on her outings.

Mothering makes letting go hard to do. The act of mothering by definition involves controlling and influencing children to develop in certain ways. Knowing when to let go of trying to mold a son or daughter is not an easy decision given that the issues involved include discipline, drugs, safety, and education. In the beginning, of course, we wield considerable power and control over our kids. As they grow up, however, this diminishes as they increasingly (and appropriately) assert their independence.

Parental letting go needs to be gradual and suitable to a child's maturity. It's tragic to wrestle with your kids in power struggles until the day they leave home. Even if you win some of the battles, you inevitably lose the war. One mother of a 14-year-old son was lucky enough to realize the error of her ways before it was too late:

I used to nag him from morning to night about his schoolwork. He wanted to get into Brown for pre-med, and I knew that if he so much as brought home an A-minus it was all over. Then last October one of the boys in his class was killed in a head-on collision. After the funeral I kept looking at my son thinking, "It could have been him." I started thinking that if it had been, our last conversation together would have been me screaming out the front door at him about his homework. Sitting quietly one day, it dawned on me that we hadn't talked about anything else in months. Did I really want to sacrifice the years I had with him like this?[3]

We need a love that "lets them go." As our children grow older, we need to let them make many of their own choices, even when it means they may suffer unpleasant consequences. When problems occur that violate our own rights or endanger our kids, we need to exercise "tough love."[4] As the time grows near for them to forge out on their own, our attention and caring is best placed on developing new forms of relationship with them as young adults and restoring a fresh relationship with ourselves as well. The loss we experience can thus be compensated by the gain of time and energy for personal pursuits and pleasures.

You may want out of the relationship. If you find it impossible to let go when someone fails to change, another admittedly drastic option is to let go of the relationship itself.

---

[3] Lee Morical, *Where's My Happy Ending?*, Addison Wesley, 1984.
[4] P. A. Ness, *Tough Love*, Abbington, 1985. This book espouses a system of dealing with out-of-control teenagers based on "natural consequences." It helps parents reclaim power and set limits appropriately under very trying circumstances.

This is a "last course" recourse for relationships with serious problems that you've tried to clear up with no success.

Of course, with children and blood relatives, ending a relationship may be neither feasible nor desirable as an alternative—most of us are not about to disown rebellious teenagers or abandon recalcitrant four-year-olds because they fail to abide by our limits. Likewise with parents and relatives, we'll tolerate a great deal before ending a relationship (and, even then, we're usually only changing the nature of the relationship, not ending it). In lifelong relationships, the best you may be able to do is set limits using appropriate muscle and, if that doesn't work, figure out how to take care of yourself, given that the person is not changing. Instead of saying, *"I can't stand the way he is!"* tell yourself, *"I can bear it that he's this way. I forgive him for not being exactly as I want him to be. I love him enough and care enough about our relationship to let this issue go."*

It's tough to stop trying to change others, especially when we're convinced that the change we're asking for will be good for both the relationship and for them as individuals. A number of years ago when I was trying to let go of foolish, fruitless attempts to change the man in my life, a subscriber to *Soft-Power!*, my newsletter, sent me the following poem. It's an excellent description of the kind of inner surrender that must occur if we are to drop futile efforts to "fix" someone:

To Let Go

To let go is not to stop caring,
It's recognizing you can't do it for someone else.
To let go is not to cut yourself off,
It's realizing you can't control another.

To let go is not to enable,
But to allow learning from natural consequences.
To let go is not to fight powerlessness,
But to accept that the outcome is not always in your hands.

To let go is not to try to change or blame others,
It's to make the most of yourself.
To let go is not to care for, it's to care about,
It's not to fix, it's to be supportive.

To let go is not to judge,
It's to allow another to be a human being.
To let go is not to try to arrange outcomes for someone else,
But to allow others to affect their own destinies.

To let go is not to be protective,
It's to permit another to face their own reality.
To let go is not to regulate anyone,
But to strive to become what you dream you can be.
To let go is not to fear less, it's to love more.[5]

You can still be assertive. I want to stress that dropping your efforts to change someone doesn't mean you never set limits or speak up about problems. You have a right to ask for what you want and to set limits regarding what's unacceptable to you—that's the whole point of this book. Letting go enters the picture when others fail to comply with your limits or requests and there's nothing more to be done about it. By letting go, you recognize that they have a right to disagree with you and (within legal constraints) do whatever they please, even when what they choose goes against your deepest desires and values.

[5] I don't know the author of this poem. It comes from literature passed out at 12-step programs (Alcoholics Anonymous, Alanon, ACA, etc.). For information on subscribing to my newsletter, see the back of the book.

Trouble Spot #5:
Letting Go of Doing It All

There's a limit to what you can do. You need to learn what it is, respect it, then let go of all the other things you're not going to do. In *Where's My Happy Ending*? Lee Morical reports the results of a survey she conducted with thousands of women. Ninety-two percent of those polled said the biggest problem facing us as women today is that we have so much choice we feel continually guilty or disappointed in ourselves for not "doing it all." Even more recently, the December 4, 1989, cover story in *Time* magazine ("Women Face the '90s") claimed that the biggest issue for women today is how to balance their work and home life so they don't burn out. As *Time* put it, "In the '80s they tried to have it all. Now they've just had it."[6]

Part of the problem is that too often we equate the fullness and worth of our life with how much we can cram into it. Lee Morical reminds us that we don't have to face life like a starving person at a smorgasbord, stuffing our faces out of the fear that we won't get any more or will end up with less than our share.

Delegation is one of the main ways to reduce what's on your plate. An ability to give work away is a cornerstone of healthy self-management. By delegating to family, staff, and other suitable helpmates, you free yourself from overflow responsibilities and obligations. How about letting the teenager down the street clean your basement instead of doing it yourself? How about teaching your kids to make their own lunches and do their own wash? How about turning over the research for your report to your secretary?

[6]"Women Face the '90s," *Time*, Dec. 4, 1989.

Most of us are unskilled and uncomfortable giving away work. We *overcontrol* by breathing down someone's back as he or she does what we've asked. We *undercontrol* by engaging in "dump and run" delegation, abandoning projects with little or no management of the results. Or we don't delegate at all —we do it all ourselves.

It's usually fear that interferes with the process. Typically we hesitate to turn the reins over to others because we're worried that if we trust them to do a project it will never get done. Or if it does get done it won't be done as well as we'd do it. Or, perhaps worse yet, it will be done better than we'd do it.

The skills of delegation deserve an entire book, and, luckily, Larry Steinmetz has written an excellent, thorough one on the topic: *The Art and Skill of Delegation*.[7] I recommend it highly even if the only delegating you do is getting your husband to buy the weekly groceries.

Delegation is but one of many ways to prune down your activity level. In *Enough is Enough: Exploding the Myth of Having It All*, Carol Orsborn suggests another.[8] She recommends that, when faced with too much to do, you distinguish between must-dos, need-to-dos, want-to-dos, and going-to-dos. For example, if you have both a busy career and a young child, you may want to be there for your child's first step but, given your situation, this may not be something that you are going to do. Nor is it something that you necessarily need to do— your child will not be emotionally scarred if you celebrate the big event a few hours after it happens. Your gut is the best guide in making these kinds of distinctions. Attending your daughter's ballet recital may feel in your gut like a must-do,

---

[7]Larry Steinmetz, *The Art and Skill of Delegation*, Horizon Publications, Inc., 1976, 3333 Iris Avenue, Boulder, CO 80301, $15.95.

[8]Carol Orsborn, *Enough Is Enough*, Putnam, 1986.

but being her class mother may not. As you engage in the sorting process, it's fine to factor in the opinions of others, but reserve the final judgment for yourself. Your must-dos won't be the same as those of your friends, neighbors, husband, or mother-in-law—and that's perfectly okay.

You do not and should not have to do it all. Stop carrying the world on your shoulders. As a note on a friend's refrigerator puts it:

> Dear Marilyn,
>
> You are not 100%, totally responsible for doing everything, taking care of everything, or taking care of everybody. That's my job.
>
> Love, God

The world will not fall apart if you decide against serving as president of the board. Your friend will not hate you if you decline an invitation to her dinner party. Your boss will not fire you if you speak up when you have to much to do (or if he or she does, it will no doubt be a blessing in disguise). Give yourself a break and treat yourself with kindness. Let go of doing it all.

Trouble Spot #6: Letting Go of Anger— Learning to Forgive

Forgiveness may be the most important area where we need to learn to let go. Forgiveness has been called "attitudinal aikido." It is an act of will (something you choose to do) and a skill (something you can learn to do and improve in with practice). When you learn to forgive you lighten your load in life. It is, therefore, a loving gift not only to others but to yourself as well.

Refusing to forgive is, in contrast, a self-destructive act. When you carry resentment and rage in your body as pent-up tension, you deplete yourself of power and place substantial stress on your physical system. Your blood pressure elevates, your stomach acidity increases, excess adrenalin rushes through your veins, your neck tightens, your back hurts. With forgiveness, all that changes as anger stops eating away at your insides.

Beyond such important health implications, there's another good reason to forgive and forget. When you cling to old gripes, you accord those you resent enormous power over you and your life. The rage you carry toward your ex-husband means he still has a hold over you. Is that what you want? Holding anger toward a boss, a co-worker, or a stranger means these individuals are to some degree running you. Is that what you want? By learning to forgive, you become a free agent again, unencumbered by excess emotional baggage.

You'll probably find it easier to forgive if you can empathize with the other person's side of a situation. As you may remember from Chapter Three, empathy does not mean you, yourself, ever did (or would ever do) what someone else has done. It just means you know what it's like, in a generic sense, to be an imperfect human being. You know from experience what it's like to act inappropriately, be thoughtless of others, lose control, seek revenge, manipulate, or punish.

To help yourself feel empathy, put yourself in the place of the person you're trying to forgive and guess at their emotions and motives. As that person, what do you guess you'd feel? Would it be anger? Hurt? Confusion? Pressure? Jealousy? Vindictiveness? What emotional dimensions can you identify with? Try to recall a time when you felt jealous or hateful or pressured yourself, even if you didn't act on the feelings or the circumstances were completely different. The realization that you too have had equally unenlightened moments can help you let go of anger, however justified it may otherwise be.

Another way to improve your ability to forgive is to stage regular forgiveness sessions. Set aside time specifically for the purpose of clearing away old resentments. To prepare yourself for the session, tape the following guided visualization in your own voice (or ask a friend to do it if you prefer hearing someone else's voice). Use a calm, relaxed tone of voice and maintain an easy pace of delivery. Take pauses as suggested in the parentheses:

Take a moment to get comfortable. Close your eyes and take a few deep breaths. *(15 seconds)* Relax your eyelids as you continue to breathe with full, relaxed breath. *(10 seconds)*

Release all physical tightening in your body. On each exhale, sigh out loud and, with each sigh, imagine the tension from all your muscles draining out through your fingers and toes. *(20 seconds)*

Identify in your mind a situation in your life where you are holding resentment or anger toward someone—anger and resentment you now want to free yourself from. Pick a situation where, although you may not be sure that you're ready to forgive, you know you want to at least begin the process. It might even be yourself that you are going to forgive. As you select someone to forgive, continue to relax your body and mind and breathe with calm, full breaths. *(20 seconds)*

Relax even further and imagine you're seated in a safe, protected sanctuary. Perhaps you're secure in a tree house or maybe you're in a cozy room complete with a fireplace and crackling fire. Perhaps you're on a beautiful stretch of beach with the ocean lapping gently on the shore. Create an atmosphere in your mind that feels completely safe, secure, and peaceful. Wherever you are, imagine yourself in a comfortable easy chair and picture a second chair facing you where the person you're about to forgive will sit. *(15–20 seconds)*

As you envision yourself in this protected spot, feel how calm you are. You are totally relaxed. You feel open-hearted, open-minded, ready to lighten up, let go, and forgive. *(10 seconds)*

Now take a moment to imagine the person you are about to forgive joining you in this place. See this person seated comfortably across from you in as relaxed and calm a state as you are yourself. They are ready to hear what you have to say. They are ready to be forgiven. *(15–20 seconds)*

Take the following few minutes of silence to tell this person what's been bothering you. This is a last chance to get the matter off your chest. Quietly yet clearly, express your hurt and anger. Do this in a way that is both completely truthful and nonabusive. Speak from your heart. Speak for yourself. *(2 minutes)*

Now invite the person you're forgiving to respond. Imagine what this person might say if he or she were to answer you honestly and nonabusively. Don't worry about whether or not the response you imagine is accurate. Give yourself free rein.

If this person were given a chance to communicate from the heart, what do you imagine would be said? *(90 seconds)*

Now tell this person that, despite what has happened, you are ready to forgive. You have decided to free yourself from the anger, resentment, and guilt you've been carrying around. Picture yourself releasing all your inner tension in a physical, visible way. Perhaps it drains out of your fingers and toes. Maybe you release the negative energy out an open window to the evening sky. Perhaps you burn a symbolic statement of your anger to ashes. Or fill a large balloon with your upset, then release the balloon so it is carried up, up, and away. *(20 seconds)*

As these upsetting emotions leave your body, feel how much lighter you are. It's as if your insides have been swept clean —washed clear. You feel free and easy—ready to move on. *(15 seconds)*

Finally, take a moment to pat yourself on the back for having had the sense, courage, and good will to forgive. *(20 seconds)*

To use this taped visualization for a forgiveness session, settle yourself somewhere where you can completely relax. Sit in a favorite easy chair that fully supports your body, or lie on a comfortable rug with a pillow under your head. Uncross your arms and legs, take your glasses off, and close your eyes. If you listen to the visualization instructions on headphones, you might want to play restful music in the background on a second tape player.

Don't be discouraged if there are no dramatic results immediately. It may be necessary to repeat the exercise several times before it "takes." Forgiveness doesn't have to happen all at once. The most lasting forgiveness can be a gradual release that in the beginning feels contrived and phony. With more serious and severe situations (like forgiving an abusive husband or incestuous parent), look on the process as a long-term project and seek the assistance of a trained therapist.

LEARNING TO "LIVE IN THE LEAP"

Without an ability to let go you are chained to your past. With it you free yourself to move on, unencumbered, into the future. But because the letting-go experience implies loss, it can be scary as well as exhilarating. If you feel more unnerved than elated at the prospect of letting go, it may help to play down the deprivation and focus instead on the many expansive and freeing dimensions of the process.

But even the possibility of liberation can be frightening. Marilyn Ferguson, author of *The Aquarian Conspiracy*, speaks of the terror of "living in the leap." To let go and live with freedom, you must at times live in the leap of the unknown. Because of this, letting go takes guts and self-trust. It also takes a certain foundation of faith. Faith (as I use the term) refers to trust in a power that is both greater than you and a part of you. With faith you become willing to surrender to a God force in the universe when things are outside your control. As a popular affirmation puts it, you "let go and let God." This sort of faith has nothing to do with formal religion. It's a world apart from the rigid patriarchal doctrine of most organized churches. Instead it is a private, quiet connection between you, your inner spirit, and the rest of all things. With a strong foundation of faith, it becomes infinitely easier to let go. In the words of poet Richard Wilbur, "Float face up, my child, and let the sea hold you."

In *Creative Visualization*, Shakti Gawain also uses a water metaphor to reflect on how you can let go as you simultaneously take charge of your life:

> Let us imagine that life is a river. Most people are clinging to the bank, afraid to let go and risk being carried along by the current of the river. At a certain point, each person must be willing to simply let go, and trust the river to carry him along safely. At this point he learns to "go with the flow" and it feels wonderful.
>
> Once he has gotten used to being in the flow of the river, he can begin to look ahead and guide his own course onward, deciding where the course looks best, steering around boulders and snags, and choosing which of many channels and branches of the river he prefers to follow, all the while still "going with the flow."[9]

The SoftPower challenge is finding the mid-zone between surrender and control where you can relax your grip on life and go with the flow while at the very same time taking command and making things happen. Trust—both self-trust and faith in a Higher Power—plays a major role in the process.

Letting go is an integral part of living and of changing. Once you become skilled at the process of inner surrender, you can release anger, guilt, and fear. You can change your stubborn ways and free yourself from unhealthy relationships.

A feeling of trust can help you to let go. With trust in yourself, you'll be ready to take risks to effect change, stand

[9]Shakti Gawain, *Creative Visualization*, Whatever Publishing, 1978.

firm in the face of opposing forces, or give in when that's the gracious or smart thing to do. With trust in a Higher Power, you'll feel protected enough to seize the initiative and try new things, yet supported enough to let go and let God when situations are beyond your control.

10

CHANGE

It's Up to You

You can start anew anytime you want. You're not stuck with how you are, who you are, or what you've got. Subatomic physics has recently confirmed what ancient mystical traditions have known for centuries: Everything, including you, is constantly shifting and transforming. The wonderful part of this all-pervasive, universal impermanence is that it means that at any given moment you can turn over a leaf and create a new beginning. Whether it's staying on a diet or learning to say no, you can do things differently starting right now. Just as your body is perpetually recreating itself, you are given a fresh start in terms of behavior and attitude every day, every minute, every second of your life. Not only *can* you change, you *are always* changing—whether you like it or not. Change is everpresent and unavoidable.

As human beings, our ability to *choose change* sets us apart from all other creatures. This distinguishing talent reveals itself early in life. You do not come out of the womb eating with a fork and knife—eating neatly is not what comes naturally. Watch a one-year-old at her birthday party and you see a face, dress, hair, and high chair smeared with cake and ice cream. Slowly over the years, however, she learns to shovel food onto a spoon instead of directly into her eager little mouth. Voila! By the time she's five, table manners have become second nature. She has succeeded (with a little help from social re-inforcement) in changing her nature.

Scott Peck gives a vivid example of how our capacity to choose change frees us from instincts and makes us unique in the animal world.

> I live in Connecticut on the shore of a large lake. To this lake every March when the ice melts there comes a flock of gulls and every December when it freezes they depart, presumably for parts south. I do not know where they go, but acquaintances have recently suggested it's Florence, Alabama. Scientists who have studied migratory birds have come to realize that with their little bird brains the gulls are actually able to navigate by the stars so as to hit Florence, Alabama, right on the dot every time. The only trouble with this is that they have relatively little freedom. It's either Florence, Alabama, or not at all. They cannot say, "Well, this time I think I'll winter in Waco, Texas, or Bermuda." But because of our relative lack of instincts, what most distinguishes us human beings is our enormous freedom. We have the freedom (if we have the financial wherewithal) to choose to winter in Alabama or Bermuda or Barbados, or to stay home or to do something totally unnatural and turn around and go in the opposite

direction up to northern Vermont to slide down icy hills
on awkward slats of wood or fiberglass.[1]

As a member of the human race, you too can choose to
winter anywhere you please. You can choose to change a lot
of other things as well. You can choose to change your mind
and rearrange your priorities. You can choose to be more
honest in your relationships. You can choose to improve your
relationship with your mother. You can choose to alter how
you hold the past. You can choose to upgrade how you feel
about yourself. You can choose to change yourself (and your
life) at will. The message of SoftPower is a message about
changing at will.

There are two big reasons why you elect to change. When
you make a decision to change things, it's usually either to
make a situation better or keep it from getting worse. As you
contemplate change, you consciously or unconsciously weigh
the benefits of experimenting against the cost of staying the
same. If the promise seems worth the risk, you forge ahead.
When there's little prospect of gain, it's unlikely you'll ever
get off the dime. Let's face it—it's easier staying with what's
charted and familiar than heading out into the unknown where
you could get lost or hurt. Changing yourself calls for living
in the leap. If you're an adventuresome soul, this will be no
problem. You'll willingly and spontaneously venture off the
beaten path. But if like so many others you are less risk-prone,
you may need a nudge from an outside force to move you out
of a rut and away from the safety of your comfort zone.

Understanding what keeps you from changing is just as
important as knowing what propels the process. For starters,

[1]M. Scott Peck, *The Different Drum*, Simon & Schuster, 1987, pp. 179–180.

self-doubt can be a sizable obstacle. When you don't believe you're capable of change, fear of failure blocks the way. Indifference is another handicap. When you don't care whether or not things change, there's no motivation to overcome stuck inertia. Pride is a third problem. When you think you have all the answers, your mind closes down to alternatives. Pride can also block the way when a decision to change implies that things weren't okay the way they were. It's hard to admit you've been wrong, especially if you've invested considerable time and energy in being a certain way. Changing yourself then represents a significant loss of effort and refusing to change becomes a way to save face and sustain belief in yourself. Your fragile ego would rather say, "*I don't care—I'm fine the way I am,*" than try and fail.

ARE YOU FLYING BLIND?

Unless you're a gull and automatic pilot always lands you in the right place, lack of self-awareness will put you at a sizable disadvantage. Unaware, you can steer yourself in wrong directions, get into ruts or go-nowhere circles, or crash into unforeseen obstacles. Anything out of your awareness (be it perceptions, thoughts, feelings, or desires) has the potential of running you into trouble. For example, unmonitored irrational thoughts can lead you to foolhardy actions. The minute you become aware of what your mind is up to, however, you take more control over the situation. Even if your mind continues to blow things out of proportion and dwell on the negative, you can disregard such thinking and elect to hold back from doing anything foolish as a result of it.

Unconsciousness can sometimes be a self-protective maneuver designed to spare you the pain of rude reality. A woman unwilling to face the consequences of divorce, for example, may deaden her feelings and "go unconscious" about how bad the marriage is. She just keeps plodding along the way she always has. If she doesn't think about it, she doesn't have to face choices that could turn her world upside down. In other circumstances, flying on automatic is a desirable thing to do because it saves you time and energy. By relegating unimportant or uncomplicated choices to a routine, you free yourself for more important matters. Productive, healthy habits make it possible for you to brush your teeth, get dressed, and drive a car without thinking. If you had to think about every single thing you did and each and every step you took, your attention and energy would be consumed by the most mundane of tasks.

Unfortunately, it's not just with the routine that we go unconscious. Some psychologists have estimated that 95 percent of all behavioral and emotional responses are habitual. This means you are probably handling even important, difficult, and complex choices in your life with unconscious, habitual responses. When unconsciousness is pervasive (and 95 percent is certainly pervasive!), your life is little more than a trance. Because you aren't paying enough attention to what you're doing, you stay in jobs you don't like, in relationships that are lifeless, and in routines that are self-destructive. In effect, you lose your free agency and live in bondage to the program. Like Scott Peck's gulls, you can only do it one way. You forfeit freedom for the party line.

Waking up begins the process of changing at will. You need to take stock of the way things are *right now*. Contrary to common wisdom, ignorance is not bliss. It's having little or no choice or making stupid, uninformed choices. To change your attitude, you must first know what your current attitude is. To change your behavior, you must be aware of what you're presently doing and not doing.

The self-awareness needed for changing at will can be gained in a variety of ways. Sometimes it's the result of feedback from others. A story from my life illustrates:

My mother used to call me a "big mouth." She had a point. I did have a tendency to butt my nose into everyone's business, speak up for underdogs whether they wanted my help or not, and drum in my point ad nauseam (*"Maria, you never know when to stop!"*). Letting go was not my strong suit.

In addition to being a Big Mouth, I was a Tomboy, Troublemaker, and Smart Aleck. Of course, this wasn't the whole story. Using the terminology of the '80s, my family was dysfunctional. I thought of it as "crazy." While there was no alcoholism, divorce, or abuse in any criminal sense of the word, the majority of my family memories are of fights, yelling, sarcasm, tension, frozen silences, long faces, and dirty looks. My toughness camouflaged a vulnerable, scared little girl using survival skills to make the best of a not-so-great situation.

Acting tough also gave me an illusion of power. From an early age I had decided to say, "No, thank you" to the ladylike forms of power that society had accorded to those of us born with double-X chromosomes. I was singularly unimpressed with the results my mother and girlfriends seemed to reap using traditional, Stage One, keep-your-mouth-shut, give-in-to-what-others-want, and make-believe-you're-stupid-to-bolster-the-male-ego forms of power. Besides, the Saturday matinee movies at the Westbury Theater made it abundantly clear that the people who got the goodies in this world were those who threw their weight around and shot their mouth off. So at the risk of killing myself falling from a tree and alienating potential boyfriends by being a "brain," I exerted what felt like power in my own scrappy way.

In my mid-twenties, I experienced a "turning point" event that changed me forever. It occurred during my first year in graduate school. The small seminar group I had been a member of for six months staged an Encounter Marathon Weekend in Santa Cruz, California. This was the era when encounter groups were "in," and all of us thought it would clear the air if we took a retreat together where we could be brutally honest with each other.

Lucky me, I was the first one to get the "hot seat" (where you had the dubious honor of receiving honest feedback from the rest of the group). Brutal honesty is what I got. Eleven people (the entire group) told me in no uncertain terms that I came across as aloof and conceited, that I interrupted others all the time, and that I had been treating them all as if they weren't worth the time of day.

With the first of the feedback, my well-developed defensiveness kicked in and I privately dismissed the criticism. *They* were the ones with the problem, not me. By the time the last person had echoed the refrain, however, I had dropped my smugness and was sitting there silently horrified that I was such an awful and unpopular person. Not even one member of the group seemed to like me! It was truly a bleak moment.

Actually, my misery lasted a lot longer than a moment. I sat there mute for several hours, virtually catatonic, while the group proceeded on its merry way to give feedback to each individual member. As I sat there, frozen within the deepest dark recesses of myself, I felt as if I didn't deserve to live. Thank God there were no bridges around or I would have jumped. I had had no idea that I was making such a negative impression on so many people!

At the lowest point, I began to experience a shift. It dawned on me that Iden (a professor in the program whom I greatly respected and admired) had befriended me. I had gone to his house socially and become friends with Wendy, his wife, and his kids. "If Iden likes me," my desperate thinking went, "I couldn't be that bad!" The memory of Iden's friendship was like a hand held out to me at the bottom of a deep, dark well. It pulled me up and out into the light again.

There were many other dramatic breakthroughs and insights that weekend, but this single episode woke me up with a start to the impact I was having on others. It brought home to me in no uncertain terms that, if I wanted my life and relationships to work, I was going to have to change.

The effect of this harsh experience was profound. For starters, I became excruciatingly aware that the group members were right. My interrupting behavior *was* obnoxious. I *was* thoughtless of others. I *did* hold myself above it all. In my determination not to be like my mother with her selfless martyrdom, I had gone the other extreme.

My newly found self-awareness, of course, was only the first step on the long road to change. Once aware, the hard part of the change process began—the part that demands persistence, self-discipline, and commitment. It took many years for me to change my ways (and I'm still working at it!). Breaking well-entrenched habits demands time and sustained effort. While occasionally you may be able to literally transform yourself overnight, usually it's a slower, more deliberate process. Like the Little Engine That Could, you chug chug chug along, affirming, "*I think I can, I think I can. I know I can, I know I can.*" It's an evolutionary affair, a slow, irregular process of repeated self-corrections.

Many experiences have the potential to wake you up to greater awareness and begin the change process. Some, like my encounter group interaction, jolt and startle you like a loud alarm clock that interrupts a sound sleep. You may not always enjoy such an awakening, but it does get you up and moving. A fight with a friend, a sickness that puts you out of commission, an embarrassing failure or mistake, the death of a loved one—any of these can startle you to attention and make you realize in a moment all sorts of things you were previously oblivious to. The fight brings home how you have been less than truthful in that relationship. The sickness forces you to face the fact that you need to slow down and set limits on the obligations you accept. The mistake gets your head out of the clouds and onto the business at hand. The death makes you realize how little time you spend with your family, how brief life is, how fast it all goes by, and that you haven't yet written your will.

Fortunately less startling wake-ups can be equally effective. The impetus to take notice and make changes doesn't have to be traumatic to work. It can be as subtle as a dream or a poem, as soft as an honest, loving comment from a friend. Self-help books, tapes, and workshops are other ways in which you can wake yourself up in gentler fashion. You see yourself walking across the pages or hear a vivid description in a seminar of someone who is unable to say no and think to yourself, "Boy, that's me!" The next day, you may still get roped into obligations, but at least now you see what's going on and that you are a part of the problem.

No matter how your awakening is triggered, becoming aware will only be the beginning. If true change is to occur, there will then be several predictable levels you'll move through as you break old habits and make new ones. Lets look at what these are. Once you know what to expect, you can smooth the path for yourself and accelerate your own change process dramatically.

LEVEL ONE
Unconscious Incompetence:
Ignorance Is Not Bliss

Before change occurs, you are usually operating on automatic pilot, oblivious to negative habits that are interfering with your success. Perhaps, like me, you have a tendency to interrupt others without realizing what you're doing. Or maybe you unconsciously pick at your nails or play with your jewelry when you're nervous. There are typically dozens of self-sabotaging habits that we engage in with little or no awareness. The more pervasive a habit is, the less aware of it we usually are. What's everywhere is invisible. Like a fish in water, you don't see what surrounds you. This means your most insidious bad habits can be the ones most dominant in your life.

Let's track a self-defeating habit that relates to limit setting through the various predictable stages of change. Assume, for the sake of example, that you indiscriminately accept every invitation or request for help that comes your way. The only thing you're aware of with regard to this tendency to overbook yourself is that your calendar is perpetually jammed and you are forever unhappy about all the responsibilities in your life. But you haven't yet put two and two together and realized that your own behavior is at the root of it all. This is classic Level One unconsciousness.

You graduate to Level Two when something happens to provoke awareness of your contribution to the problem. Perhaps you get sick and the doctor tells you to cut down on the million and one things that you're involved in. At this point, although you haven't yet changed your behavior, you know what needs to be changed. As a result, you begin to "witness" yourself as you accept invitations you have no interest in. This marks the all-important shift to conscious incompetence.

LEVEL TWO
Conscious Incompetence:
This Is Your Life—Wake Up and Take Charge!

The heightened self-awareness of Level Two can occur before, during, or after a specific behavior occurs. At the start, awareness may not hit you until a situation is over and done with. For example, it may not be until after you hang up the phone that it dawns on you that you've gone and done it again—you've agreed to do something you should have turned down. As you progress, your awareness may start to take place as an event transpires. You hear yourself saying to someone, "*Sure, that'd be great,*" all the while knowing it wouldn't be great at all. While your mouth hasn't caught up yet with your consciousness, the gap is narrowing.

Level Two can be a discouraging time because "after the fact" and "middle of the act" awareness may not seem like much progress—who wants to be aware of how much you're still flubbing it when you haven't yet done any improving? So instead of congratulating yourself on how far you've come, you may trash yourself because you're still the same. I vividly remember how uncomfortable it was for me after my encounter group experience. For weeks after, I was so painfully aware of how appallingly rampant my interrupting behavior was, I almost gave up. "What's the use," I thought, "I'll never change—I do it all the time. It's just the way I am."

It's essential to recognize during this wake-up stage of Level Two that hindsight and "mid-sight" are a far sight better than no awareness at all. They begin the process and put you on the road to change. Give yourself a big pat on the back. At least you're noticing the error of your ways. This shows you're in transition between behavior patterns. Reinforce the healthy shift with a "Good for me!" attitude and reassure yourself that eventually, you'll be catching yourself *before* the act and then real progress will have been made.

Some people, of course, get to Level Two and never budge beyond that. But even this can be an improvement over the unconsciousness of Level One. With awareness, you can at least make changes in your circumstances that could remedy a problem even if you don't make any changes in yourself. A friend, for example, knows that on Thursdays, when she works an unusually long day, she arrives home short-tempered. Because she's tired and strung out, she's more susceptible than usual to getting into hassles with her kids or husband. Once she became aware of this predictable tendency, she asked her family to treat her gingerly on Thursdays and made sure to reserve alone time for unwinding on those evenings. These coping strategies made a difference, even though she herself stayed the same.

If you decide to change *yourself*, however, by altering your attitude, emotional responses, or actions, this signals a readiness to move on to the next stage of change, Level Three.

LEVEL THREE
Conscious Competence:
Choosing to Do Things Differently

Here is where change really starts to happen. You are now motivated to take the time and trouble to go beyond merely recognizing that you're not doing something right and begin the correction process. You begin to act or think in a new way.

Levels Two and Three often occur back to back. You catch yourself doing something the old way (Level Two), then make a change and do it the new way (Level Three). For example, immediately after agreeing to a dinner date, you realize you've overbooked yourself. This prompts you to call the person back and bow out of the commitment.

Ultimately, of course, you don't want to have to go back to undo or redo actions, but in the early stages of the change process this can be good enough. Fortunately, many things in life *are* "redoable." In a lot of situations, you can say, *"I've changed my mind about Tuesday. I'm sorry if this disappoints you, but I overextended myself."*

Level Three (like Level Two) can be an uncomfortable stage of the change game. Fears of disapproval, rejection, and failure may surface and frighten you into retreat. The fears are not groundless. When you change, there are bound to be people in your life who won't like the new you—especially if the new you is saying no to them when the old you always said yes. Be prepared to weather a bit of criticism and conflict as you see the change process through to completion.

You may also have to experience some failure along the way. When you try something new, chances are you'll occasionally foul up simply because of the novelty of it. Despite the name of this stage, you are not yet competent. Like a first-time skier going down the bunny slope on her rear end, at times you'll end up looking and feeling foolish. Even when you pull off a new skill fairly well, it may still feel contrived and unnatural as you execute it. Like breaking in new shoes, it takes a while before you adapt a skill to who you are and the awkwardness and discomfort dissipate.

You need motivation, commitment, and self-discipline to make it through this challenging third level of the habit-formation process. The first of these—*motivation*—is what overcomes inertia and fuels the entire process. You need a reason to try something different, a payoff for spending the time and energy that change requires. It helps to know both what's in it for you if you change and what it will cost you if you don't change. But whether it's the stick or the carrot that moves you to action, in order to get the ball rolling you need a strong desire to have things be other than how they are.

To sustain this desire for change, you also need *commitment*—personal dedication to the change process. A well-grounded pledge to your goal grows best from passionate enthusiasm for the way you want things to be. While you may feel equally passionate about how you *don't* want things to be, it's better to direct your devotion toward the carrot (what you want) rather than what you don't want. Otherwise you can unwittingly reinforce what you'd like to get rid of by "trying too hard" against it. In *Psychocybernetics*, Maxwell Maltz tells of a 20-year study of habits that showed how effort to change often backfires and ends up deepening negative habits instead of uprooting them.[2] So instead of struggling against bad habits, conjure up clear thoughts and images of desired end results and hold to your vision.

Both your motivation and commitment sustain the last of the requirements for success at Level Three: *self-discipline*. You need a structured determination to hang in there even in the face of mistakes or failure. You don't need to act like a boot camp sergeant with yourself, but you may need to kick your own butt once in a while when you're tempted to quit trying. Be patiently persistent, determined without desperation. Get-

---

[2] Maxwell Maltz, *Psychocybernetics*, Wilshire Book Co., 1960.

ting mad at yourself for falling off the wagon of self-discipline will only work against you. Like the dieter who binges after she pigs out on cheesecake, when you are too hard on yourself about a slip-up, you're likely to say "The hell with it" and give up entirely. Get off your own back. All that's necessary to recover your course is to make the needed corrections. Much in the manner of a jetliner that lands in the right place via hundreds of minute navigational corrections, you can achieve amazing personal transformation by making repeated and continual small self-corrections. This is what Level Three is all about.

Maxwell Maltz claims it takes twenty-one days of concerted effort before a new habit is fully ingrained, so keep the faith. Virtually anything is habit forming if repeated enough times. Sustained effort is the price of excellence. There are two good ways to get the repetition you need during this stage. One is to actually execute the desired behavior over and over. Each successful experience, no matter how small, becomes a chance to breed more success. The second method is to use your mind as a private rehearsal room. You dwell mentally on how the "best you" acts and thinks. Dennis Waitley calls this "practicing within when you can't practice 'without.' " He tells of American POWs who created a mental "Hanoi Hilton" while in captivity. The prisoners spent hours each day mentally working on golf swings, playing a guitar, or drilling themselves on some other activity they had enjoyed in their former lives. Once released from the camps, the men discovered to their amazement that as a result of the imaginary practice sessions, they were able to perform at dramatically higher levels than they had before their imprisonment. Visualization does indeed pay off.[3]

[3] Dennis Waitley, *Seeds of Greatness*, Pocket Books, 1983.

If you hang in persistently through the discouragement and frustrations of Level Two and Level Three, one fine day you find that you no longer have to remind yourself to do things differently. You no longer have to monitor yourself as you execute your new behavior. It all happens automatically as situations demand. Congratulations! You've graduated to Level Four.

LEVEL FOUR
Unconscious Competence:
Back to Automatic Pilot

You're unconscious again, but now a self-serving habit is running the show. Without even thinking about it, you hear yourself say, *"I need to check my schedule before committing to this"* or *"I'm sorry but I'm not able to go with you. Next week is already packed."* There's no need to tell yourself to turn down invitations you have no time for or interest in. It just happens on its own. Your new habit has become a dependable part of your repertoire.

From time to time, of course, despite your progress you may regress to old ways. In the normal course of change, you'll typically experience a back-and-forth kind of progression. When you're under unusual stress, overtired, or feeling sick, an occasional backslide to old habits is to be expected. Accept this as part of the process so it won't be demoralizing. Such a regression is usually both specific to a particular situation and temporary. Just do what's necessary to get back on course and you'll be fine.

ARE YOU READY TO CHANGE?

You are the architect of your own future. As a Hindu proverb says, "There is nothing noble in being superior to someone else. The true nobility is in being superior to your previous self." When poet Oliver Wendell Holmes examined the multiple tiers of a nautilus shell, he saw in its ever-expanding shape a beautiful symbol of the way individuals develop themselves as they go through life. Inspired by the message of the shell, he wrote his magnificent poem "Chambered Nautilus." It speaks of the unlimited potential each of us has to develop and shape ourselves as we experience the adventure of life. Read it aloud to yourself (especially the last passage) whenever you feel powerless and stuck.

Chambered Nautilus

This is the ship of pearl, which, poets feign,
    Sails the unshadowed main,—
    The venturous bark that flings
On the sweet summer wind its purpled wings
In gulfs enchanted, where the Siren sings,
    And coral reefs lie bare,
Where the cold sea-maids raise to sun their streaming hair.

Its webs of living gauze no more unfurl;
    Wrecked is the ship of pearl!
    And every chambered cell,
Where its dim dreaming life was wont to dwell,
As the frail tenant shaped his growing shell,
    Before thee lies revealed.—
Its irised ceiling rent, its sunless crypt unsealed!

Year after year beheld the silent toil
*   That spread his lustrous coil;*
*   Still, as the spiral grew,*
He left the past year's dwelling for the new,
Stole with soft step its shining archway through,
*   Built up its idle door,*
Stretched in his last-found home, and knew the old no more.

Thanks for this heavenly message brought by thee,
*   Child of the wandering sea,*
*   Cast from her lap, forlorn!*
From thy dead lips a clearer note is born
Than ever Triton blew from wreathed horn!
*   While on mine ear it rings,*
Through the deep caves of thought I hear a voice that sings:

Build thee more stately mansions, O my soul,
*   As the swift seasons roll!*
*   Leave thy low-vaulted past!*
Let each new temple, nobler than the last,
Shut thee from heaven with a dome more vast,
*   Till thou at length are free,*
Leaving thine outgrown shell by life's unresting sea.

The rest of your life awaits you. How you live it is entirely up to you. Will you build for yourself ever statelier mansions or will you dwell in the narrow confines of self-doubt and bad habits? Which path will you take—that of expansion or that of fear?

It's Time to Come Full Circle

What better way to end our exploration of SoftPower than by returning to the beginning—to the women described at the start who were having so little success with their own power. Let's see how SoftPower could help them out:

Tina lives in Seattle. She is single, 29, and a personnel manager at a large bank. Tina has trouble setting limits with her boss, Ken. It's 4:15 on Thursday and, just as Tina is winding up for the day, Ken announces he needs her help in finishing a report due Friday morning. Tina had set aside this evening to shop and cook for a dinner party the next night but her boss seems desperate. This isn't the first time he's expected her to stay overtime without advance warning, but while she complained once about last-minute assignments, little has changed.

Tina looks up at Ken and says in a kind yet firm voice, *"I wish you had told me about this earlier, Ken. I could have postponed working on the Hamilton report and fit this job in during the afternoon. Unfortunately, I'm not able to stay past five tonight. Do you want me to call downstairs to see if Janet could lend a hand?"*

Louise is 40 years old. She is an executive vice-president for a large insurance company and the mother of a four-month-old son. Louise is upset because Karyn, the young woman taking care of her baby, plays with Greg all day instead of putting him down for an afternoon nap as Louise has asked her to do. Louise had hoped that her pediatrician would back her up on the wisdom of getting the baby used to napping at an early age but, unfortunately, he didn't. Now she's afraid of offending and perhaps losing Karyn (who is otherwise wonderful with the baby) if she orders her to follow directions on the nap. Louise's insecurity as a new mother doesn't help. So to bolster her confidence, she plans and practices what she'll say to Karyn with a good friend at the office.

The next time Louise hears from Karyn that the baby "didn't want to nap," she suggests with a friendly tone of voice that they get a cup of coffee and visit for a few minutes. As they sit in the breakfast room together, Louise calmly expresses her feelings. While inside she feels nervous, her outer demeanor is easygoing and centered.

"Karyn, I'm very happy with how you care for the baby. You give him such loving and responsible attention—that means a great deal to me. It's inevitable, however, that we'll run into occasional times when we don't to see eye to eye on how to handle Greg and, of course, when that happens we need to work out those differences.

"I know you don't see a naptime as all that important—especially if Greg doesn't seem sleepy. For me, however it's extremely important that we establish a routine where Greg gets used to spending a couple of quiet hours in his crib each afternoon. I need you to respect my feelings on this, Karyn—even if you don't agree with me personally. It's not acceptable that he stay up all day without a rest. I'll be happy to work with you on how you can manage the naptimes, but I need to first be sure I have a commitment from you to follow through on my wishes regarding this. Do I have that?"

Karyn agreed to do what Louise wanted. At that point, Louise suggested they talk over how Karyn might create a better transition for the baby to a naptime and how she could encourage Greg to settle down when he resisted. They agreed to keep track of daily progress and celebrate together when a nap routine had been firmly established.

Carolyn is an attractive 17-year-old. She lives with her mother and stepfather in Dallas. On numerous occasions, her stepdad has barged into her bedroom without knocking, sometimes catching her half-dressed. Once, in the kitchen, on the pretense of horsing around, he "felt her up." When she told him to knock it off he just teased her, saying she was too sensitive. Carolyn hasn't mentioned anything to her mother because she's afraid it would only make trouble. Instead she decided to discuss the problem with a school counselor. With his help, Carolyn got up the nerve to confront her stepfather.

"Jack, I've told you this before, but you didn't listen to me. I don't want you to touch me. Maybe you think I'm too sensitive about this, but it's how I feel. You have no right to touch my body. I'm serious. It's not a joke. If you do it again, I'm going to tell Mom what's happening."

Jack looked angry but said nothing. After that, he kept his distance and confined himself to an occasional crack about her "sensitivities." She ignored these, pleased he had finally changed.

Janice, 43, is a secretary in her hometown of Albany, New York. She has three teenagers, and a 20-year marriage to her high school sweetheart. Janice has trouble being honest with her mother. A number of times each day her mom calls the office to chat (*"Hi, it's me. What are you having for dinner?" "Chicken? Again? I thought Annie doesn't eat chicken"*). Janice knows her mother is lonely and well-intentioned, but she also knows that the constant phone calls have to end. So the next time her mom comes over for a visit she decides to have a heart-to-heart talk with her.

"Mom, I love you loads and the last thing I want to do is hurt your feelings. But I need for you to understand that I simply cannot take personal phone calls at the office—from you or anyone else. Given my schedule, it just doesn't work. How about if I try to give you a call each day when I take my break in the afternoon?"

Her mother, at first, played the martyr. *"You don't have to call me at all if you don't have time for me in your busy life."*

Janice reassured her mom that she was fine chatting each day but needed to do it on her own terms. Then she dropped the matter and suggested they start dinner. For a few days, the new arrangement worked pretty well. Her mom didn't call and Janice checked in with her at some point each afternoon. Then, one morning, she picked up the receiver to find her mother on the other end.

"Hi. I'll be out this afternoon so I thought I'd call you. Do you want me to pick up Julie's costume for her?"

Janice had her response prepared. *"Sorry, Mom,"* she said pleasantly, *"I can't talk with you now. I'll give you a call this evening."* Her mother didn't give up. *"Just give me a yes or no on what you want me to do."*

Janice knew that were she to respond to anything short of an emergency, in no time at all her mother would be back calling her a million times a day. She stood firm.

"Sorry, Mom, this isn't a time when I can talk. I'll get back with you later on this."

Joanne, in her early fifties, is a dynamic and successful professional speaker. Recently, while on the road for an engagement, she went out to dinner with John and Leslie, old friends she hadn't seen in more than twenty years. During dinner, John drank too much and became loud and unpleasant. Although he was in no shape to drive, when his wife tried to convince him to hand over the keys, he refused. The two of them proceeded to have an ugly argument while Joanne stood by awkwardly, uncertain whether to "interfere." Finally, Joanne spoke up.

"Excuse me, John, but I feel the same way Leslie does—I'm not

comfortable either with you driving. I'd like for Leslie to drive or I'll be happy to take a cab back to my hotel."

"I'm not drunk." John said, trying not to slur his words. *"This is none of your business."*

"If I climb into the car with you it is my business. It's also the business of everyone else on the road. I'd like Leslie to drive or I'll take a cab."

Leslie knew her husband wouldn't give in to anyone—Joanne included—so she tried to salvage the situation with a compromise. *"How about if you drive very slowly, John, and take it real easy?"*

"Leslie," Joanne interrupted, *"I'm not willing to drive with John at the wheel—even if he takes it easy. I'll get a cab back to my hotel."* Which is exactly what she did.

Beth is 32 and lives in a Cleveland suburb with her husband, Paul. She is unhappy with their sexual relationship but doesn't know how to ask for what she wants. Paul's style of lovemaking leaves Beth totally unsatisfied.

After complaining for months about the situation to a close girlfriend, Beth realized that if she failed to talk with Paul himself, nothing would ever change. She brought the matter up one evening while they were relaxing after dinner.

"Honey, I've been feeling some frustration with our lovemaking but haven't been very comfortable talking about it. I didn't want to hurt your feelings or make you angry. Plus you know how it's always been hard for me to ask for what I want sexually. I figured, though, that you'd want to know about my feelings. Would you be willing to talk about this?"

The conversation that followed was a bit awkward at first, but it was a start. Beth talked about her need for more "warming up" before intercourse and more cuddling afterward. Even though she felt shy doing it, she described specific kinds of foreplay that turned her on and asked Paul how he would feel if she were to ask him to continue doing something when he stopped too soon.

Slowly, Beth noticed some positive changes in the way Paul made love to her. She told him how much she appreciated his responsiveness and invited him to ask for more of what he wanted, too.

Helen is an operating room nurse in a Chicago hospital. On several occasions she suspected that a respected surgeon was physically manipulating unconscious patients in inappropriate ways. At first she couldn't believe her eyes, but after several episodes she became convinced that he was getting a few cheap thrills with unknowing patients.

In considering her options, Helen realized that it felt too risky to confront this doctor on her own. Instead she chose to share her suspicions with a member of the ethics committee at the hospital. Together they set up a plan with a senior manager of nursing to watch the physician's actions more closely. When another nurse witnessed the same kind of questionable behavior, a formal complaint was drafted and presented to the committee. At a hearing, the doctor was judged guilty of unethical conduct and subsequently dismissed from the hospital staff.

SoftPower Does Not Always Mean "Happily Ever After"

I don't mean to imply by these completed vignettes that when you speak up and set limits with SoftPower, good always prevails over evil and all works out smoothly with a few brief interactions. A decision to be honest can be excruciating, frustrating, and futile. In the end, all you may have left is your integrity and the knowledge that you did what you could in the best way you knew how, however imperfect or unsuccessful your efforts. But many times it will be easier and more successful than you expected. Resist the tendency to focus exclusively or predominately on the down side of honesty—the risks it entails, the fears that hold you back, the discomforts of expressing yourself frankly—and look instead at the other side of the coin.

There is another side. Honesty is not always painful. In fact, telling the truth can be a source of great joy. So have fun— tell the truth faster! Yes, honesty can be risky, but it also can be exciting. Yes, honesty can be scary, but it is frequently an unparalleled learning experience. In fact, in many cases, well-executed honesty from the heart is a positive turn-on. As I said at the start of this book, truthfulness enlivens relationships, clears the air, and lets everyone know where things stand. It also frees up energy, which may be why a lot of people have good sex after a fight. The truth has finally been told and this liberates you in wonderfully stimulating ways.

Honesty from the heart is also a gift to others. Who knows what your heartfelt words might mean in another person's life? The turning point that launched me on the path of self-awareness and personal growth was the direct result of honesty from others. Perhaps the truth-telling of the encounter group was extreme, but it did the job. In fact it was precisely what I needed—a gentler kind of feedback probably would not have made a dent in my well-fortified defense systems.

The Choice Is Yours—
Which Path Will You Choose?

If you so desire, you can travel your life journey on a path of self-deception and inhibition, hiding from your need to change, holding back on honesty out of fear and guilt. Or you can choose to go another way and live a life based on telling the truth to yourself and others and doing it with heart. This is the path of SoftPower.

If you take the path of SoftPower, you choose the road less traveled. You live aware and alert, in charge of your mental home, responsible for your own feelings and actions. External circumstances and the behaviors of others no longer dictate your power and your peace of mind.

If you take the path of SoftPower, you are clear and energetic in pursuit of what you want, at ease accepting what's rightfully yours, graceful yet self-assured enough to yield when necessary to the demands of the moment.

If you take the path of SoftPower, step by step you build a true and lasting power that is sustained from the inside out. You find that ultimately you lose nothing you need to have and that what counts in the long run is building into your life lots of truth, lots of courage, lots of laughter, and lots of love!

A Personal P.S.

It is my fervent hope that as you practice the principles and skills of SoftPower, you will not only use them to be clear, direct, and powerful with your partner, boss, colleagues, friends, and family; you will use them as well in ways that make a difference outside the boundaries of your own personal life.

Late in the fall of 1988 I went through a period of deep despair about the state of our world. I decided to dedicate an issue of my newsletter *SoftPower* to the topic and call it "The World Is in Trouble, Do Your Share." It was not an easy issue for me to write. The topic was so depressing, plus I felt so emotional about the message I was afraid I'd be too emotional and come across as a bleeding heart on a soap box, turning some off with my intensity. It seemed impolite—against social taboos—to speak up about the dire state of affairs we're in. Several times I told myself, "Forget about it. Write something 'uplifting' instead. It's all too morbid—nobody wants to hear that the future of our species is holding on by a thread." Where was my "positive thinking"? Norman Vincent Peale would be so disappointed. Besides, Russia and America are friends now, right?

But then I listened to Elaine Melamed, on the video *Women for America, for the World*, tell women to stop apologizing for their strong feelings about the threats that surround us. "If you're not going to be emotional about the destruction of the planet," she said, "what are you going to be emotional about?" I realized that the feelings I was experiencing were not false alarms based on faulty thinking. They were gut responses to true danger. So at the risk of being "heavy" I decided to deal with the topic anyway. I want to share my message with you as well.

I won't bore you with the details of what punctured my denial systems that fall (cover stories on trash TV, editorials on the crack crisis, articles about the exploding economic implications of AIDS, the recent rise of neofascism—small downers like that). Suffice it to say I became deeply worried about America and profoundly concerned about the world. Here we stand at the threshold of the '90s and beyond that the twenty-first century. Are we going to make it? What will be left—if anything—for our children's children?

There's no escaping it, we're in deep trouble on many fronts. All is not well, as some politicians would have everyone believe. Many of us, however, find the bad news so overwhelming (and want so desperately to believe that everything will work out), we stick our heads in the sand and go on with life as usual. In *Despair and Personal Power in the Nuclear Age*, Joanna Macy calls it leading a double life—on the one hand, we know in our bones that the earth is in the highest of jeopardy; on the other, we deal with what to make for dinner and which movie to see on Friday. Even if we remain conscious of the constant danger, we try to be upbeat, to keep a brave front for the kids.

Actually, a certain level of healthy denial is probably necessary if we are to be functional. Yet, for most, the denial is massive and unhealthy. As Macy warns:

> The fear of despair can erect an invisible screen, selectively filtering out anxiety-provoking data. Since organisms require feedback in order to adapt and survive, such evasion is suicidal. Despair cannot be banished by sermons on positive thinking or injections of optimism. Like grief, it must be worked through. It must be named and validated as a healthy, normal, human response to the planetary situation.
>
> Whether or not we choose to accord them serious attention, we are barraged daily by data that render questionable the survival of our culture, our species, and even our planet as a viable home for conscious life. These warning signals prefigure probabilities of apocalypse that are mind-boggling. Each scenario presents its own relentless logic. Poisoned by oilspills, sludge, and plutonium, the seas are dying. When the plankton disappear (in thirty years at present pollution rates, says Jean-Jacques Cousteau), we will suffocate from lack of oxygen. Or carbon dioxide from industrial and automotive combustion will saturate the atmosphere, creating a greenhouse effect that will induce plagues of cancer that will decimate populations and cause fearful mutations in the survivors. Or deforestation and desertification of the planet, now rapidly advancing, will produce giant dustbowls and unimaginable famines. The probability of each of these perils is amply and soberly documented by scientific studies. The list of such scenarios could continue; the most immediate

and likely stem from the use of nuclear bombs, by terrorists or superpowers. This presents vistas of such horror we hear the survivors will envy the dead.[1]

The source of the despair we deny, according to Macy, is "the loss of the assumption that the species will inevitably pull through, a genuine accession to the possibility that this planetary experiment may fail." She argues that it is our denial—our unwillingness to face the crushing facts as well as the self-numbing needed for such repression—that holds us back from doing our share to save the situation.

I agree. It is for this reason that I share my concerns with you. We must help each other wake up, face the facts, then stay aware. Only in this way can we empower ourselves and each other to do our share, whatever that share turns out to be. By facing the facts, we know what we're dealing with. The question here, however, is how to open up to such horrifying facts without buckling under in a state of immobilized hopelessness. And how to share grief, sorrow, rage, and dread with others without provoking political arguments or isolating yourself in the process. As Macy says, "Expressions of anguish are considered a breach of etiquette." In a culture committed to the American dream, it's hard to be public about despair —who wants to feel the powerlessness and depression inevitable when you let the full impact of the bad news in? Instead, it gets treated like toxic waste: Out of sight, out of mind.

But there's nowhere to hide. And hiding is counterproductive anyway. The anguish and anxiety we feel in the face of the perils before us are in fact normal, healthy responses. Feeling the pain turns out to be a source of enlivenment and

[1]Joanna Macy, *Despair and Personal Power in the Nuclear Age*, New Society Publishers, 1983.

empowerment. It connects us to our common humanity—not only with each other but with all past generations and with all generations yet to come. Facing the facts enables us to draw from untold wells of strength, much as a mother does who lifts a car off of her child's body.

On a recent trip to England, surrounded by profound evidence of how far we've come—from prehistoric caves to Stonehenge to King Arthur's castle to Roman ruins to present-day London, I found myself overwhelmed with sorrow at the prospect of our potential self-destruction. As Macy says, "It's hard to believe that after millions of years of the evolution of life on earth, after millenia of civilization, of spiritual and artistic geniuses, Shakespeares, Mozarts, Einsteins, we should come to this." We've come so far from caves to computers, yet we have such a long way to go—if we want to avoid coming "to this."

And there isn't much time. In *You Can't Kill the Spirit*, Pam McAllister writes, "The Doomsday Clock is at five minutes to midnight and counting." At the brink of blowing ourselves up, at the edge of destroying our environment, in the middle of moral decay, it's essential for each of us to get involved, do our share, and do it now!

I pray this message, disquieting as parts of it may be, jolts and empowers you to action. The form will vary for each of us. But, whether it's saving the whales or stopping the arms race, protecting our rain forests or dealing with AIDs, caring for the homeless or cleaning up corruption, supporting quality television or working with troubled youth—find something that lights your fire and charges your commitment to make a difference.

Working together, we have a chance to preserve this precious planet for our great-great-great grandchildren. Don't let denial and despair immobilize you. Get involved. Your energy,

your vision, your love, your checkbook, and—most of all—
your actions are desperately needed. Take a stand while we
still have Mother Earth to stand on. If not you, who? If not
now, when? Do something. The world is in trouble. You are
needed. Do your share. And, please—do it now.

Maria Arapalis

About the Author

Maria Arapakis is president of SoftPower Resources, Inc. She lives in Oakland, California, where she raised two sons as a single mother. As a psychologist, speaker, and trainer, Maria has given over one thousand programs and presentations on communication, self-esteem, and personal power. Each year she speaks to over fifteen thousand professionals around the country and abroad. Her audiotape program on limit setting has helped over fifty thousand individuals learn the art of communicating assertively. In addition to her training and speaking work, Maria publishes *SoftPower!* an every-other-month newsletter on personal power.

SoftPower® Resources
For ongoing personal support

SoftPower!
An every-other-month newsletter by Maria Arapakis

How to Speak Up, Set Limits, and Say No Without Losing Your Job or Your Friends
Four Audiotapes and workbook by Maria Arapakis

A lively, content-rich program that spells out strategies and specific words and phrases to use in difficult limit-setting situations. An excellent program to share with family members who are also interested in improving limit-setting skills.

SoftPower Presentations and Training

Maria Arapakis is available for keynote presentations and training programs on a variety of topics related to personal power, self-esteem, and assertive communication.

For more information on any of the SoftPower resources, call 303-331-0011.